O9-BTI-719

Contemporary Sermon Illustrations

Contemporary Sermon Illustrations

James F. Colaianni Jr.

James F. Colaianni Sr.
Senior Editor

Italicus, Inc.
Ventnor, New Jersey

Library of Congress Catalog Card Number 91–093066
ISBN 0-941685-04-7

For information about other Italicus Publications
including The Preacher's Illustration Service write:
Italicus Inc., Post Office Box 3102, Margate, New Jersey 08402

To Lila

ABUNDANT LIFE

101
Before Columbus set sail to cross the Atlantic, it was believed that the world ended out somewhere past Gibraltar. The royal motto said plainly "Ne Plus Ultra," meaning, "there is no more beyond here."

But then, when Columbus returned, he had actually discovered a whole new world. The ancient motto was now meaningless. In this crisis, someone made a noble and thrifty suggestion, which Queen Isabella acted on. It was simply that the first word, "ne," be deleted leaving just two words: plus ultra—"there is plenty more beyond."

Plus ultra. There is plenty more beyond if you take the first step, if you begin your journey of an eternity, with the Lord Jesus Christ. "I came that they may have life, and have it abundantly" (Jn. 10:10).

AFTERLIFE

102
A traveller sat one morning having breakfast in a lodge high in the mountains. Through the window he could see great snow-covered peaks, green forested slopes and a brilliant blue

sky. He exclaimed to the waiter that he never expected to see such beauty anywhere. Whereupon the waiter replied, "Yes, but wait till you see the other side!" That is Jesus' Word to His people. Much more is available!

More insight into the truth.

More vision for the future.

More appreciation of the glory of God!

More genuine rejoicing—unimaginable joy—in the Kingdom of God!

—Johnson, R.N., "Much More!" (Adapted).

AGING

103

These lovely lines, entitled "My Beatitude," were seen hanging in an old folks' home. They speak for old folks everywhere:

Blessed are they who understand my faltering step
and palsied hand;
Blessed are they who seem to know that my eyes are
dim and my wits are slow;
Blessed are they who looked away when coffee
spilled on the table today;
Blessed are they with cheery smile who stop to chat
for a little while;
Blessed are they who know how to bring back fond
memories of yesterdays;
Blessed are they who make it known that I am loved,
respected, and not alone;
Blessed are they who know I'm at a loss to find more
strength to bear my cross;
Blessed are they who ease the days on my journey
home—in loving ways.

— "The Friendship Book"

104/AGING
On his one hundredth birthday, a man was asked the inevitable question by a reporter: "To what do you attribute your long life?" "Haven't decided yet," the old man answered. "I'm still negotiating with a mattress manufacturer and two breakfast food companies."

105/AGING
An old man was interviewed by a newspaper reporter on his one hundredth birthday. "To what do you attribute your longevity?" asked the reporter.

The centenarian thought for a moment and began ticking off items on his fingers: "I never smoked, I never drank liquor, I never over ate, and I always rise at six in the morning."

"I have an uncle who did all those same things, yet he only lived to be sixty," the reporter said. "How do you account for that?"

"Well," said the old man, "he just didn't keep it up long enough."

106/AGING
Author Eric Johnson mailed in–depth questionnaires to senior citizens (aged 67 to 97) to compile the material for his rich and entertaining book, "Older and Wiser." The following are a few examples from the more than 2,000 responses he received.

From a seventy–year–old woman:

> I am old so why mind being called old—but (and here's the crazy part) I feel vivid! Like a tree in its most glorious, autumnal colors with all its leaves on. I know they'll fall off soon, but that makes this stage of life even more precious. I am living life to the fullest.

4 Aging

From a seventy–year–old woman:

I do not feel old inside—I feel no great change. I'm simply appalled at how old my children are.

From a seventy–two–year–old man:

The bird of time is on the wing. I'm enjoying all the questions and delights I never had time for when I worked.

From a seventy–seven–year–old woman:

Here is my message to the world: Dear Friends, When you greet us, look into our eyes. See the marvelous things we elders have experienced—joy and sorrow, success and frustration, ecstasy and desolation. Ask us how it was. Share your life's journey. Together we will bless each other with new appreciation of the oneness of life.

From an eighty–three–year–old woman:

The biggest surprise about being my age is that I am succeeding, so far, in not being a nuisance.

From an eighty–four–year–old woman:

Old age is a time to drop guilt and learn to love yourself, for yourself and your uniqueness. Then from you will flow love and concern and help for others.

From an eighty–five–year–old man:

Danged if I can think of what in my life makes me feel hopeless. Life is a bowl of cherries, and if you have to pick out a few ants along the way, that's the way it is.

From an eighty–six–year–old man:

I'm waiting with bated breath. When will I feel old?

From a ninety–six–year–old woman:

I'm glad to be alive; thank God for the blessings I have, for the memories of a full life and the ability to see things in perspective.

107/AGING

Several elderly church members were being asked to what they attributed their longevity. One wealthy old woman was asked, "Mabel, why do you think God has permitted you to reach the age of 92?"

Without hesitation, she replied, "To test the patience of my relatives."

108/AGING

A common criticism of our society is that the elderly are not treated with the reverence and respect they deserve.

> Imagine a society where older people are able to live out their lives with dignity, security, and independence. The Scandinavians call their approach—developed over a 50–year period—"Open Old Age Care." Senior citizens are encouraged and helped to live their mature years in their own homes, instead of being "warehoused" in nursing homes. One of the key features in Scandinavian open care is the "home helper," who assumes chores the resident can no longer perform—housekeeping, cleaning, shopping, cooking, dressing and personal hygiene.
>
> Helpers are mainly young people—many of them students, and middle–aged persons. These "home helpers," who receive varying degrees of training, are paid by local municipalities and are considered to be municipal employees. This approach to home care produces a sense of independence in people—and with it pride, even a healthy vanity. Interesting is the great demand among older women living alone for hairdressers and manicurists. As a sign of respect, home helpers in Sweden are trained

> not to patronize elderly patients by calling them by their first names—it must be Mr. Larsen and Mrs. Nillson.

—Szulc, T., Parade Magazine

"Do not let your love be a pretense...have a profound respect for each other...if any of the Saints are in need, you must share with them: and you should make hospitality your special care" (Rom. 12:0,10,13).

"It is precisely the parts of the body that seem to be the weakest which are the indispensable ones" (I Cor. 12:22).

109/AGING

Dr. Irving Wright, President of the American Federation for Aging Research, tells the story of a psychological test that was developed to measure the mental agility of elderly people. A young psychologist was chosen to try out the test on a 91–year–old man.

The psychologist explained that it was a verbal test and that some of the questions were easy, while others were difficult. The first question, for example, was "What two days in the week begin with T?"

"That's easy," the man replied. "Today and Tomorrow."

The psychologist paused, studied his papers, and moved to the next question.

"This one is much more difficult. How many seconds are there in a year?"

Without blinking an eye, the man said, "Twelve."

"What did you say?" asked the psychologist.

"Twelve," said the elderly man, smiling. "The second of January, the second of February..."

110/AGING
When Pablo Casals reached the age of 95, a young interviewer asked him this question: "Mr. Casals, you are 95–years–old and the greatest cellist who ever lived. Why do you still practice six hours a day?" To which Pablo Casals replied, "Because I think I am making *progress*."

"...let us run with perseverance the race that is set before us" (Heb. 12:1).

111/AGING
A four–year–old boy had received a severe sunburn and it had reached the peeling–off stage.

His mother heard him saying to himself as he was washing up for dinner, "Only four years old and wearing out already."

112/AGING
A man called a life insurance agent and said he wanted to take out a policy on his life. "Fine," said the agent, "but before we make an appointment I would like to ask a few preliminary questions. Tell me, how *old* are you?" "I'm ninety–seven–years–old," the man replied. "I'm very sorry," said the agent, "but my company couldn't possibly insure you at that age." Hearing this, the old man became very annoyed. "You folks are making a big *mistake*," he said. "If you look carefully at your statistics you'll find that very *few* men die after they're ninety–seven."

113/AGING
"To those who ask how I can write so many things that sound as if I were as happy as a boy, please say that there is in the neighboring town a *pear* tree, planted by Governor Endicott *two hundred years ago*, and it still bears *fruit* not to be distinguished from that of a *young* tree in flavor. I suppose the tree makes new *wood* every year, so that some parts of it are *always* young.

"Perhaps this is the way with some *men* when they grow old. I hope it is so with *me*."
—Longfellow, H.W.

8 Aging

114/AGING
When he was seventy years old, Ty Cobb, perhaps the greatest baseball player of all time, was asked by a reporter, "What do you think your batting average would be if you were playing these days? Do you think you would be able to approach your lifetime average of 367?" Cobb replied, "I'd probably average around 290 today."

The reporter then asked, "Is that because of today's heavy travel schedules and all the night games and the artificial turf, and all the new pitches that have been developed, like the slider?"

"No," said Cobb, "it's because I'm *seventy.*"

115/AGING
The 70–year–old pianist, Mischa Elman, was preparing to depart from the United States for his final European concert tour. As he boarded the plane he said, "When I made my debut as a twelve–year–old in Berlin, people said, 'Isn't he *wonderful* for his age!' Now, they're beginning to say the same thing again!"

116/AGING
When Konrad Adenauer, former West German Chancellor, was confined to his bed with a chronic illness, he told his doctor that he had to get better within the week because he was scheduled to make an official trip abroad.

"I'm not a magician," said the doctor. "At your age, you've got to face reality, I can't make you young again."

To which Adenauer replied: "I'm not asking that. I don't want to become young again. I just want to keep on getting older."

117/AGING
A woman wrote a letter to the "Dear Abby" column. "Dear Abby," she said, "I am forty–four–years–old and never been married. As the years go by, I feel more and more lonely. I

would like to find the right man to marry. At my age, I would like to meet a man with no bad habits." To which Abby replied, "So would I!"

118/AGING

A woman had taken her elderly, fiercely independent mother to visit a retirement complex, She hoped to convince her of the advantages of living there instead of being alone in the rambling old family home. "Mother, see how much fun they're having playing bridge," said the daughter cheerily. "When I'm their age, I'd love to live here."

"Fine," the mother replied, "I'll be sure to visit you."

119/AGING

A stockbroker urged Senator Claude Pepper (Chairman, House Committee on Aging), to buy a stock that would triple in value in a year. Pepper told him, "At my age, I don't even buy green bananas."

AGNOSTICISM

120

It has been said that when people no longer believe in God they believe in *nothing*. It might be closer to the truth to say that when people no longer believe in God, they'll believe in *anything*.

121/AGNOSTICISM

Robert Ingersoll, the famous agnostic, once visited Henry Ward Beecher, the famous minister. During his visit, he noticed a beautiful globe which pictured the stars and constellations in the heavens. "This is an exquisite thing," Colonel Ingersoll said admiringly. "Who made it?" "Who made it?" Beecher replied with pretended surprise. "Why, Colonel, nobody made it. It just happened."

AIMLESSNESS

122
If you take a glass jar with air holes at the top and you put some flies inside the jar, the flies will buzz around frantically trying to get out of the cramped container. However, if you keep the ventilated jar closed a long time, something fascinating happens. When you finally take the lid off, the flies don't escape.

Even though the lid is off and the opening is clear, the flies that are so used to circling in the cramped jar will *continue* to do so. Just when they get close to the opening and liberation, they go right back to flying the same aimless patterns that keep them imprisoned.

Often, we human beings have the same problem. We get so *used* to bearing the burden of emotional baggage from the past we begin to accept it as a way of life from which there is no escape. And we go around in circles, so to speak, repeating the laments and asking the same agonizing questions, over and over again: "If only I had done this or that!...What if I had done this or that?"

"I do not run aimlessly...as one beating the air" (I Cor. 9:26).
—Feld, L., "Fresh Start"

123/AIMLESSNESS
A pastor received a literary magazine containing an announcement about a novel by one of Europe's more esoteric authors. The book was entitled "Composition #1." The unbound work contained unnumbered pages that could be shuffled randomly like a deck of cards. The reader was encouraged to arrange the pages helter–skelter, in any order. "From *there* the story will unfold," the instructions said.

The book is a striking symbol of an attitude that has taken hold in modern society: "Just arrange your activities helter–skelter, in any order, and your life story will unfold."

For us, the Good News is that the *true* story of our life is not revealed in a series of random, aimless events. The *good* life, Jesus tells us, is revealed in the *orderly* process of obedience to the Will of God. The *good* life unfolds to the extent that we are growing into the kind of persons *God* created us to be.
—Kennedy, G., "In Search of a Plot." (Adapted).

124/AIMLESSNESS
There is a "Peanuts" cartoon in which little Lucy has set up shop as a counselor. "Advice—5 cents," the sign reads over her booth. Charlie Brown comes to her and says, "Lucy, I need *help.*" "What can I do for you?" Lucy asks. Charlie says, "I'm *confused.* I can't seem to find a *direction,* a *purpose* for my life." Lucy answers, "Oh, don't worry, Charlie. It's like being on a big ocean liner making its way through the sea. Some folks position their deck chairs to face the *bow* of the ship, and others place their chairs to face the *side* of the ship or the *back* of the ship. Which way do *you* face, Charlie?" Charlie Brown answers, sadly, "I can't even *unfold* the deck chair."

ALCOHOLISM

125
A member of Alcoholics Anonymous said that his process of recovery began on the day he decided to buy an exceptionally fine watch. In his words…

> The watch combined a chronometer, a stop watch, a few features of a calendar and an astrological observatory; it indicated the day of the month and the phases of the moon. In fact, all it lacked was hot and cold running water. I realized that if it ever needed repair it could not be taken to an ordinary repair person. It would need to be taken to its *maker.* Then it came to me that my *life* was a very complicated affair—like that *watch.* It had broken down, and was running out of control. I decided that my only chance was to take it back to its *Maker.*

AMBITION

126

A recent high school graduate visited with his pastor in order to discuss with him his plans for the future. "My ambition is to become a great architect," he said. "I want to get my undergraduate and graduate degrees from the best University in the field." "What then?" asked the pastor. "I want to become famous by designing magnificent public buildings." "What *then?"* asked the pastor. "I want to get married." "What *then?"* asked the pastor. "I want to raise a family." "What *then?"* asked the pastor. "Oh, I see what you mean," said the young man, "I will then make peace with God." "That's all well and good," said the pastor, "but you must reverse the plan. Make peace with God first and all the other things will be added. Make peace with God first so that you will be able to trust His promise to give you what you need. Make that your life's ambition."

ANGELS

127

It was little Jane's first visit to the country. The night was warm, the window was open, the insect noises were strange.

"Mummy," whimpered Jane, "it's dark here. And everything buzzes. And I'm *afraid.*"

"Don't be afraid, Janie," comforted her mother. "Remember the angels are watching over you. They are right there with you." There was a pause, and then a loud wail.

"Mummy!" cried Jane, "one of the angels just *bit* me!"

128/ANGELS

A minister's wife told of her husband standing in front of the congregation to give the benediction:

Dressed in his white robe, and with his arms outstretched, he looked just like an angel ready to ascend. I had to squelch laughter when our teen–age son leaned over and whispered in my ear, *"He'll never get off the ground!"*

ANGER

129

"Anger" is only one letter removed from "danger." And we can sympathize fully with the little fellow whose angry outburst brought him swift punishment. "Dear God," he was later heard praying, "please take away my temper, and while you're at it, take away my father's temper too."

When kept within reasonable limits, anger is a *healthy* emotion. It is not "bad" or "sinful": it is as normal and as healthy as grief, love, joy, fear, sadness. Anger is a basic part of our human equipment, found earliest in infancy, as a response, for example, to frustration or rejection.

Anger that is *denied* an outlet can be like a festering sore which poisons the body and the mind. It is the stuff of which ulcers are made. It can cause blood pressure to rise, depression to set in.

Aristotle anticipated modern psychology when he wrote: "Anybody can become angry—that is *easy;* but to be angry with the right person, and to the right degree, and at the right time and for the right purpose and in the right way—that is not within everybody's power and is *not* easy."

Perhaps then the prayer of the little fellow is not our prayer after all. We should not ask God to take away our temper. Instead, we should ask, in Shakespeare's words: "Touch me with *noble* anger."

130/ANGER

"Of the seven deadly sins, anger is possibly the most fun...

> to smack your lips over grievances long past,
> to roll over your tongue the prospect of bitter confrontations still to come,
> to savor to the last toothsome morsel both the pain you are given and the pain you are giving back.
> In many ways anger is a feast fit for a king. The chief drawback is that what you are wolfing down is *yourself*. The skeleton at the feast is *you!*"

—Buechner, F., "Wishful Thinking: A Theological ABC" New York: Harper & Row, 1973 (Adapted).

ANNIVERSARIES

131

A man entered a greeting card store and asked the clerk for a "birthday/anniversary" card. "We have *birthday* cards," the clerk said, "and we have *anniversary* cards. Why not take one of each?" "You don't understand," the man answered. "I need a card that covers *both* events. You see, we're celebrating the fifth anniversary of my wife's thirty–fourth birthday."

ANXIETY

132

Edwin Teale, the naturalist writer, tells about a period of anxiety in his life during which he could not *sleep*. One night he decided to try the old remedy for insomnia: counting *sheep*. He says he went to bed and closed his eyes, but when the first sheep came along, it stumbled and *fell*. His state of mind was such that he became totally *involved* with the situation. Would someone come along to *help* the sheep? How many *more* sheep would stumble over the fallen one? How much *money* would the shepherd lose as a result of the accident?

133/ANXIETY

The root meaning of the word, "worry," is "to choke" or "to strangle." You can strangle yourself—choke the life out of yourself—with anxious worry. But it's a bad habit that can be broken. Someone has come up with a statistic that may be helpful to anyone who is trying to break the "anxious worry" habit: 92% of anxious worry is about things that never happen.

But what about the remaining 8%? You can handle it!

"Do not be anxious about your life, what you shall eat or what you shall drink, nor about your body, what you shall put on...but seek first his kingdom and all these things shall be yours as well" (Mt. 6:25,33)

134/ANXIETY

In her autobiography, the great singer, Ethel Waters, states her faith simply, saying that the "most important thing" in her life was to have found her "living Saviour." Ethel Waters loved to sing one "spiritual" that she learned from her grandmother and which she made the title of her autobiography:

Why should I feel discouraged, why should the shadows come
Why should my heart be lonely, and long for heaven and
home.
When Jesus is my portion, my constant friend is He
His eye is on the sparrow, and I know He watches me.

"Look at the birds of the air; they neither sow nor reap nor gather into barns, and yet your heavenly Father feeds them. Are you not of more value than they?" (Mt. 6:25).

135/ANXIETY

There are many *superficial* and, therefore, *unsuccessful* ways in which modern men and women try to handle anxiety:

...Some use alcohol or other drugs. They try to *tranquilize* away their anxieties.

...Some use the method of *repression.* They try to *pretend* away their anxieties, refusing to *confront* them.

...Some use the expedient of *work.* The "workaholics"

try to *work* away their anxieties. They fear that the *anxieties* will take over to the extent that they cut down on the *work*.

...Some use the gift of *speech*. They try to *talk* their way out of anxiety. They never stop *talking*. They fear that once their *mouths* stop going the *anxieties* will catch up to them.

...Some use the quest for *money* or *power*. They try to *buy* relief from anxiety.

...Some use the *sexual* experience. They try to *fantasize* their way out of anxiety.

And the list goes on...and on...

136/ANXIETY

Shalom Aleichem is considered by many to be the greatest of the ethnic humorists. He is perhaps best known as the creator of the character, Tevye, in one of America's most heartwarming Musicals, "Fiddler on the Roof."

Although it would be inaccurate to characterize Tevye as "a man of little faith," nevertheless he constantly needles God about the way He is running things on earth. Looking up toward heaven, Tevye worries over his situation as a village dairyman: "With God's help, I *starve* to death," he complains. "And now my *horse* is lame, so *I* pull the cart. Today I am a *horse.* Where is *justice?* If I pull this cart with *two* legs, why can't the horse with *three?* Dear God, it's enough that you pick on me, Tevye...but what have you got against my *horse?* Sometimes I think when things get too quiet up there, You say to Yourself, 'Let's see, what kind of mischief can I play on My friend Tevye?'"

Also from the pen of Shalom Aleichem is the story of an elderly man who easily outclasses Tevye as a certified worrier. The old man is standing with a friend on a crowded bus. A young man asks, "What time is it?" The old man refuses to reply and the young man moves on. The old man's friend asks, "Why were you so discourteous?" The old man replies, "If I had given him the time of day, next he would want to know where I'm going.

Then we might talk about our interests. If we did that, he might invite himself to my house for dinner. If he did, he would meet my lovely daughter. If he met her, they would both fall in love—and I don't want my daughter marrying someone who can't afford a watch."

137/ANXIETY

It's now a proven medical fact that your attitude can make you ill. When you get angry, arteries tighten. Do it often enough and you'll bring on a heart attack that can be just as fatal as one brought on by physical causes. Did you know that anxiety can create an ulcer that's just as painful as one brought on by the wrong diet? And a whole host of other illnesses can be brought on by your state of mind.

To head off these avoidable conditions, the American Medical Association has made the following suggestions:

- Stop looking for a knock in your motor.
- Learn to like your work.
- Develop at least one hobby.
- Learn to like people.
- Learn to be satisfied when you can't easily change your situation.
- Learn to accept adversity.
- Learn to say the cheerful, helpful, and humorous thing.
- Learn to face your challenges and your problems with confidence and decision.

In the words of songstress Dolly Parton, "If you want the rainbow, you gotta put up with the rain."

"So do not worry: do not say, 'What are we to eat? What are we to drink? How are we to be clothed?'...Your Heavenly Father knows you need them all...So do not worry about tomorrow; tomorrow will take care of itself. Each day has trouble enough of its own" (Mt. 6:31,33,34).

APATHY

138
Do you remember the Smothers Brothers? They used to do a routine that went something like this:

> Dick asked, "What's wrong Tommy? You seem despondent."
>
> Tommy replied, "I am! I'm worried about the state of American society!"
>
> Dick said, "Well what bothers you about it? Are you worried about poverty and hunger?"
>
> "Oh, no, that doesn't really bother me."
>
> "I see. Well are you concerned about the possibility of war?"
>
> "No, that's not a worry of mine."
>
> "Are you upset about the use of illegal drugs by the youth of America?"
>
> "No, that doesn't bother me very much."
>
> Looking puzzled, Dick asked, "Well Tom, if you're not bothered by poverty and hunger, war and drugs, what are you worried about?"
>
> Tommy replied, "I'm worried about apathy." Their routine is summarized on the bumper sticker that reads, "America's Greatest Problem Is Apathy—But Who Cares?"

And comedian George Carlin reported that "Scientists have just discovered a cure for apathy. However, no one has shown the slightest interest."

APPRECIATION

139
A man recalls how, as a boy, he first realized how much his father *appreciated* his mother:

> My father, a farmer, was undemonstrative. We children used to worry that he didn't show our mother due appreciation for her kind disposition and her many efforts in helping with the demanding farm chores. One afternoon, mother was delayed at a neighbor's house caring for a sick child and did not arrive home before father, as was customary.
>
> Father returned from the field at the usual time and walked in the front room where we *six children* were playing. He stood in the doorway surveying the scene for a moment, then frowned and said, "Where is *everybody?*"
>
> After that moment, we stopped worrying if mother was appreciated.

—Blevins, E. (Adapted).

140/APPRECIATION
In Robert Bolt's very successful play and film, "A Man For All Seasons," the main character, Thomas More, gives a young man this advice:

> "Why not be a teacher?" he says. "You'd be a fine teacher. Perhaps a great one."
> The young man is not impressed. "And if I was, who would know?" he asks.
> Thomas More tells him, "*You*, your pupils, your *friends*, and *God*. Not a bad public that!"

It's very much the same public that recognizes and appreciates the qualities of a good mother or father, wife or husband. Not a bad public at all!

ASSURANCE

141

Immediately after World War II the Allied Armies gathered up many hungry, homeless children and placed them in large camps. There the children were abundantly fed and cared for. However, at night they did not sleep well. They seemed restless and afraid.

Finally, a psychologist hit on a solution. After the children were put to bed, they each received a slice of bread to hold. If they wanted more to eat, more was provided, but this particular slice was not to be eaten—it was just to hold.

The slice of bread produced marvelous results. The child would go to sleep, subconsciously feeling he or she would have something to eat *tomorrow*. That assurance gave the child a calm and peaceful rest.

We read in the Twenty–third Psalm: "The Lord is my shepherd; I shall not want." Instinctively, the sheep knows that the shepherd has made plans for tomorrow's grazing. It knows the shepherd made ample provision for it today, and will do so tomorrow as well. The Psalmist is telling us that the sheep lies down in its fold with the piece of bread in its hand, figuratively speaking.

—Allen, Charles L., "God's Psychiatry" Guideposts (Adapted).

142/ASSURANCE

Drop to your knees beside the wide road,
And pick up a stone to turn in your hand.
Now make one like it.
Then if you succeed, tell me there's no God.

Take clay and dust, and fashion a child.
With wistful brown eyes and breath in its lungs,
Make flesh–warm lips, a brain, and red blood.
Then if you succeed, tell me there's no God.

—Hammill, C.E., "Challenge" (Denver Post).

ATTITUDES

143
Victor Frankl, who spent a long time in a concentration camp, describes what it was that made life tolerable for some while others simply gave up and died. "What was really needed was a fundamental change in our attitude toward life," he said. "We had to learn...that it did not really matter what we expected from life, but rather what life expected from us. We needed to stop asking about the meaning of life, and instead to think of ourselves as those who were being questioned by life—daily and hourly."

Put that statement in a Christian context and it sounds like this: "What is needed is a fundamental *change* in our attitude toward God. What matters most is not what we expect from Him but what He expects from us. We need to stop wondering about what we can *get* out of God and instead think of ourselves as being *questioned* by God—daily and hourly." These may seem like harsh words; and yet if He is God, then doing business with Him is on *His* terms, not ours.
—Lee, H.W., "On God's Terms" (Adapted).

B

BACKSLIDING

144
During England's darkest hours of World War II an article appeared in an English newspaper, saying, "We have preferred motor travel to church–going—now there is a shortage of motor fuel. We have ignored the ringing of church bells, calling us to worship—now the bells cannot ring except to warn us of invasion. We have left the churches half empty when they should have been filled with worshippers—now they are in ruins. We would not listen to the way of peace—now we are forced to listen to the way of war. We refused to live under God's control—now we are under the nation's control.

The money we would not give to the Lord's work—now is taken from us in taxes and higher prices. The food for which we forgot to say thanks—now is unobtainable. The service we refused to give to God —now is conscripted for our country. The nights we would not spend in 'watching unto prayer'—now are spent in anxious air raid precautions."

BEAUTY

145
Our bodies are the most complex pieces of machinery that exist. Our minds are the most remarkable computers that will ever be created. Our emotions are so deep and varied that we

are capable of experiencing ecstasy, joy, grief, despair, love, and hate. We are all alike, yet each of us is unique. Each of us is a non–repeatable mystery. However, we are our own harshest critics. We have been conditioned to focus on what is wrong with us, what is lacking in us, our faults, our mistakes, and our failures, rather than to appreciate how special we are. We see our shortcomings and are blind to our strengths. The beauty and wonder of life can be seen not only in the ocean, the mountains, and the flowers, but in the twinkle of an eye of a human being.

We ask ourselves, "Does just being me bring me happiness?" Rev. Peter Fraile believes, "As humans, we're stuck with our smallness, but we should admire our greatness. Within human beings I see the amazing beauty of life."
— Wholey, D., "Are You Happy."

146/BEAUTY
Alice Freeman Palmer, once president of Wellesley, spent some time in her youth teaching a Sunday school class made up of small girls recruited from a city slum. One Sunday, the idea came to her to ask those poor children, to find in their homes something beautiful, and then tell the other children about it the next Sunday.

When the next Sunday came, one bedraggled little girl who lived in a particularly dirty tenement said slowly: "I ain't found nothin' beautiful where I live except…except the sunshine on our baby's curls."

Years later, long after Mrs. Palmer's untimely death, her husband was lecturing at a University in the West. He was entertained in a distinguished home, and his hostess fondly recalled that she had once been a member of Mrs. Palmer's Sunday school class. She said: "I can remember that your wife once asked us to find something beautiful in our homes, and that I came back saying the only beautiful thing I could find was the sunshine on my sister's curls. But that suggestion your wife made was the turning point in my life. I began to look for something beautiful wherever I was, and I've been doing it ever since."

BELIEF

147
A very able man who was a chemist and the head of a chemistry department of a large University once said to E. Stanley Jones:

> Man is combustion, chemical combustion. He flares up for a few years and then dies down to an ash.

E. Stanley Jones related this to the great Christian scientist, Dr. George Washington Carver. "You are a chemist," Jones said, "what would you say in reply to this man?" Dr. Carver answered, "The poor man. The poor man." "That is all he would say," said Jones, "but it was an adequate reply, because if you have a small view of life, a poor philosophy, you are going to be a poor person. If you believe that the end of life is only an ash, then you are going to live life as an ash. A nothing. But God has qualified us for more than that. The believer knows that, accepts that, and becomes an inheritor of God's Grace because of it."
—Jones, E.S., "Jesus, the Divine Yes," Abingdon Press (Adapted).

BETRAYAL

148
Many years ago, Indian youths would go away in solitude to prepare for manhood. One such youth hiked into a beautiful valley, green with trees, bright with flowers. There he fasted. But on the third day, as he looked up at the surrounding mountains, he noticed one tall, rugged peak, capped with dazzling snow.

"I will test myself against that mountain," he thought. He put on his buffalo–hide shirt, threw his blanket over his shoulders and set off to climb the peak.

When he reached the top he stood on the rim of the world. He could see forever, and his heart swelled with pride. Then he heard a rustle at his feet, and looking down, he saw a snake. Before he could move, the snake spoke.

"I am about to die," said the snake. "It is too cold for me up here and I am freezing. There is no food and I am starving. Put me under your shirt and take me down to the valley."

"No," said the youth. "I am *forewarned.* I know your kind. You are a rattlesnake. If I pick you up, you will bite, and your bite will kill me."

"Not so," said the snake. "I will treat you differently. If you do this for me, you will be *special.* I will not harm you."

The youth resisted awhile, but this was a very persuasive snake with beautiful markings. At last the youth tucked it under his shirt and carried it down to the valley. There he laid it gently on the grass. Suddenly, the snake coiled, rattled and leapt, biting him on the leg.

"But you *promised...*" cried the youth.

"You *knew* what I was when you picked me up," said the snake as it slithered away.

"I am afraid that just as the serpent deceived Eve by his cunning, your thoughts will be led astray from a sincere and pure devotion to Christ" (2 Cor. 11:3).

BETROTHAL

149

While some newspaper reporters have been accused of being hard–nosed cynics, at least one correspondent believes in reporting life's "little stories." The following item appeared on the UPI wire service:

> Omaha, Nebraska...A couple strolled into a local jewelry store, smiled at the clerk and shyly asked to look at engagement rings.
>
> The confused clerk stammered, then said, "I'm sorry but all our engagement rings are being cleaned right now. Can you come back later?"
>
> The couple whispered together, smiled, nodded "yes" and left the store. The boy was *eight*. The girl *seven*.

BIBLE

150

A French dramatist was asked to write the script for the first episode in a radio series of Bible study programs. When the episode was aired, the author was greatly pleased with the performance. But he also was taken aback when, during the sign–off portion, he heard the announcement: "Will Cain kill Abel?" Dear listeners, tune in next Sunday and hear the exciting conclusion to this compelling story."

151/BIBLE

A newly appointed pastor met with his daughter's teacher for the first time at the school's open house. The science teacher, with a twinkle in her eye, asked,

> "Are you a minister?"
>
> "Yes," he replied."Why do you ask?"
>
> "It was just a feeling I had after reading one of your daughter's homework assignments," she said, handing him the corrected paper. Next to the item "Define the Great Divide," his daughter had written: "When Moses parted the Red Sea."

—Burt, S.

152/BIBLE

An American clergyman was travelling in Korea by train. At a busy station, an old man boarded and sat across from him. The man was Korean and he addressed the American in his native tongue. The clergyman responded with the only Korean phrase he knew—meaning that he did not understand. A few minutes later the old man tried another sentence and the American clergyman again responded as he did before. The Korean then tried a third question, only this time the American recognized a *familiar* word. It was "Yesu" which means "*Jesus.*" The American pointed to himself and said "Yesu." The old man did the same with a delighted smile.

The Korean then unwrapped the bundle he was carrying. It was a large Korean Bible. He turned the pages and pointed to a place he wanted the American to read. Remembering that Oriental Bibles are written from back to front, the clergyman took his own Bible and counted the number of books and chapters from the back to the place that the old man had pointed to. The man had pointed to Mark 3:35 "Whoever does the Will of God is my *brother* . . ." The American searched for a suitable *reply.* He counted it out and pointed to it in the Korean Bible. It was Psalms 133:1. "Behold, how good and pleasant it is when brothers dwell in *unity*". The Korean man read it and smiled in agreement. For the rest of the journey, these two men, ages apart in culture, were brought together in a remarkable friendship as they pointed first to one verse and then another. Their separate Bibles had a common language of the *Spirit.*

—Crowe, C. M., "The Bible In An Atomic Age." (Adapted).

153/BIBLE

When calling on a family in the parish, a certain pastor always made it a point to read from Scripture. On one occasion, when he thought it was the appropriate moment, the pastor expressed his desire to read a few verses. Whereupon, the hostess said to her daughter, "Run to the bookcase, dear, and bring back the book we all *love* so well." The little girl obediently went to the bookcase and then returned with a book in her hand. It was the Sears Catalog.

154/BIBLE

"For if anyone is a *hearer* of the Word and not a *doer*, he is like a man who looks at his natural face in a mirror; for once he has looked at himself and gone away, he has immediately forgotten what kind of person he was" (James 23–24).

Here is a man who gets out of bed and looks in the mirror. He sees whiskers, disheveled hair, yellow teeth, and a dirty smudge on his cheek. But then he walks away and forgets what he saw. He goes to work in that same condition! And of course his mere looking in the mirror didn't improve his appearance one bit! No mirror can shave a man's beard, or comb his hair, or brush his teeth, or wash his face. The mirror's purpose is to show him what he *needs* to do!

So it is with the Bible! When we look into it, we see the dishevelment and the smudges sin has caused. When we look into it we see our faults, our blemishes, our weakness of faith, our jealousies, our greed, our idolatries, our backbiting, our unkindliness. But just seeing those smudges and blemishes doesn't take them away! The Bible exposes our sins, but we are the ones who have to exercise belief! It is up to us—each of us individually—to become DOERS OF THE WORD!

BLESSINGS

155

In her Book of "Useless Information," Barbara Cortland reports that when the Mona Lisa was stolen from the Louvre in Paris in 1911 and was missing for two years, more people went to stare at the blank space in the museum than had gone to look at the masterpiece in the twelve previous years.

Far from being "useless," this intriguing bit of information tells us something important about ourselves. It points to our all–too–human tendency to fail to appreciate precious things while we have them. But let one of them be taken away from us and we become painfully aware of the "blank space" in our lives, and our attention is sharply focused on that "blank space."

The walls of our lives are crowded with Mona Lisas, but too often we are unmindful of them—take them for granted. Countless blessings attend us daily and too often we are insensitive to them.

The more often and the more regularly we receive any blessing, the less likely we are to be aware of it. What is constantly granted is easily taken for granted.

"I have often thought," Helen Keller wrote, "that it would be a blessing if human beings were stricken blind and deaf for a few days at some time during their adult lives. Darkness would make them more appreciative of sight; silence would teach them the joys of sound."
—Greenberg, S., "Say Yes To Life." (Adapted).

BONDAGE

156
In the jungles of Thailand, when a wild elephant is captured, hunters tie one end of a thick chain around the elephant's feet. The other end is tied to a large banyan tree. The huge beast pulls with all its strength, but it can't budge the banyan tree. Finally, after struggling for days and weeks, the elephant *surrenders* to the chain.

At this point, they take the elephant and chain it to a small iron stake by a circus tent. The elephant doesn't attempt to pull away because it still thinks it is chained to the *tree.* It never realizes how easily it could achieve freedom. It has become a slave to habit.

BROTHERHOOD

157
Human brotherhood is not just a goal. It is a condition on which our way of life depends. The question for our time is not whether all men are brothers. That question has been answered by the God who placed us on this earth together.

The question is whether we have the strength and the will to make the brotherhood of man the guiding principle of our daily lives.
—*Kennedy, J.F.*

158/BROTHERHOOD
The following true account appeared in a New York Times feature:

> It happened to me the other day on the train as it pulled out of Times Square on its way to Queens.
>
> As the passengers sat there, two beggars appeared at each end of the car. Almost simultaneously, they started moving toward the center of the train, holding tin cups as they went.
>
> The older man, who was *blind,* wore a sandwich board that seemed to be covered with news stories of his unsuccessful attempts to get a seeing-eye dog. He declaimed loudly and clearly that he, once a promising composer, was now reduced to begging. We could see that the younger man—making his way silently between the poles—was a *double amputee.*
>
> For some reason, the passengers were being unusually generous to the *younger* man. As I heard the sound of the coins dropping into his tin cup, I wondered what would happen when the two men met at the center of the car.

As they approached, the younger man deftly moved aside and, as they passed, he took a coin from the cup in *his* lap and dropped it into the *blind* man's outstretched container, receiving the response, "*Thank* you—God *bless* you."

159/BROTHERHOOD

There is the story of a time when God's people came together to discuss God's commandment, "Remember, keep *holy* the Sabbath." They wanted to settle the question of when the Lord's Day *begins.* Some said, "The Lord's Day begins at *sunrise.*" Others said, "The Lord's Day begins at *midnight.*" And there was a third opinion: "The Lord's Day begins at sunset of the day *before.*" They weighed the pros and cons, but could not decide. Hopelessly deadlocked, they took the matter to a wise and holy woman. "When does the Lord's Day begin?" they asked. She replied: "It begins when it is light enough for you to see in another's face the face of your *brother.*"

160/BROTHERHOOD

Brotherhood is common sense saying: "Get *rid* of your prejudices in order to live *peacefully* with yourself and your *neighbors.*"

Brotherhood is good *sportsmanship* saying:"Do not make another person or another group the *scapegoat* for your own shortcomings and frustrations."

Brotherhood is *education* saying:"Beyond the development of skills and the acquiring of knowledge, we must learn how to live *together.*"

Brotherhood is *science* saying:"Humanity is *one*; there is no such thing as a superior or an inferior race."

Brotherhood is American *democracy* saying:"We hold these truths to be self–evident, that all men are created *equal,* that they are endowed with certain inalienable rights."
—Metcalf, I.E., World Call.

161/BROTHERHOOD

I looked upon my brother with the microscope of criticism, and said, "How coarse my brother is!" I looked at him with the telescope of scorn, and I said: "How small my brother is!" Then I looked in the mirror of truth, and I said: "How like me my brother is!"

162/BROTHERHOOD

Rabbi Samuel Price has recommended observance of an official "Week of Hate" instead of the traditional "Brotherhood Week."

"It would be much better," he said, "to have the week dedicated to hate: a week when we would be able to get the hate out of our systems, treat one another as badly as we know how, and then observe the remaining 51 weeks of the year as 'Brotherhood Weeks.'"

—*Arkansas Baptist.*

163/BROTHERHOOD

Leo Tolstoy, the great Russian writer, was walking along the street one day when a man in tattered clothing asked him for money. The writer searched his pockets for a coin but could find none. "I'm sorry, my brother, but I don't have anything with me," he said. The beggar's melancholy expression suddenly turned into a smile as he replied, "You have given me more than I asked for. You have called me brother."

BURDEN

164

A father and son are walking together along the beach. The little boy keeps picking up pebbles of various sizes, shapes, and colors, stuffing them into the pockets of his jeans. After a time, the boy asks his father to carry him.

By this time, with many rocks, pebbles, and stones in his jeans, the boy is too heavy for the father's arms. "Son, I am willing to carry you, but first you must take all the pebbles, stones and rocks out of your pockets."

Symbolically, this human father represents the Heavenly Father, the Creative Intelligence of the Universe. You and I are that child. We have picked up stones of doubt, rocks of fear, pebbles of resentment. We have placed them in the pockets of our consciousness—and they weigh us down. Then in our pain, our weariness, our despair, we turn to the Father within and we cry out, "Help me!" We shout for help to make it through the night or the day. The Father within us says, "Put down the rocks, My child. I want to carry you through this, but there are too many stones of fear and resentment and disbelief. I will carry you when you take them out of the pockets of your consciousness. Then the burden will be light!"
—Costa, T., "Life! You Wanna Make Something Of It?" (Adapted).

165/BURDEN
A woman got on a crowded bus carrying a heavy suitcase. There were no seats, and she had to stand near the driver, holding on to a pole next to his seat. She held the pole with one hand and the suitcase with the other. After a while, the bus driver looked at her and said, "Lady, why don't you put the suitcase down and let the bus carry it?"

Why don't you put your burdens down and let *Jesus* carry them?

BUREAUCRACY

166
The new vice–president began flaunting his title so much that one of his co–workers finally said to him, "These days v-ice–presidents are a dime–a–dozen. In fact, the title is getting so *ridiculous* that my supermarket even has a Vice–President In Charge Of *Peas.*" The new V.P. couldn't believe what he was hearing, so he called the supermarket and asked for the Vice–President In Charge Of Peas. The voice on the phone said, "Canned or frozen?"

CARING

167

Old "Aunt Maude," as everyone in her neighborhood knew her, was always looking for some reason to visit the neighborhood branch Post Office because the employees there were so *friendly*. One Christmas Season she went there to buy a couple of stamps and discovered that the lines were particularly long. As she waited patiently in the stamp line, a friend came by and said, "Aunt Maude, how many stamps do you need?" "Only two," Aunt Maude replied. "In that case," said the friend, "why not use the stamp machine in the lobby? There is no line out there." "I'd rather wait *here*," Aunt Maude replied, "the machine won't ask me about my *arthritis*."

168/CARING

"The more I feel sorry for myself, the more I go into a downward spiral. My home remedy for depression and self–pity is to find somebody to help. Going out of my way to be nice to somebody lifts me up. When I feel frustrated by what I haven't been able to accomplish, I think of all the people I have helped get through crises in their lives. When I feel *really* down on myself, one of the things I do is visit people in the hospital. It's not because I want to be reminded that some people are worse off than I; that's cruel. People are not sick in order to make me feel lucky. However, the experience of giving to somebody pulls me out of my self–pity."
—Kushner, H.S.

169/CARING

The pastor of a Church in San Antonio was making his daily rounds ministering to the poor. He stopped in front of a small, broken–down house—the home of a poor family in which there were two sons. The *younger* of the two boys was physically handicapped. As the pastor parked his car in front of the house, he was greeted enthusiastically by the *older* brother. "Wow! Your shiny, new car sure looks great," the boy said. "Where did you get it?" The pastor replied, "You know son, I don't make much money in my work and I couldn't afford to *buy* a car like this for myself. But I have a brother in Houston who makes a lot of money in the oil business. He *gave* me this car." The boy looked up at the pastor and said, wistfully, "I wish I could *be* a brother like that!" He might have said, "I wish I *had* a brother like that!" But clearly that young man was in on the secret of life's true meaning and purpose: *caring* is everything! There is no other way to make yourself rich in the sight of God! There is no other way to experience *wholeness* of life. There is no other way to spend every tiny little minute as though *eternity* were in it.

170/CARING

There was a wealthy man who, in his old age, was asked to recall the *happiest* experience of his life. He said, "It was when I was in a hospital in a strange town, seriously ill for three weeks with typhoid fever." When his listeners expressed *surprise* that this was the happiest situation of his life, he continued: "The hospital was understaffed, and overcrowded with patients. It was a difficult time for everyone. But there was *one* nurse who never let it get her down, who treated each one of us patients as if we were *royalty*. Every time she came into my room, I felt a deep sense of *peace*. I have never felt anything like it since, and I have never forgotten her. It was the *happiest* period of my life in *spite* of the physical suffering."

171/CARING

An ancient legend tells the story of a renowned rabbi who disappeared from the synagogue for a few hours each Sabbath day. His mysterious conduct was the subject of much speculation among the rabbi's students. Many of them suspected that their great mentor had discovered a secret meeting place with the *Almighty*. Consequently, one Sabbath day they agreed that one of them would secretly follow him. The designated student watched in amazement as his great teacher put on the coarse clothing of a beggar. Then he followed the older man through the back streets of the city and saw him enter a humble shack. He peered through the only window and watched in wonder as his spiritual leader tended to the needs of an elderly invalid man—changing his clothes, cleaning his room, preparing his meal. When he had seen enough, the student returned to the synagogue where the others were eagerly waiting with their questions: "What happened? Did he ascend into *heaven*?" they asked. The student answered, "Yes, if not *higher!*" In witnessing the holy man's works of *mercy*, the young student had captured a glimpse of *eternal life*.

CHANGE

172
I was a neurotic for years. I was anxious and depressed and selfish. Everyone kept telling me to change.

> I resented them, and I agreed with them, and I wanted to change, but simply couldn't, no matter how hard I tried.
>
> What hurt the most was that, like the others, my wife kept insisting that I change. So I felt powerless and trapped.
>
> Then, one day, she said to me, "Don't change. I love you just as you are."
>
> Those words were music to my ears: "Don't change. Don't change. Don't change…I love you as you are."
>
> I relaxed. I came alive. And suddenly I *changed!* Now I

know that I couldn't really change until I found someone who would love me whether I changed or not.

Is this how you love me, God?
—deMello, A., "The Song of the Bird."

173/CHANGE
In a midwestern Church, the *crib*–room is filled to capacity every Sunday without fail. As you *enter* the room, you see a large framed sign hanging on the wall over the long line of cribs. It reads, "Not all of us shall fall *asleep*, but all of us are to be *changed*." That line is a direct quote from First Corinthians, Chapter 15, Verse 51.

"Not all of us shall fall *asleep*, but all of us are to be *changed*," wrote the Apostle Paul. Not all who come to Church fall *asleep* but how many who stay awake are really being *changed?* How many really believe there is a *need* to change? How many understand that the Word of God they hear in this Church is always and without exception a *call* to change?

174/CHANGE
The famous entertainer, W.C. Fields, was a lifetime agnostic. It is reported that during his last illness a longtime friend made a bedside visit and saw that Fields was reading the *Bible*. "Bill, it's so good to see that you have *changed*," said the friend. To which Fields replied, "I haven't changed. I'm looking for a *loophole!"*

175/CHANGE
Rivers in extremely cold climates freeze over in winter. In the Spring, when they *thaw*, the sound of ice cracking is an incredibly *violent* sound. The more extensive and severe the *freeze*, the more thunderous the *thaw*. Yet, at the end of the cracking, breaking, violent period, the river is *open*. The river is life–*giving*. And notice, no one has said, "Let's not *suffer* the thaw; let's *keep* the freeze; let's keep everything nice and *quiet*." To wrench anything out of its accustomed course often is a painful

process. It does great *violence* to the existing pattern. Many people *want* change, both in the *external* world and in their own internal world, but they are unwilling to undergo the severe *pain* that often must precede it.
—Mebane, M.E..

176/CHANGE
The world–famous opera singer, Beverly Sills, gave up her career while it was still at its peak in order to take over the management of the New York City Opera Company. Ms. Sills now wears a gold chain and medallion around her neck on which are four gold letters: I.D.T.A.

It is said she was so weary of answering the question as to why she gave up her singing career to manage the opera company that she now points to the letters on the medallion to explain: I.D.T.A.—"I *did* that already."

You may be experiencing that same "I did that already" feeling. You may be growing tired of following the same old routine. You may be weary of *repeating* your activities day–after–day–after–day. But, as a loyal follower of Christ, you must always remember that whatever *else* you may change in your life, there can be *no* change in your response to Jesus' command of *love.* Day–after–day–after–day it is always "*Yes* Lord!" to Jesus' command: "Love one another as I have loved you"—*never* "I did that already!"
—Costa, T., "Life! You Wanna Make Something Of It?" (Adapted).

CHARACTER

177
A dear old Quaker lady was asked to explain her obviously youthful appearance, her appealing vivacity, and her winning charm. She replied sweetly, "I used for the lips—truth; for the voice—prayer; for the eyes—pity; for the hands—charity; for the figure—uprightness; for the heart—love." How's that for a makeup kit?

CHARITY

178
"He who has two coats, let him share with him who has none; and he who has food, let him do likewise" (Luke 3:11).

One Sunday morning, a preacher delivered a sermon on this text which he had spent long hours preparing. A friend who knew how much effort had gone into the sermon asked him later if it had gone over well with the congregation. The preacher replied, "I tried to convince them that it was the Christian duty of the *rich* to help the *poor*. But I don't think I succeeded very well. I only convinced sixty percent of them—and all of them are *poor*."

179/CHARITY
The story goes that Henry Ford Sr., having made his fortune, decided to visit Cork, Ireland, the city from which his father had emigrated.

When he arrived, he was greeted by a group of locally prominent citizens, including a committee of people who were trying to raise funds for a new hospital. Ford immediately wrote out a check for $5,000 and gave it to the committee.

The public learned of his generosity in the newspaper the next day but the figure was mistakenly published as $50,000. Embarrassed committee members promptly contacted Mr. Ford and offered to straighten the matter out.

"I have a better idea," said Ford.

He said he would write a check for the additional $45,000 if they would allow him to have something inscribed over the hospital's main entrance. They readily agreed. Ford wrote the check and chose a line from Matthew's Gospel:

I WAS A STRANGER AND YE TOOK ME IN.

CHILD–BEARING

180
A four–year–old boy and his six–months–pregnant mother were sitting side–by–side in the obstetrician's office. Suddenly, the mother clutched her stomach and let out a deep sigh. The little boy, with a worried look on his face, said, "Mom, what's the matter?" "The baby brother you're going to have soon is *kicking*," she said. The little boy thought about this for a few moments, and then said, "He's probably getting *restless*. Why don't you swallow a *toy?*"

CHILDREN

181
There was a newspaper report about a mistake that had been made in the records of the City of Houston, Texas which resulted in a two–year–old child being summoned to *jury* duty. Could it be that the mistake was inspired by the *Holy Spirit?* After all, the child *is* the final jury before whom the *adult* world ultimately must be tried.

182/CHILDREN
During the Christmas Season, a grandmother took her little granddaughter on a shopping trip. After watching her grandmother choose and buy gifts for several hours, the little girl was taken for her promised visit to Santa Claus. She made her desires known to Santa, and when she finished reciting her list, Santa presented her with a little bag of popcorn. "What do you *say?*" grandmother asked. The little girl thought for a moment, than said in a firm voice, "*Charge* it!"

183/CHILDREN
A class of second–graders in a parochial school was asked to draw a picture which showed what they would like to do if Jesus came to spend a day with them. After the students had worked on the project for a while, one little girl went up to the teacher's desk with her almost finished drawing in hand. "Miss Kelly," she said, "I have a question. How do you spell *Bloomingdale's?*"

184/CHILDREN

A new class of second–graders was asked to tell how many other children they had in their families. The teacher asked, "Have you any brothers or sisters?" One little boy answered, "No, ma'am, I'm single."

—Muller, H.L.. (Adapted).

185/CHILDREN

A little boy, in Church for the first time, sat fascinated as the members of the choir entered in their flowing, white robes. In a loud voice the child cried out, "Look mommy, they're all going to get their hair cut."

186/CHILDREN

The teacher asked her pupils to write essays on *anatomy.* One little boy wrote:

> Your *head* is kind of *hard* and your *brains* are in it and your *hair* grows on it. Your *face* is in *front* of your head, the place where you *eat.* Your neck is what keeps your head off your *shoulders,* which are sort of like *shelves* where you hook the straps to your *overalls.* Your *arms* are what you have to pitch a *softball* with and to reach for the *muffins* at breakfast. Your *fingers* stick out of your *hands* so you can *scratch,* throw a *curve,* and add *arithmetic.* Your legs are what you have so you can *run* to first base; your feet are what you run *on,* and your toes are what gets *stubbed.* And that's all there is of you, except what is *inside.* But I've never *seen* that.

– Prochnow, H. (Adapted).

"You created my inmost being; You knit me together in my mother's womb. I praise You because *I am fearfully and wonderfully made*" (Psalm 139:13–14).

187/CHILDREN

A mother took her children on a cross–country vacation to California to visit their grandparents. They flew out and back on a 747 jet. Flying over the Rockies, the kids looked down at the Grand Canyon. They spent three days at Disneyland and finally went to Yosemite National Park where they spotted two big bears.

The vacation provided all sorts of new and exciting experiences for the children. Yet, when the vacation ended, upon arrival at the airport, the five–year–old son rushed up to his father who was waiting at the gate. "Daddy, guess what?" he shouted. "Granddad can take his *teeth* out!"

188/CHILDREN

Trying to instill a sense of confidence in her children, a mother began a family ritual, starting with her first baby. As soon as he was old enough to respond, she asked her son, over–and–over again, "Billy, why do I love you?" He would then answer, "Because I'm *Billy*."

When the mother's second child, *Amanda*, was old enough, she tried the same dialog. "Why do I love you?" she asked her daughter. Without hesitation Amanda responded, "Because I'm *Billy*."

189/CHILDREN

A little boy announced excitedly to his birthday party guests: "I'm six years old today!"

"Six years old! Wow! Imagine that!" his grandfather said. "But, you're not even as tall as my *cane*."

"How *old* is your cane?" the little boy asked.

190/CHILDREN

Many behavioral scientists have come up with an interesting theory on aging. The theory hypothesizes that human behavior is cyclic. We start as babies, but slowly learn social customs and norms and eventually act like adults. However, in the twilight years, we regress back into child–like modes of behavior and thought processes. For instance, many people who are very old and nearing death sleep in the fetal position. When someone is near death, they are often said to be closer to God. And when a baby is born he is said to be a bundle from heaven. And if all this is so, then isn't being child–like the closest any of us will ever get to our Creator?

"Truly, I say to you, unless you turn and become like children, you will never enter the Kingdom of Heaven." (Matthew 18:3).

191/CHILDREN

A little girl was moving with her family from California to Cleveland, and was very excited. The night before their departure she said her prayers as usual and finished off with, "God bless Mommy and Daddy and my little brother, Tommy. And this is goodbye, God—we're moving to Cleveland."

192/CHILDREN

A young boy in Cleveland went with his father to the Western Union office one day to send a telegram. The boy listened to the conversation between his father and the Western Union attendant but he didn't ask any questions.

That night, as his mother was putting him to bed, he turned from a kneeling position as he finished his prayers and said to his mother:

"Mommy—what are prayers anyway?"

"They are messages sent to *Heaven,*" she explained briefly.

"Well...do I pray at night because the *rates* are cheaper?"

193/CHILDREN

"Henry" was a man who always made the wrong choices. If he bet on a baseball game, the team he chose would lose. If he chose between two elevators, the one he entered would stall between floors. If he chose one line at the bank over another, his line would never move. One day, Henry had to take an airplane trip to a distant city. He was pleased to learn that he could not choose between planes. There was only one plane that could get him to his destination on time. With no choice to make, he would come to no grief, Henry reasoned. Shortly after takeoff, the engines caught fire. It became obvious that the plane would crash. Immediately, Henry began praying to his favorite saint: St. Francis. "Dear St. Francis", he cried out, "you know I have never made a right choice in my life. But this time I had no choice. Why then am I being punished in this way?" Suddenly, a giant hand swooped down from the heavens and snatched Henry from the falling plane. A heavenly voice said, "Henry, my son, I can save you, if you have sincerely called upon me." "Oh, yes, I have in truth called upon you, St. Francis." "Then tell me Henry," said the heavenly voice, "*which* St. Francis? St. Francis of *Assisi* or St. Francis *Xavier?*"

194/CHILDREN

A little girl from Minneapolis came home from Sunday school with a frown on her face. "I'm not going back there anymore," she announced with finality. "The Bible lessons aren't fair!" "Why not?" asked the astonished mother.

"Because," said the little girl, "the Bible is always talking about St. Paul, and it never once mentions Minneapolis."

195/CHILDREN

The Boys Choir of Harlem operates out of a dilapidated former school building in a crack dealing neighborhood. Yet the group has often succeeded in its mission of teaching youngsters to sing like angels and act like men.

Walter Turnbull, the 43 year–old founder/director, is determined to help each boy. If a kid is having trouble, musical or personal, Turnbull, a former opera tenor, won't give up. In a city where a large percentage of blacks entering high school do not graduate, 98 percent of the chorus goes on to college.

"Introduce a child to what beauty is at age ten," Turnbull declares, "and he will look for it the rest of his life!"

CHILDREN OF GOD

196
Once upon a time there lived a very wise king who had a son. The king feared that his son would be spoiled by the adulation of the courtiers and servants of the court, so he sent the prince to a peasant couple to be brought up as their own son. The child knew nothing of his royal birth, or of his father's riches and power. He worked and studied and played like any other peasant child. It was not until he had grown into a strong, self–reliant young man that the king sent for him, and revealed his heritage and true position in life.

This plot has been used for many famous tales. But it is one that carries an important message with it, because most of us are like that child. Brought up in ignorance of our divine heritage, we think that we are poor and powerless. Emerson says

that Jesus Christ alone, of all those who have lived upon this earth, appreciated the worth of man—the greatness of man and his unlimited possibilities. Remember that the Lord Jesus said, "...I came that they may have life, and have it abundantly." (Jn. 10:10).

Again and again Jesus reminded us that we, too, are sons and daughters of the divine: children of God!
—Fischer, W.L., "The Nature of Our Creation" (Adapted).

CHRIST PRESENCE

197
I am daily impressed that we are but a tiny dot on the edge of a star cluster in a universe that has *millions* of star clusters just like it. But that leads me to dwell less on our *unimportance* than to marvel at a God who *cares* for us as if He had nothing else to care for.

I know that Jesus walks with us along our pilgrim journey, but doesn't have us on a leash, for God tenders maximum *support* but minimum *protection*. When our journey ends, while we do not know *what* lies on the other side, we know for sure *who* is there—"For neither death nor life can separate us from the love of God which we see in Christ Jesus our Lord."
—*Coffin, W.S. (Adapted).*

CHRISTIAN LIVING

198

Do more than touch—Feel!
Do more than look—Observe!
Do more than read—Absorb!
Do more than hear—Listen!
Do more than listen—Understand!
Do more than exist—Live!

CHRISTIAN MINISTRY

199
A page from the diary of an unknown Christian:

> I've spent so many days when I haven't lived the kind of Christian life I'd like to, so last night when I said my prayers, I asked God to help me live a really Christian life today. This morning when I woke up, I thought of it again, but even before I got out of bed, the telephone rang. It was my next–door neighbor. She'd had a terrible toothache all night, and when she called the dentist this morning, he told her to come right down. She had just one slight problem: her little boy Billy was in bed with the measles. Of course I said that I'd be right over. So I gave Billy his breakfast and took care of him. There went my morning.

But I still had the rest of the day. As I was finishing up the lunch dishes at noon and thinking of what I could do in the afternoon that would really be of service to God, there was a knock at the door. It was a friend who has been in and out of a mental hospital for the last few years. She had a couple of dresses over her arm, and she asked if I would help her shorten them. I got out my pins and we went to work. The time passed quickly as we drank coffee and visited while we sewed. There went my afternoon.

It was supper time before I had a chance to think of my resolve again—to live today the kind of Christian life I've always wanted to live. As I peeled potatoes, I tried to think of some big, important thing I could do in the evening that would really be serving God. But before I could think of anything, my husband George came in the back door and said, "We're having company this evening! I met a fellow named Carl today who just moved into town—down the street a few blocks. He's had a lot of trouble finding a job because he has a prison record. He has excellent recommendations from the last place he worked—he'd worked there ten years since his time in prison, but he can't find anybody who'll take him on with his prison record. Automation tossed him out of his job. "I thought we could get acquainted with Carl and his wife tonight, and maybe I can find a place for him down at the plant. I hope it's o.k. with you that I invited them." "Sure," I said. "Sure, it's fine." They came, and I did enjoy the evening. George had phoned the man's former employer earlier in the day and was pleased with what he heard. I was glad when George offered him a job. But now it's bedtime. Another day has passed—another day in which I haven't lived the kind of Christian life I'd like to be living.

I want so much to serve you, God. But how can I with all these interruptions?

—Jurgensen, B., "You're Out of Date, God?" (Adapted).

200/CHRISTIAN MINISTRY

When the Rev. Sabine Baring–Gould, author of the hymn, "Onward Christian Soldiers," was pastor of the North Devon Church in England, he used to delight in taking visitors 'round the church and churchyard and pointing out to them the things of special interest.

He never failed to show them the tomb of a predecessor of his, of many years before, which was set just inside the churchyard wall. The tombstone had been erected by grateful members of the parish and it listed the ways in which the pastor had faithfully fulfilled his ministry of caring, loving service.

When Baring–Gould asked visitors if they noticed anything unusual about the stone, the more observant would remark, "Why, yes! There is no name on it! Who was he?"

"That's the point," said Baring–Gould. "Generations of school boys have sat on the bank above the stone, and their feet have

gradually worn away the inscription of the name on the top line. So, we don't know who he was, only what he did!"

People may not remember who we are, but if there is some piece of service, some word of encouragement, some deed of mercy that we have contributed to their lives, that is our true memorial.
—*"The Friendship Book."*

201/CHRISTIAN MINISTRY

What would happen if we all agreed to read one of the Gospels until we came to a place that told us to do something, then went out to do it, and only after we had done it began reading again? Why don't we do what Jesus says? How exciting life would become were we to begin living according to His way of life!

Friends would say we had "lost our minds."
Acquaintances would say we were "peculiar."
Those who dislike us would say we were "crazy."

But Someone Else, who had these same things said about Him, would smile. And the joy and peace in our own hearts would tell us who was right.

There are aspects of the Gospel that are puzzling and difficult to understand. But our problems are not centered around the things we don't understand. Our problems are centered around the things we do understand, the things we could not possibly misunderstand.

This, after all, is but an illustration of the fact that our problem is not so much that we don't know what we should do. We know perfectly well…but we don't want to do it!
—The Compact Treasury of Inspiration, "By Invitation of Jesus" (Adapted).

202/CHRISTIAN MINISTRY
Every week night between 11pm and 4am, Betty Baker comes down Broadway into Times Square driving her mobile canteen, handing out hot chocolate and granola bars to the girls she calls her "kids." Her "kids" are teenage prostitutes working the dangerous New York City streets. They call her "Ma."

Betty Baker came from Scotland in 1946 to a home in the coal fields of Kentucky. That experience softened her and hardened her: "Sweet as honey, tough as nails." Three years ago, Betty Baker, a major in the Salvation Army, chose to become a missionary in the asphalt jungle of Manhattan. Over the years, "Ma" Baker has become a link, however fragile, between her "kids" and a promised land which has failed to line up to its promises.

"Ma's" presence often is their only reminder that they are worth something to somebody, that somebody really cares.

Ma Baker never preaches to her "kids". And when a familiar face is no longer at the curbside she usually doesn't know whether the girl went up, down, or out. But, over the years, many of the girls, one at a time, have left Times Square after announcing, "Ma, I'm going home."

And so tonight, and any night, Major Betty Baker will load her mobile canteen in the Bowery. She'll head through the jungle of crack-cookers and dope dealers and hoods for hire. She'll move through the avenues of the most depraved and the most menacing until she gets to the most miserable of them all: her kids. The seedy girls in long stockings and short skirts, high heels and deep, shadowed eyes who have made a thousand compromises with their consciences. And there, with a cheery Scotch-Irish grin, Ma Baker will stand on the staircase between heaven and hell—serving.
—Harvey, P., Los Angeles Times, 1988 (Adapted).

When the scribes of the Pharisee party saw him eating with sinners and tax collectors, they said to His disciples, "Why does he eat with tax collectors and sinners?" When Jesus heard this He said to them, "It is not the healthy who need the doctor, but the sick. I did not come to call the virtuous, but sinners." (Mk. 2:16-17).

203/CHRISTIAN MINISTRY
Residents in an Argentine city set their watches by a clock that sits atop a pedestal in the downtown section. Lettered across each face of the four-sided clock is a reminder far more important than the time of day. It reads: "Es la Hora de Hacer El Bien." ("This is the hour to do good.")

204/CHRISTIAN MINISTRY
"All things are Mine...*Come*" (Matthew 11:26)
"All things are Mine...*Believe*" (John 3:35, 36)
"All things are Mine...*Go*" (Matthew 28:16-20)

205/CHRISTIAN MINISTRY

One afternoon in 1953, reporters and government officials gathered at a Chicago railroad station to await the arrival of the 1952 Nobel Peace Prize winner.

As he stepped off the train—a giant of a man, six-feet-four, with bushy hair and a large moustache—cameras flashed and the officials approached him with hands outstretched, telling him how honored they were to meet him. He thanked them, then, looking over their heads, asked if he might be excused for a moment. He walked through the crowd with quick steps until he reached the side of an elderly woman who was having trouble trying to carry two large suitcases.

He picked up the bags in his big hands and, smiling, escorted the woman to a bus. As he helped her aboard, he wished her a safe journey. Meanwhile, the crowd tagged along behind him. He turned to them and said, "Sorry to have kept you waiting."

The man was Dr. Albert Schweitzer, the famous missionary-doctor who had given his life helping the poorest of the poor in Africa.

Said one of the reporters, "That's the first time I ever saw a sermon walking."

206/CHRISTIAN MINISTRY

The Sandwich Man leaves his home in the Eltingville section of Staten Island, New York, at about 5:10 a.m. By 5:40 he is making his rounds of the card-board condos—the cartons and scraps of wood that are shelters for the homeless near City Hall.

He is carrying two shopping bags filled with sandwiches, and as the men and women spot him, they call out, "Hey, sandwich man!"

Within minutes, Mike Christiano has given each person two sandwiches, usually bologna or American cheese. Only then does Mike start his workday as an administrator for the city's Emergency Medical Service.

He says he started his sandwich service by accident. "I was a court officer in Brooklyn, and I used to see this guy on the street with a white beard and long white hair.

"One day, I said, 'Why don't you come in and clean up?' When he came out of the shower, he looked like he was ready for first Communion. I thought, If I can do that for him, I can do anything."

That was 15 years ago. Now, Mike and a group of volunteers make up to 200 sandwiches each week night.

Why does he do it? Ask Mike and he will answer, simply, and humbly, "I know God wants me to do *more*."

CHRISTIAN WITNESS

207
The celebration of the 250th anniversary of the founding of Harvard University was climaxed by a great parade through the streets of Cambridge, Massachusetts. The parade was led by the President of the University, followed by dignitaries from the Alumni, then the current Senior, Junior and Sophomore Classes. Finally, at the end of the parade, came members of the Freshman Class, carrying a large banner which read: HARVARD UNIVERSITY HAS WAITED 250 YEARS FOR US!

The world has been waiting countless years for YOU! The Church has been waiting 2000 years for YOU! Now is YOUR time to parade your ideals and hopes and dreams and creativity and FAITH down the streets of your earthly pilgrimage!

CHRISTIANITY

208/CHRISTIANITY

E. Stanley Jones once met a bright Russian actress. "I suppose you are a religious man?" she asked. "Yes," replied Jones, "I suppose I am." "Ah," she said, "you are religious because you are weak. You want someone to hold your hand. You want God to hold your hand." Jones, of course, strongly objected. He didn't want God to wipe the tears from his eyes; he wanted God to give him a handkerchief so he could wipe tears from other people's eyes. He did not want God to hold his hand; he wanted God to give him a strong arm with which he could reach down and lift up the fallen and the outcast. Seeing that she was off the track, the actress countered, "But you are an idealist?" "Yes," said Jones, "I suppose I am." And she waved him away in dismissal. "Good–bye, then, I am a realist," she said.

"That started me thinking," Jones said. "Am I a realist or just an idealist? Is Christianity a beautiful idea, or is it real? Does it work?"

209/CHRISTIANITY

Christianity does not offer *escape* from problems; it offers a life in which troubles are faced and *overcome.*

Christianity does not instill a desire to *abandon* the world; it instills a desire to *win* the world.

Christianity does not advocate one's *withdrawal* from life; it equips one to pursue a *better* life.

210/CHRISTIANITY

It has been said that there are three levels of life, each with its own predictable results. On the lowest level you repay good with evil. This is the *demonic* level. On the next level, you repay good with good and evil with evil. This is the *legalistic* level. On the highest level, you repay evil with good. This is the *Christian* level. The results are as follows:

If you repay good with evil then you become evil and eventually perish as an evildoer.
If you repay good with good and evil with evil, then you are an eye-for-an-eye and a tooth-for-a-tooth person. This means that your conduct is determined by what others do; that you have no moral code or standard of your own; that you are merely an echo. A modest example is the teenage girl whose mother always introduced her to new acquaintances and "my fifteen-year-old daughter." This upset the teenager and she asked her mother many times not to introduce her in this manner. But the mother couldn't seem to break the habit. One day, the daughter brought some new friends from school home with her. They were in the kitchen talking when the mother appeared. Whereupon the daughter said to her friends, "I want you to meet my fifty-year-old mother."

If you repay evil with good, it leads to your own life-enrichment and to the possible ennobling of the evildoer. And even if the evildoer is not redeemed, you have been spiritually enriched.

211/CHRISTIANITY

Syndicated newspaper columnist Sidney J. Harris tells the story of visiting a certain friend. Each night the friend would go to the same newsstand to buy a newspaper. And he always had a cheerful greeting for the newsdealer. He would say something like, "Nice to see you. You're looking good. How's business?" But the newsdealer's response was always curt, even sarcastic. After observing these encounters for several nights, Sydney Harris said to his Quaker friend, "You are always so *kind* to that fellow. How can you be so friendly toward him when he is so nasty to you?" To which the Quaker replied, "Why should I let *him* decide how I am going to act?"

212/CHRISTIANITY

In an ancient legend, two brothers in a village in Central Europe were caught stealing sheep. Their punishment for the crime was to have the letters "ST" branded on their foreheads. "ST": Sheep Thief! They were to carry that mark for the rest of their lives. For *one* of the brothers, life went from bad to worse. Some years later he died in jail. However, the *other* brother was deeply *repentant*. He found the Lord Jesus. He turned his life around. Not only did he grow in *self*-respect but also he became an extremely *caring* person and earned the respect of *others*. Years went by. A stranger came to the village. He noticed the "ST" on the man's forehead and asked one of the younger citizens what it meant. "I really don't know the details," the young citizen replied. "It happened many years ago. But I think the letters "ST' on his forehead are an abbreviation for the word *'Saint.'"*

CHRISTMAS

213
Once there lived a king who had power over all nations and peoples. His courts were of richest splendor; his tables were heavy with finest food. Music and laughter and gaiety floated from his castle. Clouds wrapped it in ethereal majesty. Peasants —in their valley of violence and hunger—stopped and looked at the castle for a long while, wishing they might know the king. But none were able to reach it.

In the cold of winter, the king's tailor entered the royal chambers with the latest additions to the king's wardrobe. He had selected the finest materials and woven them into the most beautiful garments that eyes had ever seen.

But the king was not pleased with what he saw, and he ordered his tailor out. "I'll make my own clothes," he said. The door to the throne room was shut and locked. Weeks passed. The royal court waited with keen anticipation to see what the king would make for himself. They knew they were bound to be blinded by the glory of it. Finally the awaited day arrived. The door opened and the king appeared.

Everyone, especially the tailor, gasped in surprise. His Majesty was dressed in the simplest, cheapest, most unkingly garments imaginable. He had the choice of the world's finest materials, but he had chosen to wear the clothes of a beggar.

He spoke quietly to them all: "I am going into the valley!"
—Daves, M. (Adapted).

214/CHRISTMAS

The only cards that really count
Are that extremely small amount
From *real* friends who keep in touch
Just because they *love* us much.

Some ways indeed are very *odd*
By which we hail the birth of God
We raise the *price* of things in shops
We give plain boxes *fancy* tops
And stuff which traders cannot sell
Thus parcel'd go extremely *well*

We dole out bribes we call a *present*
To those to whom we must be *pleasant*
The time draws *near* the birth of Christ
a present that *cannot* be priced
Given two thousand years ago
Yet if God had *not* given so
He still would be a distant *stranger*
And not the Christ-Child in the manger.
—Betjeman, J. (Adapted).

215/CHRISTMAS

The Sunday School teacher was telling her class about the birth of the Baby Jesus. When she came to the part about there being no room at the inn, one boy shot up his hand and said, "Well, I blame Joseph. He should have made a *reservation*!"

216/CHRISTMAS

We all associate mince pies with Christmas. But do you know why? Apparently in the 14th century mince pies were oval or cradle-shaped, like a manger, and often an image of the baby Jesus was outlined on the pastry. The filling was made with game, poultry, beef, eggs and spices. The pies were intended as reminders of the manger in which Jesus was born, and as they were eaten, people thought about the Holy Child.

Today some people make a silent wish when they take their first bite of a mince pie. It may sound a little superstitious, but that's okay if it helps to remind them not only of the origin of *mince pies*, but also the real meaning of *Christmas.*

217/CHRISTMAS

When the Puritans ruled the country, they strongly disapproved of setting aside *any* special day—except Sunday, "the Lord's Day". So they passed an act of Parliament to *cancel* Christmas 1652. To show they *meant* it, they decided that Parliament would convene on Christmas Day just as on any other day of the year. *Everything* was banned—from *mince-pies* to *Church* attendance.

Writer John Evelyn and his wife *defied* the ban and *went* to Church on Christmas Day. He recorded what happened: As they were receiving communion, a party of *musketeers* broke in. They waited till the service was over, then *arrested* the worshippers. However, they were soon let go because the authorities were unsure of how to punish people for going to Church.

No one is likely to try cancelling Christmas again, but for *many*, perhaps, the real Christmas already is cancelled. Perhaps the true *cause* for celebration already has been *forgotten.*

Rejoice and be merry in songs and in mirth!
O praise our *Redeemer*, all mortals on earth!
For this is the birthday of Jesus our *King*,
Who brought us *salvation*—His *praises* we'll sing.

Cancellation or renewal—which will it be? *Christ* at the center or *Visa/MasterCard?*

—Batchelor, M., "Mary Batchelor's Everyday Book." (Adapted).

218/CHRISTMAS

It was the day before Christmas and little Bobby was in his room trying to be good. He was being so quiet that his mother called into him, "Bobby, what are you doing in your room?" "Nothing," Bobby replied, "with you and God and Santa Claus *watching* me all the time, I can't do anything."

219/CHRISTMAS

A Christmas Thought

If there had never been a *Christmas*
  or the Holy Christ Child's *birth*,
Or the angels singing in the sky
  of promised *peace* on earth—
What would the world be *like* today
  with no *eternal* goal?
What would the temporal *body* be
  without a living *soul?*
What would give us courage
  to push on when hope is dead,
Except the *Christmas* message
  and the words our *Father* said:
"In *love* I send My only Son
  to live and die for *you*,
And through His resurrection
  you will gain a new life *too*."

—Rice, H.S.

220/CHRISTMAS

Last minute gifts that money can't buy:

Keep a promise!
Keep a secret!
Let someone have the last word!
Return a smile!
Share a dream!
Let someone in line—in front of you!

Listen to a child!
Listen to an adult!
Say something nice to someone you like!
Say something nice to someone you don't like!

221/CHRISTMAS

Just as stories with morals sometimes backfire, so do the attempts of teachers to instill ideas of charity and sacrifice for others in their students. One girl seemed remarkably enthusiastic when her teacher suggested she could share her toys with the less fortunate. "I'm going to give all my toys to the underprivileged children," she said. "Then my room will be clean and empty," she added, "and Santa Claus will have to bring me all *new* toys."

222/CHRISTMAS

It was near Christmas time when a child told his Sunday School teacher, "There are some poor kids next to us who have no daddy, no toys, and no Aunt Jane."

The teacher asked, "Wouldn't you like to give them something?"

"Yes," he said. "Let's give them Aunt Jane."

CHRISTMAS GIVING

223

Several years ago, a little Christmas story was published with the unusual title, "The Secret of Snootbaum." It began,

> Thirty-five years ago my eight-year-old brother John and I stood arguing loudly at the back of Woolworth's. We were on a Christmas shopping expedition, and I was convinced that I knew exactly what kind of gifts would please our mother.

We were arguing in front of a large display shelf filled with ugly plaster-of-paris poodle dogs that John had decided would be the perfect gift for Mom. They were grotesque. Each stood about two feet tall and came in a garish variety of colors: shocking pink, brilliant bluc, and flashy yellow. John had his heart set on a blue one. "I'm going to buy Mom one of those for Christmas," he said.

"She'll hate it," I stated flatly. "What in the world will she do with such an ugly thing?" Tact was not one of my strong points.

"She'll put it out where everyone can see it. She'll love it; I know she will."

"Ha," I snorted with ten-year-old wisdom. "She'll be ashamed to have it in the house."

"No, she won't," he argued. "She'll love it because I do."

Nothing I said made any difference, and he walked out of the store proudly carrying what to me was the most hideous gift possible. I was sure that Mom would make fun of the ugly poodle, and I thought that John had really made a fool of himself.

I can still remember the smile of delight on Mom's face when she unwrapped that ugly blue dog. I can still hear her tell John that it was exactly what she wanted for Christmas. I can still hear Dad chuckling and saying that "John sure has a knack for giving Christmas gifts."

Personally, I didn't understand it. No matter how you looked at that dog, it was ugly. Yet it was given the name Snootbaum and for years occupied a place of honor on the hearth of our fireplace.

It was 25 years later that I finally began to understand. My daughter Laura was seven at the time, a little girl who loved animals passionately—sheep, dogs, cows, goats, pigs, and horses. A large bag of plastic animals could occupy her for hours as she sat on the floor pushing them this way and that, weaving stories about them. That year she and her Dad went shopping for Christmas presents. What caught her eye for me was a six-inch statue of two pigs hugging each other. One's snout is cuddled on top of the other's, and their hooves are tucked cozily under their chins. A slogan on the base of the statue reads, "Ain't love grand?"

Indeed it is, Laura! Indeed it is! When I look at that small statue now, I don't see two silly pigs. I see a little girl who went shopping with her *heart*. The pig statue becomes more precious to me as the years go by because when I look at it, I remember a little girl who gave from her heart a gift that was really her. And I can remember a little boy saying, "*Mom will love it because I do.*"

Walt Whitman once said, "When I give, I give *myself*." It is a characteristic of children more than adults. In this Christmas season I want to remember that my gifts are more meaningful and more precious when I give of myself than when I give for the lavish display or to impress. A gift of the *heart* is what lasts in the memory. My brother John and my daughter Laura knew this at a young age. It took me a quarter of a century to unlock the "Secret of Snootbaum." But I finally understand!

—Pirtle, C., "Scope," Augsburg Publishing (1984)

CHURCH

224

Several years ago, while on tour in Russia, an American Bishop decided that he would attend as many Church services as he could. After one service, a young Russian girl approached the bishop and asked him to describe the Church in America. He replied by reciting a litany of optimistic statistics and projections on Church membership and financing.

Satisfied that his dissertation on the state of the Church in America was thorough, the Bishop was surprised at the young woman's response. With all sincerity she asked him, "But what *difference* does it make? What difference does it make to the *people*?"

What difference does it make if you measure the state of the Church in terms of *quantity* (How many members?) instead of *quality* (What difference does Church membership make in your *life-style*?).
—Bristol, L., "What Difference Does it Make." (Adapted).

"If we live by the Spirit, let us *walk* by the Spirit"(Gal. 5.25).

225/CHURCH

The preacher was more than ordinarily eloquent and everyone, but *everyone*, was moved to tears. Well, not everyone exactly, because there, in the front pew, sat a gentleman looking straight in front of him, apparently quite *unaffected* by the sermon.

At the end of the service, someone said to him, "You *heard* the sermon, didn't you?"

"Of course I did," said the stony gentleman. "I am not *deaf*." "What did you think of it?"

I thought it so moving I could have cried."

"And why, may I ask, did you *not* cry?"

"Because," said the gentleman, "I belong to another parish."
—deMello, A., "Taking Flight" (Adapted).

CHURCH-GOERS

226
First plant two rows of PEAS: Prayer and Perseverance.
Then plant two rows of Lettuce: Let us be faithful, and Let us follow Christ.
Then plant two rows of Turnips: Turn up for Church, and Turn up with a smile.
—*"The Friendship Book"*

227/CHURCH-GOERS
At a detention center in California one Sunday morning, a group of detainees were being shepherded to the Catholic and Protestant chapels. One young man did not enter either chapel, but continued walking toward the main gate. When a guard caught up with him and asked where he was going the man replied, "I was told I could go to the church of my choice, and the church of my choice is in New York."

228/CHURCH-GOERS
A married couple introduced themselves to their new pastor. "We thought we'd try your denomination," said the husband. "This is our fourth Church in three years," said the wife. "That's fine with me," said the pastor. "It doesn't do any harm to change the labels on empty bottles."

229/CHURCH-GOERS
"Guide To Ecclesiastical Birdwatching" is the title of a little book written by a pastor after he helped evict a sparrow that had managed to fly into church but couldn't find its way out. "I returned to my office," the author said, "to reflect on the theological significance of the event. Could it be that there are a number of funny birds fluttering around the premises?" Upon further reflection, he discovered there were at least 25 such birds. He described two of them as follows:

The Sickly Swallow: The Sickly Swallow is prevented from attending church by sniffles, sinus, sunburn, stings, suspicious spots, slivers, sprains, stress, sties, showers, sunshine, squalls, snow and other such sufferings.

His symptoms always appear on Sunday, are most acute early in the morning, and invariably abate shortly after noon. The bird may hasten the healing process by a ride in the country, a trip to the beach or a little work in the garden. By evening he usually feels well enough to go bowling or take in a movie.

During the course of the week, this bird's health improves until by Saturday he's as fine-fathered as they come, fairly bursting with health. But come Sunday morning, he suffers the usual relapse and wakes up with another one of those terrible sinus headaches.

The Late Loon: Although it has not yet been established scientifically, it is conjectured that the Late Loon is allergic to invocations. He always arrives at church after the morning service has started, usually during the Old Testament Scripture lesson, but sometimes after the offering.

At weddings he arrives just in time for the kiss and the reception. At committee meetings he shows up in time to bring up a matter that has already been discussed and voted upon. The Late Loon and his family come to potluck suppers when everyone else is already eating dessert, so they must perch along and eat the food that they, themselves, have brought.

Because the Late Loon was late at his own wedding, the fledglings that bunch in the balcony are already taking bets that he'll be late for his own funeral.
—Koopman, L., "Guide To Ecclesiastical Birdwatching."

CIVILIZATION

230
When I was stationed on Midway Island, the Pacific "Island Paradise," 1700 sailors, dependents, civil-service workers and

contract employees lived free from worry in the harmony of an especially close-knit community. We had no automobiles, no traffic jams, no pollution and no crime. Our children loved school, where the average student-teacher ratio was 15 to 1. The teenagers tried to find ways to contribute to the community, rather than seeing what they could get away with. Good health was in abundance. Everyone over three years of age rode bicycles for transportation. We had 300 or more beautiful, sunny days a year.

Yet, when the Navy ordered a major cutback on the island in 1978 and we had to come back to the mainland, people would invariably comment, "Gee, I'll bet you're glad to be back in *civilization.*"
—Meador, L.K. (Adapted).

COMPASSION

231
Helen Keller early in her life, lost the ability to see, hear or speak. She was less than two years old when she was stricken with the disease that left her in this disabled condition. And yet, through the help of Anne Sullivan, her teacher at the Perkins Institute for the Blind, she became one of the most sensitive, most alert, most aware persons in contemporary life.

Before Helen Keller was born, in a mental institution just outside of Boston, Mass., a young girl known as "Little Annie" was locked in the building's "dungeon." Doctors felt that the "dungeon" was the only place for those who were "hopelessly" insane, and in Little Annie's case, they saw no hope.

There was an elderly nurse working in the institution who was nearing retirement. This nurse believed that there was hope for all God's creatures and so she started taking her lunch into the dungeon and eating outside of Little Annie's cage. She felt that she should try to communicate some love to the little girl, and perhaps give her some hope.

At times, Little Annie had bouts of violence. At other times she seemed to ignore the whole world. One day, the elderly nurse brought some brownies to the dungeon and left them outside of Little Annie's cage. When she returned, the brownies were gone. From then on, whenever she visited Little Annie's cage, the nurse would leave her some brownies. Soon, the doctors noticed that a change was taking place in Little Annic and, after a time, they decided to move her upstairs. Finally, Little Annie, the "hopeless case," was permitted to return to her home. But the institution had meant so much to her that she soon returned. She felt that she could use her own experience to be of some help to the other patients.

Many years later, England's Queen Victoria presented Helen Keller with the highest award bestowed upon a foreigner. When asked how she accounted for her remarkable accomplishments in life, Helen Keller responded without hesitation: "Had it not been for my nurse, Anne Sullivan, the name of Helen Keller would have remained unknown."

Little Annie, the girl in the dungeon, had grown up to be nurse Anne Sullivan. To nurse Anne Sullivan, Helen Keller was one of God's very special persons. She loved her and disciplined her and taught her and worked with her and prayed for her until the flickering candle that was Helen Keller's life became a beacon that helped light up other people's lives. Helen Keller influenced and encouraged and inspired millions. After her own life had been touched by "Little Annie."

232/COMPASSION

Jeff Wheelwright, a part–time volunteer serving meals to the homeless, reflects on his daily journey to work in New York City:

In the morning, coming back into Grand Central Terminal on my way to work, I watch my people moving aimlessly among the streams of commuters. I pick out the familiar faces, the lost expressions.

You know, you could do that too—pick out a familiar face, make a one-way connection to a fellow human. It's simple. Just break stride long enough to identify a homeless person. You don't have to address the one you choose, or hand him money. Just remember him. Will he be in the same spot the next morning? Look around for him. If you miss him for a day or two, you'll wonder whether he's all right. When you see him again, be glad. Think kindly; say a prayer for him. Give him a window into your heart.
—*"New York Times"*

COMMERCIALISM

233
Little Johnny was crying bitterly at the far end of the shopping mall. Quickly, his sobs drew a small crowd. An elderly woman stepped from the crowd and asked, "Are you lost, little boy?" The little fellow looked all around at the crowd that had gathered, stopped his sobbing and said, "Yes, ma'am, I'm *lost.*" Then, raising his voice, he said, "Will somebody please take me to the men's store at the south end of the mall where my wonderful father has just got in his winter stock of spring overcoats, suits, neckties, shirts, hats and raincoats which he will sell cheaper than anyone else in the mall!"

COMMITMENT

234

A centipede was happy quite,
Until a frog in fun
Said, "Pray, which leg comes after which?"
This raised her mind to such a pitch,
She lay distracted in the ditch,
Considering how to run.

Don't be like the theoretical centipede in your response to Jesus' call. Don't try to analyze in your *head.* Rather, receive it in your *heart*—and start *following*!

Before taking her first steps, a baby bear asked the mother bear "Do I move my front foot left first or my right front foot? Or do I put both front feet out together and then both my back feet? Or do I move my two right feet first and then the two on the other side?" The mother bear said to her cub, simply, "Leave off the *thinking* and start *walking*!"

COMMUNICATION

235

An elderly couple was celebrating their fiftieth wedding anniversary. Their children, grandchildren, and great-grandchildren, as well as the townspeople, really rose to the occasion and recognized them in every conceivable way. The mayor gave them the key to the small town; there was a brunch at the country club; an afternoon tea; a banquet that evening, and all the townsfolk as well as all the kinfolk came by to offer their congratulations. Finally, at about ten o'clock that evening, the public celebration was over. As was his custom, the husband headed for the kitchen to prepare the buttered toast with jam and the small glass of milk which he and his wife always enjoyed just before retiring.

Perhaps it was due to exhaustion from the long day, but when the husband called his wife into the kitchen for their little snack, she broke into tears. Concerned, the husband rose, walked around the table, embraced his wife, and asked her what the problem was. Teary-eyed, she said: "For all the years we've been married, every night when we had our snack you gave me the end piece of bread—and I never complained. But on this very special night I thought you would be gallant enough to offer me the best piece instead of the heel." The husband was shocked. "Why, sweetheart," he said, "I thought you understood that the end piece is my favorite part of the loaf. All these years I thought I was giving you the best piece!"

236/COMMUNICATION

A women went to her pastor for counseling concerning her marriage. After a few preliminaries, the pastor said he had a few questions that would help identify the problems. "Please answer the questions as openly as possible," he said. When the woman agreed, the pastor began the questioning. "Do you have any grounds?" To which the lady responded, "Why, yes we do, we have about ten acres just north of town." "No, ma'am," the pastor replied, "that's not what I mean. What I mean is do you have...well, do you have a grudge?" "Oh no," she replied, "but we do have a nice little carport!" "No, ma'am," said the pastor, "that's not what I mean. One more question: does your husband beat you up?" "Beat me up? Oh no, I get up before he does just about every morning!" Completely frustrated, the pastor then said, "Lady, you're not listening to me. Just tell me why you are having trouble with your husband!" "Well," she said, "the man just doesn't know how to communicate!"

237/COMMUNICATION

An out-of-work man knocked on the door of a house in an affluent suburb. "Mister," he said when the homeowner answered, "I'm down on my luck, and I need some money for food. But I'm not asking for a handout. I'm willing to work for it. Do you have any odd jobs I could do for you?"

"Well, let's see," the man said. "I do have a porch at the side of the house that needs painting. Can you do that?"

"Sure," the man said. "I can paint."

"Okay, fine," the homeowner said. He went away and returned in a few minutes with a pail of yellow paint and a large brush. "Here," he said, "when you're finished painting the porch, I'll give you $20."

"It's a deal," the man said. Then he went around to the side of the house with the paint. In fifteen minutes, he was back knocking at the front door again.

"What," the homeowner said, "finished already?"

"Oh, sure," the worker said. "It was easy."

"Well," the man said, handing him a twenty-dollar bill, "here's your money. I'm really amazed. I never knew anyone who could paint a porch in fifteen minutes."

"It wasn't hard," the hobo said. "And by the way, it isn't a *Porsche.* It's a *Mercedes!*"
—*"Sales Upbeat" (Adapted).*

238/COMMUNICATION
A woman was driving home from an optometrist's office wearing contact lenses for the first time. As she tried to adjust her eyes to the new lenses, she drove through a red light. Whereupon a policeman ordered her to "pull over." The officer asked to see her driver's license. "Aha," he said, "your license says that you must wear *eyeglasses* while driving. Where are your eyeglasses?" The woman said, "I have *contacts.*" To which the policeman firmly replied, "Lady, I don't care who your *connections* are, I'm still giving you a ticket."

239/COMMUNICATION
The keynote speaker at a sales convention was introduced as "The most gifted business man in the country...a self-made man who has earned one hundred million dollars in California oil." As the keynote speaker arrived at the podium, he appeared a bit shaken. "The facts as reported are essentially *correct,*" he said, "but I feel compelled to state that it wasn't *oil*...it was *coal*; and it wasn't *California*, it was *Pennsylvania*; and just to keep the record straight, it wasn't one hundred *million*, it was one hundred *thousand*, and it wasn't *me*, it was my *brother*, and he didn't *make* it, he *lost* it!

240/COMMUNICATION
During the last days of the Christmas rush a frenzied clerk, overwhelmed by the last-minute shoppers, was making out a sales slip. As the customer gave her name and address, the clerk, surveying the maze of confusion about her, remarked, "It's a madhouse, isn't it?" "No," the customer replied frostily. "It's a private residence."
—*Goodyear, L.*

241/COMMUNICATION

The great classical composer, Igor Stravinsky, wrote his "Ebony Concerto" expressly for the "Woody Herman Herd," one of the swingingest jazz bands ever. At rehearsals, difficulties in communication arose between Stravinsky and the jazzmen.

One day he said to the band, "I want a sudden *sforzando* followed by a *subito decrescendo."* He got blank stares.

Whereupon, Woody Herman called in his longtime arranger, Neal Hefti. "Maestro," Hefti said to Stravinsky, "tell me exactly what you want and I'll try to get it across to the boys. "I want a *sudden sforzando* followed by a *subito decrescendo,"* Stravinsky repeated.

"Gotcha," Hefti said. With that he turned to the musicians and said, "*Bend* it, boys!"

—Previn, A., quoted by Don Freeman in San Diego Union

242/COMMUNICATION

Matthew, a 3 1/2-year-old boy, was eating an apple in the back seat of the car, when he asked, "Daddy, why is my apple turning brown?"

"Because," his father explained, "after you ate the skin off, the meat of the apple came into contact with the air which caused it to oxidize thus changing its molecular structure and turning it into a different color." There was a long silence. Then Matthew asked softly, "Daddy, are you talking to me?"

—Cooke, S.

COMMUNISM

243

Former President, Ronald Reagan, often repeated this joke about Communism:

> An elderly woman entered the Kremlin and insisted on seeing the General Secretary. Mikhail Gorbachev agreed to meet her and asked, "What can I do for you?"

"I have one question," she said. "Was Communism invented by a politician or a scientist?"

"A politician," he said.

"That explains it," the woman replied. "A *scientist* would have tried it on *mice* first."

COMMUNITY

244
In a little town in Central Europe, "Jacob the Tailor" felt that he had been mistreated in the synagogue. And so he withdrew from the community and isolated himself from his friends and neighbors. Weeks went by until, finally, the Rabbi called on him. After a polite greeting, there was a heavy silence. Then the Rabbi said, "Let's sit in front of the fire." So the two men sat in complete silence. An hour or so later the Rabbi picked up the fireplace tongs, pulled out a coal and placed it on the hearth, *away* from the fire. Still no word was spoken. The two men just sat and watched the glowing, burning piece of coal become darker and darker until finally it was black and cold and dusty with ashes. A few moments later, Jacob the Tailor spoke. "I *understand*," he said. "I'll come *back* to the synagogue." Not a word had been spoken, but the point had been made: we withdraw from the community, we isolate ourselves from our neighbor, and we *die*. We *need* one another.

245/COMMUNITY
Bach's Christmas cantata, *For Us a Child Is Born*, is an example of the liturgical progression of Advent-leading-to-Christmas. The opening chorus of the cantata is set as a flurry of *rumors*, or spreading *gossip*, rather than a formal announcement. It is followed by the bass aria responding with words reminiscent of Advent's meaning: "In the darkness I am lost; for I know not how to find what I search for, what I long for..." The cantata follows this pattern of proclamation/response until the final chorus, which is a grandiose statement of *praise*: "Alleluia!" We

praise God because through Christmas our humanity is salvaged from the *wreck* we have made of our potential.

Moreover, we are not saved for a *solitary* existence; rather, we are brought into a new *community*, to live in communion with others who also receive the love and grace of Christmas. The long story of God's interaction with people is that the *new* humanity has always turned isolating *individualism* into *community*. We are given new life as part of the *whole* "People of God."
—Grant, J.E., "Advent Calls Us to a New Humanity."

246/COMMUNITY
Social scientists are asking us to take notice that as our technological resources *increase*, our sense of community *decreases*:

> Until fairly recently, it took considerable effort of *will* to interact with fellow humans, scattered as they were in extended rural areas. But an intimate sense of community nevertheless existed; and although "isolated" in the *modern* sense, these communities reflected man's need for *direct* human contact. The appearance of the telephone allowed *faster* communication, but the effort to meet face to face at the church or the general store began to wither—and with it the sense of *community*.
>
> A great paradox of our time is that while technology offers us instant *communication*, we use it to *isolate* ourselves from each other. We face a world without insight into the *social* nature of man.

—Shneour, E.A., "Isolation In A Communication Society" (Adapted).

COMPASSION

247
The great Japanese Christian, Kagawa, tells how a Christian missionary helped him to understand the love of God. While Kagawa was spending a sick period alone during his student

days, a man knocked at the door. He requested the visitor not to enter. "Do not come in! I have a contagious disease." But the missionary entered, and went to Kagawa's side and said: "I have something more contagious than disease. I have come with the love of God."

248/COMPASSION

The nurse escorted a tired, anxious young man to the bedside of an elderly man. "Your son is here," she whispered to the patient. She had to repeat the words several times before the patient's eyes opened. He was heavily sedated and he dimly saw the figure of the young man standing beside his bed. He reached out his hand and the young man tightly wrapped his fingers around it, squeezing a message of encouragement. The nurse brought a chair next to the bedside. All through the night the young man sat holding the old man's hand and offering gentle words of hope. The dying man said nothing. As dawn approached, the patient died. The young man gently placed on the bed the lifeless hand he had been holding. Then he went to notify the nurse. The nurse began to offer words of *sympathy* to the young man. But he interrupted her. "Who *was* that man?" he asked. The startled nurse replied, "I thought he was your *father*." "No, he was *not* my father," he answered. "I never saw him before in my *life*." "Then why didn't you say something when I took you to him?" asked the nurse. He replied, "I sensed that he really *needed* his son, and that his son just wasn't *here*. Then I realized he was too sick to tell whether or not *I* was his son—and I knew how much he needed *me*."

249/COMPASSION

Mayor Fiorello LaGuardia of New York City was one of America's most colorful public figures. He was famous for donning his fire hat and riding to fires on the big "hook-and-ladder" fire trucks; for joining police vice-squads conducting raids on dens of iniquity; for taking entire orphanage populations on excursions to big league baseball games. During a newspaper strike, "The Little Flower," as he was affectionately called, went on the radio and read the Sunday Comics to the children of the city.

Once, he showed up at "Night Court" and dismissed the presiding magistrate for the evening. Then, as was a mayor's prerogative in those days, he took over the bench himself. On that bitter cold night, a pitiful, shivering, old woman was brought before him to answer the charge of stealing a loaf of bread. LaGuardia asked the woman if she had anything to say. She told him that her family had been in dire straits for weeks: her sick daughter's husband had deserted her and their four children; the daughter was penniless and the children were without food; they were in a hopeless situation. Hearing this, LaGuardia asked the shopkeeper who had accused the woman if he would withdraw the charge. The shopkeeper refused. "It's a bad neighborhood," he said. "She's got to be punished to teach other people around here a lesson." The mayor said to the woman, "I'm afraid I must punish you. The law is the law, and there are no exceptions. I hereby sentence you to a ten dollar fine or ten days in jail. As he spoke, the mayor reached into his pocket, withdrew a bill and tossed it into his famous wide-brimmed hat which he always wore in public. Then he said:

Here's the ten dollar fine which I now remit; and furthermore I'm going to fine everyone in this courtroom fifty cents for living in a town where a person has to steal bread so that her grandchildren can eat. Mr. Bailiff, collect the fines and give them to the defendant.

Next day, the newspapers ran the story of $47.50 being turned over to an ill–clad, hungry grandmother who had stolen bread to feed her starving grandchildren and her sick daughter. The total had been collected from some seventy persons in court that night waiting to answer charges of petty crime and traffic violations, and a handful of police officers. It was further reported that the police officers gave their mayor a standing ovation.

250/COMPASSION

A beautiful insight into the true nature of Christian Evangelism is contained in the following true–life episode recounted by a man whose life is dedicated to helping the handicapped...

The other day I was with a friend. We were going into a church where an old lady was sitting at the door begging. We did not have any money with us. My friend got down on her knees in front of the old lady, looked directly into her eyes and said: "I am sorry but I do not have any money." But she said this with such tenderness that the eyes of the old lady lit up as if for the first time someone had really looked at her, seen her. We went into the church and prayed with her. On the way out she looked gently and gratefully at my friend, for she had just lived a moment of deep joy. It is good to give a check for the poor whom we do not know. It is even better to touch the wounded person who is close to us, saying by our gestures and facial expressions: I am concerned about you. I want you to live!

251/COMPASSION

During World War II, an American warship in the Pacific was transporting some wounded Japanese prisoners. The medical officer in charge took such excellent care of the prisoners that his fellow–officers protested. One of them said, "Why don't you just let them die the way they let our men die?" The medical officer replied, "I don't play by their rules. I am a Christian. The Japanese war lords tell their soldiers that all Americans are beasts. One day, these prisoners will return to their country knowing they had been lied to. They will be able to say that they were treated with compassion by persons who cared for them as human beings. I'm going to do my best to replace the hatred in their hearts with the love of Christ. That's the only way we're going to ever have peace in this world."

252/COMPASSION

A young lad arrived home from school much later than usual. His anxious mother asked him where he had been. The boy replied, "On my way home I saw a little girl crying because a wheel had come off her tricycle. I stopped to try to help her." "But, my dear, you couldn't fix your own bike when a wheel came off. How could you help that little girl?" To which the boy replied, "Well, I couldn't fix her trike, but I could help her cry."

COMPETITION

253

A bright, young pre-med sophomore at Stanford University was rewarded by his parents for having done so well in school. They gave him a trip to the Far East for the summer vacation between his sophomore and junior years. While there he met a guru who said to him, "Don't you see how you are poisoning your soul with this success-oriented way of life? Your idea of happiness is to stay up all night studying for an exam so you can get a better grade than your best friend. Your idea of a good marriage is not to find the woman who will make you whole, but to win the girl that everyone else wants. That's not how people are supposed to live. Give it up; come join us in an atmosphere where we all share and love each other." The young man had completed four years at a competitive high school to get into Stanford, plus two years of pre-med courses at the University. He was ripe for this sort of approach. He called his parents from Tokyo and told them he would not be coming home. He was dropping out of school to live in an ashram.

Six months later, his parents got a letter from him: "Dear Mom and Dad, I know you weren't happy with the decision I made last summer, but I want to tell you how happy it has made me. For the first time in my life, I am at peace. Here there is no competing, no hustling, no trying to get ahead of anyone else. Here we are all equal, and we all share. This way of life is so much in harmony with the inner essence of my soul that in only six months I've become the number two disciple in the entire ashram – *and I think I can be number one by June*!"
—Kushner, H. "Who Needs God" (Adapted).

CONCEIT

254
During the Civil War, Lincoln attended the funeral of an Army General. The man had been talented, but extremely *vain* and *conceited*. Lincoln looked around at the very large turnout, then remarked to a friend: "If the General had known how *big* a funeral he would have, he would have died years ago."

CONSEQUENCES

255
A pig ate his fill of acorns under an oak tree and then started to dig around the tree. A crow remarked, "You should not do this. If you lay bare the roots, the tree will wither and die." "Let it die," said the pig. "Who cares, as long as there are acorns?"

CONTENTMENT

256
Once upon a time there was a stonecutter. Each day he went up to the mountains to cut stones. And while he worked, he sang. Though he was a poor man, he desired no more than he had, so he had not a care in the world.

One day he was called to work on the mansion of a nobleman. When he saw the magnificence of the mansion, he experienced the pain of desire for the first time in his life and he said with a sigh, "If only I were rich! Then I would not have to earn my living in sweat and toil as I do now." Imagine his astonishment when he heard a voice say, "Your wish has been granted. Henceforth, anything you desire will be given to you." He did not know what to make of the words until he returned to his hut that evening and found in its place a mansion as magnificent as the one he had been working on. So the stonecutter gave up cutting stones and began to enjoy the life of the rich.

One day, when the afternoon was hot and humid, he happened to look out his window and saw the King go by. He thought, "How I wish I were a King myself, sitting in the cool of the royal carriage!" His wish was promptly carried out and he found himself reclining in the comfort of the royal carriage. But the carriage turned out to be warmer than he had expected it to be. He began to marvel at the power of the sun, whose heat could penetrate even the thick walls of the carriage. "I wish I were the sun," he said to himself. Once again his wish was granted, and he found himself sending out waves of heat into the universe.

All went well for a while. Then, on a rainy day, he tried to pierce through a thick bank of clouds and could not. So he got himself changed into a cloud, and rejoiced in his power to block out the sun. But when he turned into rain, he became annoyed because a mighty rock blocked his path and he had to flow around it. "What?" he cried. "A rock more powerful than I? Well than, I wish to be a rock." As he began to rejoice in his fine new figure, he heard some strange clipping sounds coming from below. He looked down and saw a tiny human being cutting chunks of stone from his feet. "What?" he shouted. "A puny creature like that more powerful than a mighty rock like me? I want to be a man!" So he found he was once again a stonecutter going up into the mountain to cut stone, earning his living with sweat and toil, but with a song in his heart because he was content to be what he was created to be and to live by what had been given to him.

Moral: Nothing is as good as it seems before we get it.
—deMello, A., "The Heart of the Enlightened" (Adapted).

CONVICTION

257
Deborah, a beautiful 38-year-old former model and mother of two teenage boys was dying of cancer. She already had undergone surgery, but some of the cancer either had evaded the

scalpel or had grown anew in the area where chest, neck and arm meet. Because the woman was in an extremely weakened condition, the surgeon called in a consulting physician to help in determining whether or not Deborah would be able to withstand further surgery.

After examining the woman, the consulting physician told her that he was going to recommend *against* the surgery. "You don't think I'm strong enough to survive it?" she asked. The doctor replied: "In my professional opinion, weighing your condition against the risk of the surgery, and the potential benefits..." Then he broke off his response. He was unable to finish telling the woman that he could see no hope for her. But Deborah had other ideas. "I want you to *change* your recommendation," she said. Then she pointed to a silver goblet standing on the night table. "My father gave me this cup when I was a little girl," she explained. "Read the inscription." The doctor read the inscription aloud—a phrase from the 23rd Psalm: "My cup runneth over." Then Deborah said:

> My father told me that the cup of life is never half-empty or half-full; it's always overflowing with possibility. He said that it didn't matter what terrible things were happening; if I had conviction, if I believed in myself, my cup would never run dry; my cup would always be a source of life, inspiration, strength, love and everything else I could possibly need.

Then Deborah took hold of the water pitcher on the night table and poured water into the cup until it flowed over the brim and splashed on the table top. She said, "My cup runneth over with *conviction*. It will *never* run dry. I will *have* the surgery and somehow I will *survive*, and I will live to see my two boys become men. You doctors take care of my body. *God* and I will take care of the rest."

Deborah *had* surgery, and she *did* survive, and she *lived* to see her two boys become men. Was her survival a "statistical quirk?" or "spontaneous remission?" or "a tribute to the genius

of the surgeon?" asks the consulting physician. "Perhaps," he replies. "I've seen enough patients to know, however, that the ones who are convinced that their cups run *over* do better than those who see their cups running *dry.*"
—Fox, A., M.D. "Making Miracles." (Adapted).

COOPERATION

258
An organist was performing a concert on an antique organ. The bellows were hand-pumped by a boy who was behind a screen, unseen by the audience. The first part of the performance was well received. The audience was thrilled by the organist's ability at the keyboard of that old instrument. After accepting the applause and taking his bows, the musician walked off-stage triumphantly. As he was passing the boy behind the screen he heard him say, "We played well, didn't we?" To which the organist replied, "What do you mean, '*we*'?"After intermission, the organist again seated himself at the console and began to play. But nothing came out. Not a *sound!* Then the organist heard a voice from behind the screen say, "Now do you know what '*we*' means?"

CORRECTION

259
A young American teacher once was invited into the cockpit of a 747 bound for Hawaii. There he saw a little black box. "This little black box," the pilot explained, "is a computer which we call *Fred.* Every time the 747 goes off course, Fred, who serves as the navigator, tells us how many degrees the plane is off course. Fred then communicates this information to another computer called *George* who steers. Every time Fred communicates a necessary *correction* in course, George adjusts the plane's steering in the *right* direction."

The pilot pointed out that the 747 is "off-course" about 90 per cent of the time, during the 5 1/2 hour flight to Hawaii. And every few seconds something like this conversation occurs:

Fred says, "Hey, George, we're 10 degrees starboard off course. *Correct.*" George responds, "Thank you, Fred. Will do." George corrects. Then Fred says, "We're five degrees port off course. *Correct.*" George responds, "Thank you, Fred. Will do!"

Imagine how their conversation would go if Fred and George were *human beings.* It would not take long for George to say something like, "Darn it, Fred, why don't you shut your big mouth and quit telling me what to do. Yap, yap, yap. Always *correcting* me. Always telling me what to *do.*"
—Fields, R., "Chop Wood, Carry Water." (Adapted).

COURAGE

260
Jason Ellison, a 15 year-old who suffers from progeria, an extremely rare disease which greatly accelerates the aging process, wrote the following in a school essay:

> "When I look in the mirror, I see a person like no other around me. I see someone who is bald, has a crooked nose, no front teeth, no eyebrows, no eyelashes and pointed ears. Someone who has bent legs and a very tiny body for his age…
>
> "I want people to look at me and see past my looks and see who I *really* am. Not a freak but a *wonderful* human being who loves life and his fellow man. I think this is who I am. Although my looks are so different, I did not choose to look the way I do or to have a life that could be over tomorrow. I am just here to love *life.*"

At age 15, Jason has already lived beyond the average life expectancy of a progeria patient, who usually dies from congestive heart failure or stroke by age 13. Jason is four feet tall and weighs just 41 pounds. The "Future Leaders of Idaho" awarded Jason a trophy for being their number one salesman. Selling candy, teas and tablecloths on weekends at area shopping centers, Jason's rapid-fire sales approach was hard to resist.

Once, at dinner, Jason asked his mother and stepfather what they were going to do with him when he died. Then he blurted, "Why can't you just bury me out back by the apple trees so I can be near you guys?" Jason will have to live another 13 years to be the oldest progerian on record. He says, "I think there's an *afterlife*, and maybe you don't have any *body* to cart around. It's a *better* place to be."

—*"Who I Really Am," Life Magazine, October 1989 (Adapted).*

261/COURAGE

On the first day of school, the teacher was asking each of the 1st–graders to tell his name and what he wanted to be when he grew up. One little boy spoke up importantly: "I'm Jimmy. When I grow up I'm gonna be a lion tamer. I'll have lots of fierce lions and tigers, and I'll walk into the cage." He hesitated, then went on: "But I'll want my mother with me."

—*"Christian Observer"*

262/COURAGE

Professional football players often become highly emotional on the playing field, and they often respond with "colorful" language when penalized by a game official for an infraction. Art Holst, a veteran National Football League referee, remembers the Sunday when a Kansas City Chiefs end named Fred Arbanas was tackled so hard that his artificial eye popped out. The whistle was blown and, after a brief search, the missing eye was found, and Arbanas popped it back into place, declined the coach's offer to send in a substitute and was eager and ready to resume play. Whereupon Referee Holst said to Arbanas, playfully, "I'm impressed with your *courage*. But what would you do if you lost the *other* eye?" "That's easy," snapped Arbanas, "I'd become a *referee*!"

CREATION

263
A little girl had worked hard all week long on her project for science class. She was determined to finish on Friday so she could bring the masterpiece home to her mom. As the girl was greeted at the door by her mother she said, "I'm sorry I'm late, Mom. We were working on our science display, and I had to stay to finish the *Universe.*"

264/CREATION
A reporter wired his editor with news of a major, exclusive story. The editor replied, "Send six-hundred words."

The reporter wired back, "Too important, can't be told in less than twelve-hundred words."

The editor responded, "Story of creation of world told in six-hundred words. Try it!"

CREATOR

265
Many years ago, in France, a famous astronomer concluded a lecture, saying, "I have swept the universe with my telescope, and I find no God." Whereupon, a famous musician replied from the audience: "That statement is as unreasonable as for me to say, 'I have taken this violin apart. I have examined each piece with a microscope, and I find no music.'"

CRITICISM

266
There is an old story of a woman who made artificial fruits so perfectly that people could not tell them from the real fruit. But she had some critics who would find fault with the shape of the fruit, the color, and other things. One day as the critics

stood before a table on which she had placed several pieces of fruit, they criticized one particular apple. "It looked too artificial," they said. When they had finished, the woman picked up the apple, cut it in half, and began to eat it. It was a real apple.

CROSS OF CHRIST

267

On the bottom of the swimming pool in the YMCA at Monmouth, Illinois, the builders placed a beautiful tile emblem symbolic of the spiritual, mental, and physical nature of man. At the center of the emblem is the Bible, opened at John 17:21. When a boy could not make out the wording, he swam to the bottom and read it. "It says John 17:21, but what is that?" he asked the lifeguard. "That they all may be one," the lifeguard answered. The boy's reply was prophetic: "You sure have to go through a lot to find that out." We need only to look at the Cross of Christ for absolute confirmation of that reality.

268/CROSS OF CHRIST

There was a woman whose husband loved her very much, and during her convalescence from a severe illness he carried her from room to room. On sunny days he would carry her onto the porch or out into the garden. He waited on her constantly. One day, the physician told him, "If you keep this up, she will never walk again. She likes being carried, and she will never even try to walk."

The husband saw the point, so when he went home that night he watched as she walked tremblingly and stumblingly. He even let her fall and painfully pick herself up. It would have been so easy to rush to her side and keep her from falling. That is what we want God to do. We blame Him when we fall, and we blame Him for not rushing to our sides to pick us up and take away all the pain. No one can ever imagine what it cost God to refrain from intervention as His own beloved Son was put to death. But God's holding back was not weakness. The Cross of Christ became the power of God unto salvation.
—Allen, C.L., "Joyful Living"

269/CROSS OF CHRIST

Once, when the famous missionary, Dr. David Livingstone, was in Africa, he wrote home to England requesting more workers. In reply, he received this message: "We would like to send more workers to you, but they first want to know if there is a good road into your outpost." To which Dr. Livingstone is said to have replied: "If you are offering to send workers who will come only if the road is easy, I can't use them. I need workers who are ready to pick up their crosses and follow Christ. The road to Calvary was far from easy."

270/CROSS OF CHRIST

In George Bernard Shaw's play about Joan of Arc, when Joan is about to be burned at the stake, she turns to those in authority who have condemned her and says: "I will go out now to the *common* people and let the love in their eyes comfort me for the hate in yours. You will be glad to see me burned. But as I *go* through the fire, I shall go through it to their hearts, forever and ever." Exactly! That's *exactly* what the great God Almighty has done through the Crucifixion! He has come through it to *our* hearts, forever and *ever*, to bring us from death to *life*. Of that we are *convinced!*

271/CROSS OF CHRIST

The Wounded Christ is looking down upon us with *death* in His bleeding hands and feet, but *life* in the light of His burning eyes.

> The Wounded Christ is demanding from us all—every individual man and woman—a *choice*—love or indifference.
>
> The Wounded Christ will not let us alone; He will *not* go away!
>
> The Wounded Christ is going to drive us to a *decision*.
>
> The Wounded Christ will not let us have His world for a *playground* or a *battlefield*.

The Wounded Christ is going to insist that we *tend* it for him, or else there will be *darkness* over all the earth from the sixth hour to the ninth—and that may be a *thousand years*.

CRUCIFIXION

272

A well–known preacher was invited to deliver a sermon in the chapel of a college for the deaf. He described it as a "Preacher's paradise, because you get two laughs for every joke: when you reach the punch line one laugh comes from those who can hear, and a few seconds later, when the sign language interpreter catches up, you get a second laugh." He said he noticed that on several occasions during the sermon the sign language interpreter, in a very graceful way, would point to the palms of her hands. Later he learned that pointing to the palms of the hands is the sign for Jesus Christ. How appropriate! Of all the signs that might have been chosen for Jesus, they chose the nailprints to symbolize who He was.

The New Testament writers take the same approach, saying to us that somehow the Crucifixion sums it all up. If you really want to get close to Jesus, if you really want to know who He was and what He was doing, you do it through the Crucifixion.

D

DEATH

273
A parable for the bereaved:

> Before you came into this world you were an unborn baby. We all were. Well, in going from this world into another one we are still unborn babies so far as that other world in concerned.
>
> Now a baby not yet born, still tucked under his mother's heart, might say to himself, "This is a wonderful place. It's warm. I'm fed, I'm taken care of, I'm secure. This is a great world where I now am. I like it." And then someone might say to him, "But you're not going to stay here. You have to move on. You're going to die out of this place. You're going into another world." That baby would look upon the process of birth as if it were death, since it would be the end of the pleasant state he was in. And he would protest, "I don't want to die. I understand it here and feel secure. I want to stay." What to us is birth, to him is death, and he resists it. But the day comes when he does die to that life and is born into our world.
>
> What happens to him? He is cradled in loving arms. Soft hands hold him gently. A kind face looks down at him, and he loves that face. Everybody that comes near loves him. He is the king of the world he surveys.

There he begins to grow, and he finds life good. Oh, he has some struggles and hardships, but he loves God and people love him. And he loves this world with its seasons, its beauty, its human companionship. Finally he gets to be an old man and he is told, "You have to die." He protests, "I don't want to die. I love this world. I like to feel the sun on my face, and the cool rain. I like our dear, human ways. I love the faces of my wife and children. I've lived here a long time. I don't want to die." But he does die to this world and is born into the next.

Now can you believe that all of a sudden the character of God and the constitution of the universe are going to be changed so that person will be born into a place of gloom and terror, or will be left in a state of nothingness? That is preposterous! He will awaken to find himself young again. Loving faces will greet him; loving hands will touch him. More beautiful sunlight will surround him; sweeter music will sound in his ears. All tears will be wiped from his eyes, and he will say, "Why was I so afraid of this thing called death, when, as I now know, it is life?"

So much depends on your point of view! You can think of death as a dark door, or a dark valley—or you can think of it as a rainbow bridge stretching between two marvelous worlds, a bridge which all our departed loved ones have crossed and which we too will cross one day to be reunited with them.

—Peale, N.V., "Let Not Your Heart Be Troubled." (Adapted).

274/DEATH

In "Whistle Down the Wind," a motion picture of the sixties, a group of children find a tramp in a barn. Through a combination of circumstances they become convinced that he is Jesus Christ, come back to earth. Then the children's little kitten gets very sick. Immediately, they ask their "Jesus" to cure the animal. But the kitten dies and this becomes a terribly traumatic experience for these children: Why did Jesus let their kitten die? And, as so often happens with children when a pet animal dies, they go on to ask the deeper question, "Why do people die. What is this whole business of death?" The children want an answer. They decide that the best place to get it is the church. With high expectations they run to the nearest church where they find the pastor sitting on the patio, having his afternoon tea. Unceremoniously they pop the question: "Why? Why does Jesus let people die?" The clergyman quickly responds with what he considers to be a correct, pious, orthodox answer. He erupts in a cloud of theological words—precise words. Then he sits back, very self-satisfied. As the children walk away, one little boy turns to his older sister and says, "He doesn't know either, does he?"

When little children begin to ask the question, "Why does Jesus let people die," they do so with high expectations. This is natural! This is human! And they are entitled to an answer. But their high expectations will not be satisfied with the theological formula or philosophical appeals to reason. What they need to know is that, even in death, God is sending a message of love and concern in a very special way. They need to know in their hearts that the love of God conquers all—even death. They need to know that in their hearts that the love of God transforms death into new life.

275/DEATH

Many years ago, a play appeared on Broadway based on the Gospel story of Lazarus, who died and after three days in the tomb was raised from the dead by Jesus. In the play, Lazarus' experience of death takes him out of the limitations of time and space and he comes to know the *greatness* and the *fullness* of life. His whole perspective changes, and when he returns from the dead he is able to view man's puny affairs with a *cosmic* insight—and it is all so funny that Lazarus *laughs.* He laughs *uncontrollably* at the way men and women worry and struggle and chase after shadows.

"Why are your eyes always fixed on the ground in *weariness* of thought, or watching one another with *suspicion?*" he cries out. "Throw your gaze *upward*—to *eternal* life! To the *fearless* and *deathless!* To the *stars!* O brothers in God...*laugh* thine everlasting laughter!"

To know that life is for *living*!

To know that life is lived from within *out!*

To know that life is so very much *more* than that which begins with birth and ends with death!

To know *this* truth, *really,* know it, is to be *free...*
free from *anxiety,*
free from *fear,*
free from the awful resistance toward *death,*
free from the awful *grief* over death!

—*Butterworth, E., "Life Is For Living" (Adapted).*

276/DEATH

If I should leave this world Without a warning,
And not even whisper a fond farewell,
Grieve not for one more message
From the lips that God has stilled.
But just remember me with *love*
And *prayers* for my soul's journey
To that fair land beyond life's tears.
For I have believed with all my *heart*
In its existence, and I know
That God is good, for he has come to me
Through the life of Him whose very *garment*
I have sought to touch.
It may be lonely, and I hope you miss me
Just a little, because I have loved so *deeply*
My own family and faithful friends.

Forgive me if I have ever hurt you
And *remember* me for what I longed to *be.*
Have *faith* that I am nearer than
Your dreams and fondest longings,
For the God of love shall keep all
kindred spirits
Close together, though the misty
vale between
This world and that to come.
Keep us from each other's sight
For a few precious moments.
Whisper softly that you love me
And it shall linger on within my soul
Until you come. Say *not* goodbye,
For on some bright tomorrow
We shall meet again!

277/DEATH

A very talented court jester was summoned by his king each morning to entertain. When the king was feeling blue, the jester would help lift the king's spirits. For his many years of fine service, the jester was presented with a golden staff. As he presented his gift to the jester, the king declared, "Here is the greatest buffoon that ever lived." Years later, as he lay dying in his bedchamber, the king once again summoned the jester to his side. As the jester stood before him, the king stated that he felt he would soon be leaving on a long journey. The jester asked if the king would be gone a long time. The reply was, "Yes." "Have you made the necessary *preparations* for your long journey your majesty," the jester asked. Sadly, the king responded "No." With that, the jester took up his gold staff, gave it to the king and said, "It is a greater fool then *I* who would take such a great journey unprepared."

278/DEATH

A Roman Catholic Priest, who was close to dying, wrote the following in his diary:

> At nearly every funeral I conduct, I say something to this effect: "Death is such an overwhelmingly powerful

experience that it opens us to the deepest, most powerful ideas and questions and convictions about *life* and especially *our* own individual lives, our dreams and purposes, ideals and hopes." And, of course, it's a crying shame that for so many people the only time those profundities surface is at the time of the death of a friend or relative. *How we need to take hold of life and its tremendous and terrific power—right now, today*!

279/DEATH

Death is "more friend than foe":

In the first place, death is not the enemy we generally make it out to be. Consider only the alternative—life *without* death. Life without death would be *interminable*—literally and figuratively. We'd take days just to get out of bed, weeks to decide what to do next. Students would never graduate, and faculty meetings and PTA meetings and church meetings and all other kinds of meetings would go on for months. Chances are, we'd be as bored as the ancient Greek gods and up to their same silly tricks. Death *cannot* be the enemy if it is death that brings us to *life*. Just as without *leave-taking*, there can be no *arrival*; just as without growing *old*, there can be no growing *up*; just as without *tears*, no *laughter*, so without *death*, there could be no *living*. So let us pause to thank our Creator who so organized things that "all mortal flesh is as the grass" (Prov. 40:6).

—Coffin, W.S. (Adapted).

280/DEATH

Two ships sailed in a harbor: one going out on a voyage, the other coming into port. People cheered the ship going *out*, but the ship sailing *in* was hardly noticed. Seeing this, a wise man remarked: "Do not rejoice for a ship sailing *out* to sea, for you do not know what terrible dangers it may encounter. Rejoice rather for the ship that has reached *shore*, bringing its passengers safely home.

And so it is in the world. When a child is born, all *rejoice*; when someone dies, all *weep*. But it makes just as much sense, if not more, to rejoice at the *end* of a life as at the *beginning*. For no one can tell what events await a newborn child, but when a mortal dies he has successfully *completed* a journey.
—A "Talmud" Lesson

281/DEATH
An ancient Chinese Fable:

> Once upon a time, a great king went hunting with his closest companions. They paused at the top of a hill from which they could see for miles around. As the king surveyed his domain, with its rich fields and bustling cities, tears came to his eyes. He thought of his palaces and friends, the honor and wealth that belonged to him, and the love of his people. "To think that one day I must *die*, and leave all this *behind!*" the king lamented. The nobles with him started thinking, and soon they began commiserating with their king: they, too, would lose palaces, riches, and honors when they died.
>
> "Imagine if we could live *forever*!" the king said. "Aye," his nobles agreed, their eyes bright at the thought of immortality. One lord among them laughed. "We should never have to leave all this," the king went on, ignoring the interruption, but the noble laughed again. This happened several more times, until the king himself demanded the reason for the mirth. Then the lord bowed. "I cannot keep my joke from you, Majesty," he confessed, "although I hesitate to say it." The lord paused and went on.
>
> "I imagined what it would be like if we all lived forever, and if there were *no* death," the lord explained. "Why then, the *First King* would still live among us, and the *Great Sage!* The *Immortal Emperor*, and the *Fearless General*, too! Compared with them, I and my fellow lords would be fit only to be *rice-planters*, and you,

Majesty, would be a *clerk!* Imagining that, I could not help laughing!"

The other lords held their breaths, fearing the king's wrath. After a tense moment, the king laughed. Then he told the laughing lord, "Whenever I bewail my death again, whenever I say, 'Imagine if we could live forever,' you are to cry out, 'A *clerk!* A *clerk!*'"

DECADENCE

282

Once the great Roman Empire was the most powerful on earth. Yet, that great empire sank down to failure. What were the causes? Historian Edward Gibbon, in his story of The Decline and Fall of the Roman Empire, gives these five reasons for that failure:

1. The rapid increase of divorce; the undermining of the dignity and sanctity of the home, which is the basis of human society.
2. Higher and higher taxes and the spending of public monies.
3. The mad craze for pleasure; sports becoming every year more exciting and more brutal.
4. The building of gigantic armaments, when the real enemy was within: the decadence of the people.
5. The decay of religion—fading into mere form, losing touch with life and becoming impotent to warn and guide the people.

Does any of the above sound familiar?

DECEIT

283

On a crowded city bus, early morning commuters listened in as a woman with a small boy in tow argued with the bus driver.

At issue was whether the child was old enough to be required to pay the fare. The woman maintained he was not.

The bus driver argued with the mother for several minutes and then turned to the boy. He asked, "How old are you sonny?"

Looking to his mother for approval the boy replied, "Five years old."
The bus driver then turned to the mother and said, "Okay, I'll let him ride free this time, but I'll bet I know what he'll be when he grows up."

"What?" asked the woman in surprise.

"Either a liar or a giant!" snarled the driver.

284/DECEIT
Many a youth has been tempted by the seemingly glamorous life-style and enormous salaries that sports figures command today. While most realize that a professional multi-million-dollar sports career is a realistic goal for only a very *few* gifted athletes, there are some youngsters (and adults as well) who fall prey to outrageous advertising claims.

One such example was seen recently on a match book advertisement. The matchbook cover read: How to earn three million dollars! (See Inside Cover)

On the inside of the matchbook there appeared an advertisement for a pair of boxing gloves for $19.95.

DECISION

285
A man who made a great deal of money in New York and who resided there for many years bought a burial plot in a New York cemetery. Later, he retired and moved to Florida, and after several years, he bought a burial plot there. A few months later

he became gravely ill. His relatives gathered at his bedside to offer their farewells. In a very delicate manner one of them asked, "Sir, we think that you will be with us for a while but, just in case, do you want to be buried in the cemetery in *New York* or in the burial plot you own here in *Florida?*"

The sick man raised his head and said, *"Surprise me!"*

DEPENDENCE

286

An insurance executive would jog to his office in the morning, and jog back home at night. But the routine began to bore him. A friend suggested he find something to keep his mind occupied, like rolling a hoop as he ran the five miles to the office, and then rolling it back at night. One evening he walked out to the parking area and discovered his hoop had been *stolen.* He called the police, but they weren't very sympathetic.

"It's not *important* enough for us to file a report," explained the policeman on the phone.

"That's easy for you to say," said the runner. "But *how am I going to get home?*"
—*The Runner's Handbook*

DEPRESSION

287

A distraught, suicidal man went to see a psychiatrist. He was desperate. He poured out his deep anguish, pain, and loneliness. He said he wanted to kill himself. The psychiatrist listened intently as the man talked about his disappointments and failures.

When the patient stopped speaking, he looked expectantly at the doctor. The psychiatrist said, "I want to recommend something that is a bit out of the ordinary, but I think it could help. I have heard that a clown is performing at the theater downtown. I hear that people are rolling in the aisles and that their laughter can be heard for blocks. I recommend that you buy a ticket, attend that show, and see that clown. I have a hunch you too will get caught up in the laughter and enjoyment and discover that life is still worth living."

The man looked down. "I can't go see that clown," he said.

"Why?" the psychiatrist asked. "Why won't you give it a try? Why not be a part of life before you try to end it?"

The man wept, "I can't go see that clown because I *am* that clown."

DETERMINATION

288
An ambitious young man had been trying for months to be granted an interview with a major computer manufacturer. After making dozens of attempts he finally managed to get the Personnel Director to take his call. The young job seeker asked if he could get into their well-known training program. With dozens of qualified candidates already in his files, the Personnel Director replied, "I'm sorry but I can't interview you *now*. Why don't you call back in about five years." The young man replied, "Morning or afternoon?"

DEVIL

289
There is an old legend about St. Martin of Tours and his encounter with a mysterious visitor.

One day as St. Martin sat in his prison cell, a knock suddenly came at the door. Instantly a majestic figure entered his cell.

St. Martin asked, "Who are you?"

"I am the *Savior,*" was the reply. St. Martin needed *proof.*

"Then where are the prints of the nails?" he questioned.

With that, the devil *disappeared!*

290/DEVIL
The following scenario was presented by Dick Bothwell in an article published in the "St. Petersburg Times":

Scene: The Pearly Gates, years in the future. Norman Vincent Peale and Billy Graham are at the head of the admitting line. St. Peter is checking their credentials when suddenly a beautiful woman marches up and gives the saint a familiar "Hi, Peter!" St. Peter gives her a beaming welcome and drops everything to make sure the young woman is properly settled into her heavenly home. Meanwhile, the two famous preachers are left cooling their heels for forty-five minutes.

Seeing this, the gentlemen become a bit irate. Billy Graham asks just why this woman should be given the red-carpet treatment, while he and Dr. Peale, who rendered great services on earth, are virtually ignored. St. Peter patiently explains, "Down on earth," he says, "Helen drove a little sports car. She cut in and out of traffic, drag-raced at intersections, tailgated and ran stoplights. Gentlemen, she scared the devil out of more people than the two of you put together!"

DIAGNOSIS

291
Pianist Arthur Rubenstein was fond of telling this story about himself. Never at a loss for words (he could speak eight languages), Rubenstein was stricken with a stubborn case of hoarseness:

The newspapers were full of reports about smoking and cancer, so he decided to see a throat specialist. After being examined, he searched the doctor's face for a clue, but he only told Rubenstein to come back the next day. The pianist went home filled with fear. He couldn't sleep all night.

The next day there was another long examination and then an ominous silence. "Tell me, doctor!" Rubenstein cried out. "I can stand the truth. I've lived a rich, full life. What's wrong with me?" The doctor looked him straight in the eye and said, "Mr. Rubenstein, you talk too much."

DIRECTION

292

When he was eighty-eight-years-old, the late Supreme Court Justice Oliver Wendell Holmes once found himself on a train. When the conductor came by, Justice Holmes couldn't find his ticket, and he seemed terribly upset. He searched all of his pockets and fumbled through his wallet without success. The conductor was sympathetic. "Don't worry, Mr. Holmes," he said. "The Pennsylvania Railroad will be happy to trust you. After you reach your destination you'll probably find the ticket and you can just mail it to us." But the conductor's kindness failed to put Mr. Holmes at ease. Still very much upset, he said, "My dear man, my problem is not 'Where is my *ticket?*' The problem is, 'Where am I *going?*'"

293/DIRECTION

There still exists *today* many rural areas of the country where unpaved roads outnumber paved ones. Worn by the wheels of traffic, over time deep grooves will form in the compacted earth of the road's surface. Once an automobile has steered into one of these "tracks" in the road, a driver will find it very difficult to steer out of it. On one such dirt road in Iowa there is posted a warning sign that reads:

CHOOSE YOUR RUT WELL,
YOU'LL BE IN IT FOR THE NEXT
TWENTY MILES.

294/DIRECTION

Humorist Woody Allen has warned: "Now more than any time in history, mankind is facing a crossroads. One path leads to despair and utter *hopelessness*, the other to total *extinction*. Let us pray that we have the wisdom to choose correctly."

Woody Allen's words to the contrary notwithstanding, the *Good* News is that the path *God* intends us to follow leads to the inexpressible joy of eternal life in His community of Love.

"...as it is written, 'What no eye has seen, nor ear heard, nor the heart of man conceived, what God prepared for those who love Him.'" (I Corinthians 2:9).

295/DIRECTION

An elderly woman who was in the habit of passing out religious pamphlets, boarded a bus one day and handed a leaflet to the driver. It was titled: "Whither Goest Thou?"

The bus driver smiled at her sympathetically, reached for a pencil and dashed off his answer: "Out Madison Avenue."

296/DIRECTION

The captain of one of the great ocean liners engaged in transatlantic traffic had worked up to his exalted position by slow stages—beginning as a cabin boy years earlier. He was one of the most respected men on the seas. His second–in–command, who had served under him for years, watched and emulated his every move. But one thing about his superior puzzled him: every morning his chief went to his cabin, opened the drawer of his desk, took from it a slip of paper, read it over and over with great concentration, returned it to the desk, and locked the drawer.

Finally the captain retired, and his second-in-command took charge. The first thing he did was to open the drawer of the desk to find out what was on that slip of paper his captain read so carefully every day. He found the slip of paper and read the single sentence on it: "Left side is *port;* right side is *starboard*."

DISASTER

297
The owner of a sprawling lake–front estate in Connecticut grew tired of his daily commute from the airport to his home. Figuring he could cut his travel time in half, he installed pontoons on his plane so he could land on the lake—right in his own backyard.

On his next trip, out of habit he began to make his usual approach down the *airport* runway. Then he thought to himself, "Am I *crazy?* I can't land here without *wheels!*"

Immediately, he pulled the nose of the plane up, narrowly escaping *disaster.* Then he continued on to the *lake*, and landed the plane on its pontoons without incident.

As he sat in the plane, visibly shaken, he said to himself, "I don't know what got into me. That's the *dumbest* thing I've ever done!" And with that, he opened the door, stepped out of the plane—and into the *lake.*

DISCIPLESHIP

298
"The harvest is rich, but the laborers are few" (Mt. 9:38).

A famous Christian preacher was scheduled to deliver a sermon in a cathedral with a seating capacity of over three thousand. Long before the sermon was to begin, the cathedral was packed—standing room only and loudspeakers hooked up so the sermon could be heard by thousands more standing outside. "Just look at that crowd," said the cathedral rector to the famous preacher. "How many disciples would you say are out there?" To which the preacher replied, "Three or four, perhaps."

299/DISCIPLESHIP
Once upon a time, there was a piece of iron which was very strong. Many attempts had been made to break it but all had failed. "*I'll* master it," said the ax; and his blows fell heavily on the iron but every blow made his edge more blunt until it ceased

to strike. "Leave it to *me*," said the saw; and it worked backward and forward on the iron's surface until its jagged teeth were all worn and broken. Then it fell aside. "Ah!" said the hammer, "I *knew* you wouldn't succeed. *I'll* show you the way." But at the first fierce blow, off flew its head and the iron remained as before. "Shall *I* try?" asked the small, soft flame? "Forget it," everyone else said. "What can *you* do?" But the flame curled around the iron, embraced it, and never left it until it melted under its irresistible influence.

As Jesus' disciples, our mission is not to *break* hearts but to *melt* hearts—under the irresistible influence of God's infinite Love.

DISCOVERY

300

In his book entitled "A Kick in the Seat of the Pants," author Roger von Oech, a pioneer in the study of creativity, writes about the importance of re-setting our "mental channel" in order to help achieve a particular goal. If it is our intention for example to laugh when we really feel like crying, we can set our "mental channel" to look for things that make us happy. This principle is the same for achieving any goal:

> Take a look around where you're sitting and find five things that have blue in them. Go ahead and do it.
>
> With a "blue" mind-set, you'll find that blue jumps out at you: a blue book on the table, a blue pillow on the couch, blue in the painting on the wall, and so on. Similarly, whenever you learn a new word, you hear it six times in the next two days. In like fashion, you've probably noticed that after you buy a new car, you promptly see that make of car everywhere. That's because people find what they are looking for. If you're looking for conspiracies, you'll find them. If you're looking for examples of man's good works, you'll find that too. It's all a matter of setting your mental channel.

It is our "mental channel" that steers us in the direction we want to head. If we were to paraphrase von Oech's statement to fit our laughter instead of tears goal, it might read like this:

> Take a look around where you're sitting and find five things that make you smile. Go ahead and do it.
>
> With a "smile" mind-set, you'll find that things that cause you to smile jump out at you: a childhood toy, a favorite picture, your pet, and so on. In addition, when you smile, things seem to smile back. In other words, if you look for smiles you'll find them. It's all a matter of setting your mental channel.

"Seek first His kingdom…" (Mt. 6:33). If you're really looking for it, you'll surely find it! It's all a matter of setting your "spiritual channel".
—Klein, A., "The Healing Power of Humor" (Adapted).

DREAMS

301
An elderly man had horrible nightmares, the same event happening over and over in his dreams. He would dream that an enormous green dragon was chasing him, and he would become frantic. Then, just about the time the dragon was catching up to him, he would awaken in a cold sweat.

One night, he did not awaken in time and the dragon caught him. There he was in the clutches of this dragon, steam jetting from its nostrils (just like in a horror movie). The old man was in sheer panic. So he looked up at the dragon and screamed, "What are you going to do with me?"

The dragon replied, "I don't know, old man. *It's your dream!*"
—Costa, T., "Life! You Wanna Make Something Of It?"

"In the days to come—it is the Lord who speaks—I will pour out My Spirit on all mankind. Their sons and daughters shall prophesy, your young men will see visions, your old men shall dream dreams." (Acts 2:17).

E

EARLY CHRISTIANS

302
The story is told of a small dog which had been struck by a car and was laying wounded by the side of the road. A doctor driving by noticed that the dog was still alive. He stopped his car, picked up the dog and took him home with him. There he discovered that the dog had been stunned, had suffered a few minor cuts and abrasions, but was otherwise all right. He revived the dog, cleaned up the wounds and was carrying the animal from the house to the garage when it suddenly jumped from his arms and scampered off. "What an ungrateful little dog," the doctor said to himself. He thought no more about the incident until the next evening when he heard a scratching at his door. When he opened it, there was the little dog he had treated, with another hurt dog.

That is a story of the "ripple effect." Throw a stone into a lake and the water ripples out, and the circle widens. One of the great characteristics of the first Christians was their ripple effect. Something had happened to them that so filled them with joy they just could not contain it. It was contagious. It spread out among the people in a ripple effect. And the circle grew wider and wider. The reason those early Christians were so filled with joy was that this Jesus who had lived among them, this Jesus who had given them such hope, this Jesus whom they had seen die on a hill outside Jerusalem, this Jesus whom they had seen put into a tomb—this Jesus was alive!

EASTER

303

In Thornton Wilder's play, "Our Town," one of the characters says:

> ...everybody *knows* that something is eternal. And it ain't houses, and it ain't names, and it ain't earth, and it ain't even stars...Everybody knows in their *bones* that something is eternal—something that has to do with *human beings*. There's something way down deep that's eternal about every human being.

On Easter we come to celebrate that "something way down deep that's *eternal* about us human beings." Easter is telling us that the Resurrection Power of God not only *was* revealed, but is *being* revealed. Easter is not only a past event to be *memorialized*, it is an eternally *present* reality. The Resurrection Power of God is working way down deep in us now to sustain us on our journey to *abundant* life. The Resurrection Power of God is revealing to us now that all the problems we can think of already have been *solved*.

304/EASTER

One Good Friday, a severe earthquake hit Alaska. Many buildings were totally destroyed, including the Church of All Saints. Consequently, on Easter Sunday, parishioners of All Saints went to nearby St. Mary's Church which had sustained only minor damage. In the church that Easter Sunday, two lists were posted for the people to sign. One was headed, "We Need." The other "We Have To Share." No one signed the first list, but the majority of families signed the second. On it they listed the items they were willing to share: clothing, food, fuel, skills, etc. Many who signed the "share" list had lost most of their possessions in the disaster, yet they offered to share the few things that had been spared. It was a remarkable example of the spirit of the *first* Christians to hear the Good News of the Risen Christ.

305/EASTER

Easter brings us the Good News of Christ's glorious Resurrection. It also brings us a mandate:

...to care about the human problems most people ignore

...to speak up for the downtrodden who are powerless to speak for themselves

...to call for forgiveness when others call for blood

...to share our resources without asking "What's in it for us?"

...to be loyal to the Rule of God when others have sold out to the idols of money and possessions.

306/EASTER

Often, to the eyes of man, it is midnight. And midnight means the *end!* But, to the eyes of Faith, midnight begins with the dawn and ends with Easter morning when *life* springs forth out of the empty tomb and the dead are more alive than ever before: their eyes open to *new* light; their spirits gifted with new *life!*

307/EASTER

In every grave on earth's green soil is a tiny seed of the Resurrection life of Jesus Christ, and that seed cannot perish. It will germinate when the warm south wind of Christ's return brings back the spring-tide to this cold sin-cursed earth of ours. And then they that are already in their graves and we who shall lie down in our own, will feel in our mortal bodies the power of His Resurrection and will come forth to a life that is immortal and unending.

308/EASTER

Shortly before his death, the legendary film producer Cecil B. DeMille, wrote this beautiful meditation:

> One day as I was lying in a canoe, a big black beetle came out of the water and climbed up into the canoe. I watched it idly for some time. Under the heat of the sun, the beetle proceeded to die. Then a strange thing

happened. His glistening black shell cracked all the way down his back. Out of it came a shapeless mass, quickly transformed into beautiful, brilliantly colored life. As I watched in fascination, there gradually unfolded iridescent wings from which the sunlight flashed a thousand colors. The wings spread wide, as if in worship of the sun. The blue-green body took shape. Before my eyes had occurred a metamorphosis—the transformation of a hideous beetle into a gorgeous dragonfly, which started dipping and soaring over the water. But the body it had left behind still clung to my canoe. I had witnessed what seemed to me a miracle. Out of the mud had come a beautiful new life. And the thought came to me, that if the Creator works such wonders with the lowliest of creatures, what may not be in store for the human spirit?

309/EASTER

In a cartoon called "The Family Circus," two children have discovered their Easter baskets and are busily enjoying the contents. One of the children asks, "Who colored all these eggs?" The other child replies, "The Easter Bunny."

"Who gave us the jelly beans?"
"The Easter Bunny."
"And the chocolate rabbit?"
"The Easter Bunny."

Clearly, for those two little ones, *nothing* was impossible for the Easter bunny. Then the family went to Church. They heard the preacher say, "They came to the tomb and saw that the stone had been rolled back. Who could have done this?" To which the two children cried out in unison, "*The Easter Bunny.*"

310/EASTER

Several years ago in Moscow, during a period of heightened governmental hostility toward the Church, a well-known Soviet educator was delivering a lecture in which he attempted to prove that Christian Faith was obsolete. At the conclusion of his talk, he asked if anyone in the audience would like to try to refute his arguments. For several moments there was only silence. Then, slowly, the village priest arose and moved toward the platform. "Remember," the lecturer said, "you have only five minutes." The priest replied, "What I have to say will be brief." Then he looked out over the crowds and , in a clear, firm voice he pronounced the Russian Easter greeting: "CHRIST IS RISEN!"

311/EASTER

How long will we come before the Lord
with *tired* spirits and *droning* voices?

How long will we try to praise Him
with our *noiseless* songs?

How long will we try to worship Him
with *bored* faces and *dull* senses,
offering Him tin
when we could be offering Him *gold*?

Oh Lord, you love us!
Why aren't we dancing
to your Good News music?

"She saw that the stone had been rolled away!"
Why aren't we *singing*?
Why aren't we c*rowning* Him Lord of Lords?

312/EASTER

The pyramids of Egypt are famous because they contained the mummified bodies of ancient Egyptian rulers. Westminster Abbey in London is renowned because in it rests the bodies of many English notables. Arlington Cemetery in Washington, D.C. is revered because it is the final resting place of many American heroes. But the Tomb of Jesus is *empty*. There is no epitaph on Jesus' tomb that begins with the words, "Here lies..." There is no epitaph inscribed in gold or cut in stone.

Rather, Jesus' epitaph is spoken from the mouth of an angel: "HE IS NOT HERE...HE IS RISEN!"

EDUCATION

313
I am a survivor of a concentration camp. My eyes saw what no person should witness. Gas chambers built by learned engineers. Children poisoned by educated physicians. Infants killed by trained nurses. Women and babies shot and killed by high school and college graduates. So I'm suspicious of education. My request is: help your students to be human. Your efforts must never produce learned monsters, skilled psychopaths, or educated Eichmanns. Reading and writing and spelling and history and arithmetic are only important if they serve to make our students human.
—Ginott, H.

314/EDUCATION
In a New York City elementary school, a class of fifth graders were encouraged by their teacher to discuss their feelings about nuclear weapons. The class was called "General Studies" and some of the students complained that the subject was covered in other classes. "This is boring," one student moaned loudly. "And besides, we learned this in American History."

"This is *not boring,*" the teacher replied, "and what we are talking about here is not American History, it is current events."

"Current events?" a girl challenged. "We learned current events *last* year!"

EGO

315
The famous film actor, Gregory Peck, and a friend once walked into a crowded restaurant and had to stand with others waiting for a table.

"Tell them who you are," urged the friend.

"If you have to tell them who you are, you aren't anybody," replied Peck.

316/EGO
The editor of the obituary column of a major midwestern paper was notorious for being unable to acknowledge his *mistakes.* His ego just wouldn't allow him to admit that he was ever *wrong.* One day he received a call from an irate subscriber. "You printed my name in yesterday's *Obituary* Column," the subscriber complained. "Oh, is that so?" replied the editor, suspiciously. "And exactly where are you calling *from*?"

317/EGO
Bill Johnson, well known for his over-inflated ego, was *constantly* reminding his employees, family and friends of his many accomplishments in life. As President of a successful business, Bill was quick to seize *any* opportunity to tell his workers how he *single-handedly* took over a company on the brink of bankruptcy and turned it almost overnight into a profit-making machine. To his friends, Bill constantly boasted about having the most talented and attractive children in the neighborhood. At home, Bill *always* had the last word. In fact, Bill was so *full* of himself that he had a custom wall plaque made to hang over his fireplace which read:

Bill Johnson is God.

After returning from the office one evening, Bill discovered a small note his wife had placed Below the plaque. *It* read:
ONE SMALL STEP FOR BILL JOHNSON,
ONE GIANT STEP FOR *ATHEISM.*

ELITISM

318
The social activist Julia Ward Howe once asked Senator Charles Sumner to use his influence to intercede for a constituent who

desperately needed help. The Senator responded, "Julia, these days I've become so busy and involved in so many different things that I no longer have time to direct my attention to the concerns of individuals."

Julia replied, "Senator, that is quite remarkable! Even God hasn't reached that stage yet!"

EMPATHY

319

The mother of a fifteen–year–old named Doug became increasingly worried when her son's temperature kept rising until it reached 105 degrees. Doug was taken to the hospital where blood tests revealed leukemia. Then Doug developed pneumonia, and for ten days his mother stayed with him in his hospital room.

One night Doug was afraid and asked his mother to sleep in his bed by his side. Through her tears, she had to tell him she couldn't; I.V. tubes were attached to his body, the bed was small, and there was no room.

The doctors were frank, telling Douglas that for the next three years he would have to undergo chemotherapy. He would go bald and probably gain weight. Learning this, Douglas became even more discouraged; although he was told that there was a good chance of remission, he was smart enough to know that leukemia can be fatal.

On the day Douglas was admitted, his first time in a hospital, he looked around his room and said to his mother, "I thought you get flowers when you're in the hospital." Hearing this, an aunt called to order an arrangement. The voice of the salesclerk was high-pitched, and she sounded young. The aunt imagined an inexperienced clerk who would be unaware of the arrangement's significance. So the aunt said, "I want the planter especially attractive. It's for my teenage nephew who has leukemia." "Oh," said the salesclerk, "Let's add some fresh-cut flowers to brighten it up."

When the arrangement arrived at the hospital, Douglas was feeling strong enough to sit up; he opened the envelope and read the card from his aunt. Then he saw another card. His mother said it must have been meant for another arrangement. Douglas removed it anyway. The card said: "Douglas I took your order. I work at the flower shop. I had leukemia when I was seven years old. I'm 22-years-old-now. Good luck. My heart goes out to you. Sincerely, Laura Bradley." Douglas's face lit up. For the first time since he entered the hospital, he had been inspired. He had talked to so many doctors and nurses. But this one card was the thing that made him believe he might beat the disease.

This story was reported in the Chicago Tribune by Bob Greene. Mr. Greene said that when he spoke to the salesclerk who had written the note to Doug, she said:

"When Douglas's aunt told me that the boy had leukemia, I felt tears coming to my eyes. It reminded me of when I first learned that I had it. I realized what the boy must be going through. I wanted him to know that you really can get better. So I wrote the card and slipped it into the envelope. I didn't tell anyone. I haven't been working here very long, and I was afraid I might get in trouble."

"It's funny," wrote Greene, "Doug was in a hospital filled with millions of dollars of the most sophisticated medical equipment. He was being treated by expert doctors and nurses with medical training totaling hundreds of years. But it was a salesclerk in a flower shop, a woman making $170 a week, who, by taking the time to care, and being willing to go with what her heart told her to do, gave Douglas hope and the will to carry on. The human spirit can be an amazing thing, and sometimes you encounter it at its very best when you aren't even looking."

320/EMPATHY

A distinguished surgeon was addressing a class of medical students on the subject of "*Muscle* Healing." After a long discussion of a certain surgical technique, he proposed the following case to his students: "The muscle in the patient's *right* leg has contracted until it is shorter than the muscle in his *left* leg. Therefore, he *limps*." Then, pointing to one of the students, he asked, "What would *you* do in such a circumstance?"

"I'd limp too," the student said.

ENCOURAGEMENT

321

Pinchas Zuckerman, one of the world's great violinists, was conducting Master Classes at the Aspen Music Festival. Aspiring young musicians from all over the world had come to perform in the presence of the famous virtuoso performer. Before an audience of mostly musicians and music critics, the young artists took the stage in turn. After each performance Zuckerman would analyze the playing, offer suggestions and kindly advice, and then compliment the artist with some encouraging words. Then he would pick up his *own* violin to demonstrate techniques that he thought would be helpful to the young performer. Toward the end of the program, a young artist gave a brilliant performance that came close to matching the virtuosity of the great Zuckerman. After the applause subsided, Zuckerman once again picked up his violin and tucked it under his chin. After holding that position for several seconds, he lowered his instrument without having played a single note. Then, without a word, he returned his violin to its case. Shouts of "Bravo!" were heard from the audience. Then an outbreak of deafening applause—in appreciation of the Master's supremely encouraging compliment of *silence.*

ENEMIES

322
On his one hundredth birthday, a man was interviewed by a reporter who asked: "What one thing are you most proud of?" The man replied, "Well, here I am, one hundred years old and I don't have a single enemy in this world." To which the reporter replied, "That is truly remarkable, sir. What made it possible for you to say you haven't an enemy in the world?" "Well," said the old man, "I've *outlived* every last one of them."

ENTHUSIASM

323
"Nothing great was ever achieved without enthusiasm," wrote Ralph Waldo Emerson. We are all born "wide-eyed," so to speak. We delight in the enthusiastic wonder of an infant who hears the jingle of keys, or sees for the first time some colorful toy. Often we are inspired by persons of advanced years who still maintain a youthful air—a spirit of enthusiastic wonder for the blessings of life. At age 90, Pablo Casals, the great cellist, would begin his day by playing Bach. As the music flowed through his fingers, his stooped shoulders would straighten and joy would appear in his eyes. Music, for Casals, was a wondrous experience that made life a never ending adventure. Poet and author Samuel Ulman wrote, "Years wrinkle the skin, but to give up enthusiasm wrinkles the soul."

How do you rediscover the enthusiasm of youth? The answer lies in the word itself. Enthusiasm comes from the Greek, and it means "God within." And the experience of God's loving presence within engenders proper love of self and, from that, love of others.

324/ENTHUSIASM

A businessman began doing volunteer work in rehabilitating former mental patients. He often visited a large mental institution where he interviewed patients who were about to be discharged, helping them to explore job opportunities. On one such visit he encountered a man who was going to be discharged in two weeks. The patient was busy building a brick wall in front of one of the buildings. After a long conversation the businessman asked, "Would you like to come and do some brick work for me at my plant?" The patient

enthusiastically replied that he would like that very much. "Fine," said the visitor, "I must go now but I'll return Monday and speak to the superintendent about it." Then, as he turned and began to walk toward the gate, the visitor was struck by a brick thrown at his head. Stunned, he fell to the ground. When he looked up he saw the patient happily waving to him as he shouted, "You won't forget Monday, will you?"

EPITAPH

325

The following epitaph appears on an old grave-marker in an English country-churchyard:

> Remember man that passeth by,
> As thou is now so once was I;
> And as I am now so must thou be:

Underneath this someone wrote:

> Prepare thyself to *follow* me.
> To follow you I'm not *content*,
> Until I learn of where you *went*.

326/EPITAPH

Benjamin Franklin, who had a great fondness for *books*, wrote an epitaph for himself which he hoped would be placed on his grave.

It read:

> The body of Benjamin Franklin, like the cover of an old *book*, its contents torn out and stripped of its lettering and gilding, lies here for the worms; yet the work itself shall not be lost, for it will, as he believed, appear once more in a new and more *beautiful* edition, corrected and amended by the *Author*.

Benjamin Franklin was *right*: "The work itself shall *not* be lost!" *Benjamin Franklin* shall not be lost! *You* shall not be lost! *I* shall not be lost! God, our Father, will *not* abandon us. Christ our King promises us *new* life in His eternal Kingdom of Love. And Christ our King asks us for a genuine Faith *response* to that promise. *Now!*

ETERNAL LIFE

327
A New York City woman who was preparing for a trip abroad wrote of her experience in acquiring a passport:

> I went to get my passport in Rockefeller Center. The place was packed, hundreds of people waiting in a long, long line that inched along slowly, slowly. I had a newspaper to read, but there was no place to sit down.
>
> The experience was tedious, and after two hours or so I was feeling quite grouchy. When I got close to the front of the line I spotted a bit of graffiti penciled in on one of the building's columns. It made me feel a lot better, even happy. This is what it said:
>
> *BE GRATEFUL THAT YOU ARE GOING SOMEPLACE.*

Over-and-over again, as they speak to us of "eternal *life* with God" and the "coming *Kingdom* of God, the New Testament writers are telling us:

> *Be Grateful That You Are Going Someplace.*

ETERNITY

328
The obstetrician was not at home. His five-year-old daughter answered the doorbell. "Is your daddy in?" asked an excited stranger. "No, he's gone," the little girl replied. "When will he return?" "I don't know. He's out on an *eternity* case." The little girl was right. Every child is an eternity case—the heir of all that has gone before, the molder of all that is to be.
—Greenberg, S., "Say Yes To Life."

EXAMPLE

329
'Twas a sheep, not a lamb, that went astray,
In the parable Jesus told:
A grownup sheep that had gone astray
From the ninety-and-nine in the fold.

And why for the sheep should we earnestly long,
And as earnestly hope and pray?
Because there is danger if they go wrong,
They will lead the lambs astray.

The lambs will follow the sheep, you know,
Wherever the sheep may stray.
When the sheep go wrong, it will not be long
Till the lambs are as wrong as they!

And so with the sheep we earnestly plead
For the sake of the lambs, today;
If the sheep are lost, what a terrible cost
Some lambs will have to pay.
—Anonymous

330/EXAMPLE
An old sailor gave up smoking when his pet parrot developed a persistent cough. He was worried that the pipe

smoke that frequently filled the room had damaged the parrot's health.

He had a vet examine the bird. After a thorough checkup the vet concluded that the parrot did not have psittacosis or pneumonia. It had merely been *imitating* the cough of its pipe-smoking *master.*

"With toil and labor we worked night and day . . . to give you in our conduct an example to imitate" (II Thes. 3:8,9).
—deMello, A., "The Heart of the Enlightened."

331/EXAMPLE
The late comedian, Sam Levenson, often told stories about his childhood school days. He recalled that his over-protective mother accompanied him on his very first day in school and insisted on talking to the teacher before leaving him. Levenson said that among other things, his mother told the teacher that if he misbehaved she should punish the boy next to him. "My little boy learns by example," she explained.

EXCELLENCE

332
A struggling young writer once got up enough courage to ask a famous old literary figure to critique a story he had written. Three days passed and the writer heard nothing. He approached the celebrity and asked what he'd thought of the piece. The old man looked up from his desk, tapped the manuscript with his finger and said, "Is this the *best* you can do?"

Disappointed, the young writer took back his manuscript and agonized over every passage. When he had finished rewriting, he again left the work with his critic. Several days later, he approached the famous man and asked for his opinion. And again, he heard the question, "Are you sure this is the very best you can do?"

> For a second time, the young man retrieved his manuscript and spent many sleepless nights trying to perfect it. And once again he stepped forward to get the famous man's opinion. "Are you positive that this is the best you can possibly do?" asked the old man.
>
> Disheartened but stubborn, the young writer replied, "Yes, sir, it is."
>
> "Okay," said the famous man. "Now I'll read it."

"Wake up; revive what little you have left...so far I have failed to notice anything in the way you live that my God could possibly call perfect, and yet do you remember how eager you were when you first heard the Message?"
(Rev. 3:2).

EXPECTATION

333
A wealthy Oklahoma oil baron died after a protracted illness, and his attorney gathered the entire family for the reading of the will. Relatives came from near and far to see if they were included in the bequests.

The lawyer ceremoniously opened the will and began to read:

> "To my cousin Nancy, I leave my ranch.
> "To my brother George, I leave my bank.
> "To my neighbor and good friend, Oscar, I leave my oil stocks.
> "To my uncle Stanley, I leave an office building in Tulsa.
> "And finally, to my cousin Willie, who always wanted to be remembered in my will, 'Hi, Willie.'"

EXPLOITATION

334

There is a marvelous story about the great composer, Guiseppi Verdi. Verdi disliked hand organs with a passion because most of the time they sounded out of tune, and worst of all, when the person turning the handle would get tired, the tempo would slow down. And if there was anything Verdi couldn't stand, it was out-of-tune, tired-tempo music. When he died, three hundred hand organs were found stored in Verdi's basement. He had bought them and hidden them away in a one-man crusade to rid the world of hand organs. According to a biographer, Verdi was walking down the street one day when he came upon a disheveled-looking organ grinder doing his thing, and a flea-bitten monkey holding a tin cup. As Verdi passed by, he tapped the organ grinder vigorously on the shoulder, saying, "The tempo! Pick it up, man, Pick it up!" Then he continued down the street holding his hands over his ears. A few days later, Verdi happened upon the same organ grinder, but with a whole new look. He was wearing a new suit. The organ was polished. The monkey had been given a bath and looked healthy and happy. As Verdi moved closer to the unexpected scene, he saw a big sign the man had attached to the organ. It read, "Master Musician. Studied with Verdi."

EYE FOR AN EYE

335

Moses Mendelssohn, the eighteenth-century philosopher, was walking down a Berlin street one day when he accidentally bumped into a stout Prussian military officer. "*Swine!*" bellowed the officer, as he glared menacingly at Mendelssohn. The wise philosopher knew that returning the insult might subject him to physical abuse. Consequently, he merely tipped his hat in a manner which suggested that the officer had just *introduced* himself, and replied, "*Mendelssohn.*"

F

FAILURE

336
It has been told that Thomas Edison made 1,000 unsuccessful attempts at inventing the light bulb before finally succeeding. When asked how it felt to fail 1,000 times, Edison replied, "I did not fail 1,000 times. The light bulb was an invention with 1,001 steps."

337/FAILURE
"For it is when I am weak that I am strong" (2 Cor. 12:10).

Learn to look at your failures as experiences in *growth!*

> Failing doesn't have to mean you've accomplished *nothing*— it may mean you can *learn* something.
>
> Failing doesn't have to mean you're *disgraced*—it can mean you were willing to *try*.
>
> Failing doesn't have to mean you don't "*have what it takes*"—it can mean you have to do something in a *different* way.
>
> Failing doesn't have to mean you've *wasted* your life—it does mean you have a reason to start *afresh*.
>
> Failing doesn't have to mean you are *inferior*—it does mean that you, like everyone else, are not *perfect*.

And that's all right! By not being perfect you are acknowledging your membership in the human family.

FAITH

338

An elderly woman named Maude had a window seat on a big "747" jetliner that had just taken off for Rome. She had been scrimping for years to fulfill her dream of travelling to Europe and visiting the exotic places she'd read about all her life. But it was her first flight and she was terrified! "O Lord, what am I doing up here?" she kept repeating to herself. Even the stately presence of the four bishops seated behind her didn't help. With fear and trembling, she finally opened her eyes and peeped out the window just in time to see one of the plane's four engines break loose from the wing and disappear into the clouds below. Maude sounded the alarm: "We're going to die! We're going to die" she cried out. The chief stewardess immediately consulted with the pilot, then announced to passengers the news that everything was under control. "The captain assures you", she said, "that he can fly the airplane back to New York and land safely on three motors." But poor, panic-stricken Maude continued to cry out, "We're going to die! We're going to die!" The stewardess went to her and said, "Don't worry, my dear, God is with us. Besides, we still have there motors, and there are four bishops on board." To which Maude replied, "I'd rather have four motors and three bishops."

339/FAITH

There is a beautiful allegory in which "Knowledge" is depicted as a strong, handsome knight making his way over the great tableland of the earth. With each step, he tests and makes certain of the ground beneath his feet. Beside him and just above the ground moves the white-winged angel, "Faith." Side by side they go until they come to the verge of a vast precipice. Here the path stops suddenly, and Knowledge can go no further. But the white-winged angel, Faith, rises majestically from the ground and moves on across the chasm, leaving her companion behind.

340/FAITH

It was on the eve of the great 1938 New England hurricane that a man living in the Stamford, Connecticut suburbs decided to fulfill a long-standing desire. He walked two miles to the Abercrombie and Fitch department store in downtown Stamford and bought a fine barometer. Delighted with his acquisition, he hurried home and proudly hung it on his living room wall. But what he saw made him very angry: the barometer reading indicated "Hurricane!" Convinced that he had been sold a defective instrument, he walked back to Abercrombie and Fitch, handed the barometer to the sales clerk, and snorted, "Fine barometer you sold me. I put it up in my house and what do you suppose it registered? 'Hurricane!'" To which the sales clerk replied, "No problem, sir. We'll replace it with a perfect one." Again, the man headed for home with his new barometer. When he arrived, he discovered that his house had been blown away by a hurricane!

God is reliable, trustworthy, perfect and unchanging. If you should try to second-guess God or exchange God or replace God or improve upon God, you are courting disaster.

341/FAITH

Someone has said that Christian Faith is a "4-F" experience:

Faith in Christ
Fellowship with Christ
Fidelity to the Word of Christ
Fruitfulness in the service of Christ

342/FAITH

An atheist fell off a cliff. As he tumbled downward, he caught hold of the branch of a small tree. There he hung between heaven above and the rocks a thousand feet below, knowing he wasn't going to be able to hold on much longer.

Then an idea came to him. *"God!"* he shouted with all his might.

Silence! No one responded.

"God!" he shouted again. "If you exist, save me and I promise I shall *believe* in you and teach *others* to believe."

Silence again! Then he almost let go of the branch in shock as he heard a mighty voice booming across the canyon. "That's what they *all* say when they are in trouble."

"No, God, no!" he shouted out, more hopeful now. "I am *not* like the others. Why, *already* I have begun to believe, having heard your voice for myself. Now all you have to do is *save* me and I shall proclaim your name to the ends of the earth."

"Very well," said the voice. "I *shall* save you. Let *go* of that branch."

"Let go of the branch?" yelled the distraught man. "Do you think I'm *crazy*?"
—deMello, A., "Taking Flight" (Adapted).

343/FAITH
In his book "Fearfully and Wonderfully Made," Philip Yancey says:

> A certain bridge in South America consists of interlocking vines supporting a precariously swinging platform hundreds of feet above a river. I know the bridge has supported hundreds of people over many years, and as I stand at the edge of the chasm I can see people confidently crossing the bridge. The engineer in me wants to weigh all the factors: measure the stress tolerances of the vines, test the wood for termites, survey all the bridges in the area for one that might be stronger. I could spend a lifetime determining whether the bridge is fully trustworthy. But eventually, if I really want to cross, I must take a step. When I put my weight on that bridge and walk across, even though my heart is pounding and my knees are shaking, I am making a statement—declaring my *position.* In the Christian world I sometimes must live like this, making choices

which contain inherent *uncertainty*. If I wait for all the evidence to be in, for everything to be settled, I'll *never* move. Often I have had to act on the basis of the *bones* of the Christian faith, before those bones were *fully* formed in me and before I understood the *reason* for their existence. Bone is hard, but it is *alive*. If the bones of faith do not continue to *grow*, they will soon become *dead* skeletons.

—Brand, P. and Yancey, P., "Fearfully & Wonderfully Made." (Adapted).

FAMILIARITY

344

One day, when G.K. Chesterton was packing his bags in his London apartment, a friend came in and asked where he was going. Chesterton surprisingly replied that he was on his way to *London*. Somewhat taken back by this answer, the friend reminded Chesterton that he already was *in* London. To this however, the essayist replied with a characteristic twist, "No," he said, "that's where you're wrong. I no longer *see* London. Familiarity has closed my eyes. The real meaning of travel is to come home again and see it as though for the first time. So I really am on my way to London though I'll go by way of Paris, Rome, and Dresden."

FAMILY

345

"If the family were a *container*, it would be a *nest*, an enduring nest, loosely woven, expansive, and *open*.

"If the family were a *fruit* it would be an *orange*, a circle of sections, held together but separable, each segment *distinct*.

"If the family were a *boat*, it would be a *canoe*. It would make no progress unless *everyone* paddled.

"If the family were a *sport*, it would be *baseball*: a long, slow, *nonviolent* game that is never over until the last out.

"If the family were a *building*, it would be an old but *solid* structure that contains human history and appeals to those who see the carved moldings under all the plaster, the wide plank floors under the linoleum: the *possibilities*."
—Pogrebin, L.C. (Adapted).

346/FAMILY
Mother Teresa of Calcutta is a living legend of love for the poor and the oppressed and the homeless and people dying in the streets. Not only is she *directly* involved with people in need, but also she manages to find time to travel all over the world to find *support* for this ministry. On one such trip she gave a talk at the National Presbyterian Church. Author Coleen Evans said she was so deeply *moved* by Mother Teresa's talk that she would have done *anything* for her. "What can we do to *help* you?" Coleen Evans asked. Mother Teresa turned to her quietly and said, "Love your *family*." Coming from this *great* Christian woman who is totally involved in a ministry to the poor all over the *world*, this was an *amazing* response. It is evident that Mother Teresa knows her *Gospel!* Mother Teresa knows that "anyone who aspires to greatness must serve the needs of *all*." Mother Teresa knows also that it all begins with our becoming as little children again in our *family* and *other* close relationships.

347/FAMILY
From Bob Greene's Chicago Tribune column:

> My parents have stayed married for 35 years. While we, their children, have been free to roam and explore every possibility of life, they have lived in the same town this whole time. We assumed that we would always have a home town and our parents would always be there. They weren't allowed to leave. That was how the rules were.

Meanwhile, we children went out to get lost or get away or get famous—whatever we wanted—and they stayed, having given us that freedom. I don't know what it is that we were trying to accomplish in our disordered lives, but they certainly accomplished what they set out to do: they raised a family—35 years and a family raised.

The three of us children never once doubted that our parents were there to turn to if we needed help, and we live with the knowledge that of all the things we may accomplish, nothing can possibly be as impressive as the memory of the house we grew up in and what it represented. That is what my parents have accomplished in this life: they have given us a hometown and a house and the memories of the years we were a family in it.

348/FAMILY

In a big urban center, the *motherhouse* of the Sisters of Saint Francis is across the street from a Franciscan *monastery*. All telephone calls to both places come through the switchboard in the motherhouse. One day, the man at the switchboard heard a caller say the following: "Sister, this is Brother. Father wants to talk to Mother."

349/FAMILY

An artist desperately desired to paint the most beautiful picture in the world. He went to his *pastor* and asked, "What is the most beautiful thing in the world?" "*Faith*," said the pastor, "is the most beautiful thing. You can see it in every Church, in every Community of the Faithful. You can find it at every altar." The artist then asked a young *bride* the same question. "*Love*," she replied. "Love builds poverty into riches, sweetens tears, makes great treasures out of little gifts. Without love, there is not beauty." Then the artist asked a *soldier*, "What is the most beautiful thing in the world?" "*Peace*," said the soldier. "War is ugly. Wherever you find *peace*, you find beauty." The artist thought: "Faith, Love and

Peace. How can I paint them?" Then he returned to his household and, entering the door, he saw faith in the eyes of his *children*. He saw love in the eyes of his *wife*. And there, in his home, he saw the *Peace* that Love and Faith had built. So he *painted* the picture of the "most beautiful thing in the world." And when he had finished, he called it "*Home*."

350/FAMILY

A young lad asked his mother: "Were you, dad and I all born in the same place?" "No," the mother replied, "I was born in *Virginia*; dad was born in *Oregon*; and you were born in *New York City*." The boy seemed puzzled. "What's wrong?" the mother asked. The boy said: "I was just wondering how God managed to get the three of us *together*."

351/FAMILY

Two high school students were discussing their report cards. One of them asked, "What did your parents say when you brought home all F's?" "They didn't say anything to me," the other replied, "They were too busy arguing about *which* side of the family I took after."

FATHER AND SON

352

A small boy was out walking with his father. The boy looked up at the electric wires stretched between poles and asked his dad, "How does electricity go *through* those wires?" "I really don't know," the father said. A few blocks further, there was the sound of distant *thunder*. "Dad, what makes the lightening and thunder," the little boy asked. "I never really understood how that works," the father answered. The boy continued to ask questions, none of which the father could explain. Finally, as they neared home, the boy said, "Dad, I hope you didn't mind my asking you all those *questions*." To which dad replied, "Of course not, son. If you don't ask questions how are you going to learn?"

353/FATHER AND SON

As Charlie Moore was reaching retirement age, he was suddenly transferred by his company to a distant city. There, he decided to fulfill a long-standing ambition: he joined the company softball team. During his first game, whenever he came to bat he heard a loud voice yelling, "Way to go, Mr. Moore!"..."You can do it, Mr. Moore!" Charlie was amazed that someone would know his name in this strange city. After the game, he located his wife and son and asked if they knew who the person was in the stands who was yelling encouragement. The son replied, "Dad, it was me." "But why were you calling me *Mr. Moore*," the father asked.

"I didn't want anyone to know we were *related*," said the son.

God, our Father, wants *everyone* to know that we're related to Him!

"Father...the world has not known Thee, but I have known Thee...and I have made known to them Thy Name"
(Jn 17:25,26).

354/FATHER AND SON

There was an amusing bit of dialog some years ago between "Lamont" and "Fred Sanford" on the television show "Sanford and Son." Fred Sanford, (played by Redd Foxx) raised his son Lamont, with only the occasional help of his late wife's sister. In one episode, Fred tries to impress upon Lamont that he made many sacrifices and worked very hard over the years to raise him in the best environment possible. "Didn't you learn *anything* all these years being my son?" he asks. "*Who* do you think I'm doing this all for?"

"*Yourself*," came Lamont's immediate reply.

Fred says, "Yeah, I guess you *did* learn something."

355/FATHER AND SON

A father and his teenage son were frequently at odds over those things that fathers and sons often disagree: homework, friends, lifestyle, curfew, the family car, etc. It seemed that the two could hardly say anything to each other without getting into a shouting match. Finally, the father proposed that they go on a camping trip—just the two of them—to a mountain a few hundred miles away. The young man agreed.

For a week, father and son forded swift streams together, climbed over huge boulders together, trampled through thick brush together, slept under starlit skies together—and *talked, talked, talked.* They began to know each other as never before. They began to see each other, not just in their usual roles of domineering father and rebellious son, but as genuine human persons, each with his own individual hopes and fears and loves. The trip up the mountain became a *turning-point* in each of their lives. In the years that followed, they continued to disagree on many things, but on different terms. When a problem loomed, one or the other would say, "Remember the *mountain*!" An ordinary mountain became their *glory* mountain. What began as a common camping trip had been transformed into a *mountaintop* experience.

FATHERHOOD

356

Three men sat expectantly in the hospital waiting room. A nurse from the maternity wing entered the room. She said to the first man, "Congratulations! You're the father of twins." "That's a wonderful coincidence," he exclaimed. "I'm a member of the 'Minnesota Twins' baseball team." Then the nurse addressed the second man: "Congratulations! You're the father of triplets." "Wow!" said the new father, "another wonderful coincidence. I work for the '3M Company'." The third man jumped to his feet. "I'm leaving," he said. "I work for '7-Up.'"

357/FATHERHOOD

"You are my Father, my God, and the Rock of my salvation" (Ps. 89:26).

"...yet I am not alone, because the Father is with Me" (Jn. 16:32).

From his book "Papa My Father," Leo Buscaglia recalls an afternoon many years ago when he was supervising an educational program for disabled children.

> I was observing in a classroom for mildly retarded fourth graders. I sat beside six children and their teacher in their reading group. They were reading a story about a little duck that had no father. As with all good children's books, this one was filled with repetitive phrases. The refrain was always. "But the little duck had no *father*."
>
> The teacher, having learned the best technique from her prestigious school of education, read carefully, distinctly, and with feeling.
>
> "Martha," she asked a lovely little girl in the group, "tell us. Did the little duck have a *father?*"
>
> The child answered without a moment's hesitation, "*Yes.*"
>
> The teacher paused for a moment, slightly taken aback by the little girl's response. "Martha, let me read to you again from the story, and listen very *carefully* this time."
>
> She then repeated several parts of the story, each time accentuating the familiar refrain. "The little duck had no *father*."

This time, *certain* of success, she again asked Martha, "Did the little duck have a *father?*"

The entire reading group now had fallen into a tense silence while Martha reconsidered the question. After several moments she responded very matter-of-factly, "Yes."

"Now listen carefully, Martha. I'm going to read from the story once more." She again read from the book, "The little duck had *no-o-o-o* father." The entire group, and poor Martha, who was now a captive in her teacher's arms, jumped at the sound of the exaggerated "no!"

"Now," the teacher asked again sweetly, regaining her control, "did the little duck have a *father?*"

Martha's large brown eyes had filled with tears. The entire group waited in anxious silence. Finally she answered again, "Yes, the little duck had a *father.*"

At this point the teacher totally lost control. "Martha, you disappoint me. You're simply not paying attention! It says again and again in the story that the little duck had *no* father."

Now the tears in Martha's eyes overflowed and ran in streams down her cheeks. "But, teacher," she said, "*everybody* gots a father."

FATHER'S DAY

358
Leo Buscaglia reminds us that for many children, *this* Father's Day may be a painful reminder that not every family situation reflects the *ideal*:

In a short, informal activity to prepare second graders for the celebration of Father's Day, a group of children were asked to respond to the question, "What do you love about your dad?" Their answers were sometimes poignant and often reflective of the fact that non-traditional roles of fatherhood are fast becoming accepted as the norm.

"I love my father, Bob, because we have fun together on weekends, and I love my new father, Al, because he plays with me and fixes me breakfast every morning."
"I love my dad but I don't know where he is. I know he's somewhere because he sends us money all the time, but I don't ever see him."

"I love my dad because he loves me and my brother and my mom and he hugs and kisses us a lot."

"I love my dad because he always brings us things when he visits us on weekends."
—Buscaglia, L., "Papa, My Father." (Adapted).

359/FATHER'S DAY

A Gift For Father

My child handed me an incomprehensible splash of color on a crumpled sheet of paper and I tried so very hard to fathom the mystery spread before me.

"What is it?" I asked. "A cat? A dog? A hat?"

"Can't you see? Oh, Dad!" he exclaimed as he turned it upside down. "It's a fish, and there's its head and here's the tail." Then he added with a twinkle in his eye, "Daddy, I made it especially for *you*!"

I told him it was *beautiful*. I told him I *loved* his big surprise. And a million dollars could not buy the look of *wonder* in his eye.

FEAR

360
Seeking a handsome settlement for injuries he had sustained when his wagon was run off the road by a truck, a farmer took his case to court. An attorney for the defense grilled him. "Did you indicate to the defendant immediately after the accident that you were hurt?"
"Well," said the farmer, "sort of."

"Please answer my question," repeated the attorney. "Did you say you were hurt and, if not, why not?"

"Let me explain," said the farmer. "You see, when that big truck hit my wagon, it knocked me off the road and into a ditch. My horse was knocked across the road and broke his leg. My dog was pinned under the wagon. Your client took one look at the yelping dog and the agonizing horse, ran to his car, and got a big pistol. Then, he came back and shot my horse. Then he went over and shot my dog. Finally, with his pistol still smoking, he came to where I lay bleeding in the ditch and asked, "Are you hurt?"

FEMININITY

361
One of the things that has come out of the feminist movement is an attempt to get believers to think of God's attributes in feminine as well as masculine terms. Said one well-known preacher: One Sunday I preached a sermon on the "Attributes of God" to a very large congregation. During the week I received a large number of telephone calls and letters complaining that every time I mentioned God I did so in strictly masculine terms. There were objections to my

exclusive use of the masculine pronouns—He, Him and His—whenever I referred to God.

The following Sunday, I preached a sermon on "Satan" to the same congregation. Again, in all my references to the devil I used the masculine pronouns: he, him, his. And I got no complaints!

FORBEARANCE

362

"...if anyone hits you on the right cheek, offer him the other as well" (Mt. 5:39).

Imagine that someone placed an offering before you and you did not pick it up. Or imagine that someone wrote a letter to you but you did not open it. Or imagine that the telephone rang and you did not answer it. Try to do this whenever you are abused or insulted or diminished in some way, and you will not lose your serenity (your peace of soul).

—deMello, A., "The Heart of the Enlightened."

FORGIVENESS

363

"Why do you keep talking about my past mistakes?" said the husband. "I thought you had forgiven and forgotten."

"I have, indeed, forgiven and forgotten, said the wife. "But I want to make sure you don't forget that I have forgiven and forgotten."

Sinner: "Remember not my sins, O Lord!"

Lord: "What sins? I forgot them long ago."

—deMello, A., "The Song of the Bird."

"Love keeps no record of wrongs." (1 Cor. 13).

364/FORGIVENESS

Some years ago, a pastor in Boston was being harassed by a woman in his congregation. She started false rumors about him. She wrote vicious letters about him to his bishop and others. She initiated petitions to have him removed. After several months of this, the woman moved to another city and not long afterward was converted to Christ. Part of the process of her conversion was to realize the terrible wrong she had done and all the pain and suffering she had inflicted on her pastor in Boston. Consequently, she wrote him a long letter explaining what had happened to her and how deeply she regretted what she had done to him. The pastor immediately sent her a telegram with three words on it: "Forgiven! Forgotten! Forever!"

365/FORGIVENESS

A dying old man lay fearful in his bed that God would not forgive him for a sin he committed earlier in life. The nurse who was caring for him was aware of his fear and tried to comfort him. "What was your occupation?" she asked. "I was a stone–cutter all my life, and an excellent one," the man said. To which the nurse replied: "That was *your* job. *God's* job is *forgiveness.* And He is *excellent* at it. God is as good at His job as you are at yours. You have *nothing* to fear."

366/FORGIVENESS

In his book "Making Miracles," Arnold Fox recalls seeing his father's Last Will and Testament for the first time.

> I'll never forget my father's Last Will. Only in his early seventies when felled by a stroke, he had lived a life that was often difficult. He was a man given to quick anger and bitter memories. I remember going with him to the farmers' produce market in Philadelphia when I was a child, where he would purchase fruit and vegetables to sell. On one occasion some men deliberately cheated him, leaving him with nothing during the hard days of the Depression. Dad was furious; he swore he'd never forgive them. He calmed

> down as he aged, though as far as I knew, he never forgave those who had hurt him. Dad had a lot to forgive, and a lot to be forgiven for.

The day after he died, my mother gave me my father's Last Will and Testament. This is how it began:

> My Last Will: All of them owe me no more. I *forgive* them. May they forgive *me.*

I forgive them, and ask that they forgive me: The perfect formula for peace of mind and soul!

"...forgive and you will be forgiven." (Lk. 6:37).

367/FORGIVENESS

Forgiving, which begins with *self*-forgiveness, can become a constant, ongoing process—*a way of living.* It means letting go of past resentments and bitterness, and *moving on.* Of course, it's not always easy, but it's *worth* every difficulty. And there is nothing mushy or softheaded about loving and forgiving. As Doctor Jonas Salk puts it:

> The end result of forgiving is to release the power in the *nucleus* of the individual—a power much greater in its *positive* effects than atomic power in its *negative.*

The point is this:

> If we can be courageous one more time
> than we are fearful,
> *Trusting* one more time than we are anxious,
> *Cooperative* one more time than we are competitive,
> *Forgiving* one more time than we are vindictive,
> *Loving* one more time than we are hateful,
> we will have moved closer to the next big breakthrough in our human growth, and closer to the next big breakthrough toward our human potential.

368/FORGIVENESS

A man went to his pastor a week after his mother's funeral, in the clutches of overwhelming guilt and remorse. He confessed that he had never really had a good relationship with his mother and, as a result, had not given her the kind of care in her dying days that she deserved. But, of course, she was dead, and there was nothing now that he could do. The pastor shared with him the Good News of *forgiveness:* that there was something bigger in the world than he was; that the something bigger was the reality of *grace* and *mercy.* He invited him to *accept* the gift of forgiveness—not because he *deserved* it but because it was God's *nature* to give it. Then the pastor said, "I know of an elderly woman in our congregation who has no children and is very concerned about how she is going to negotiate her last days. Not in order to *earn* God's forgiveness, but as a sign of the fact that you have *received* this gift, I think it would be wonderful if you would start doing for this woman what you cannot do for your own mother now." The suggestion made sense to the man and he began to do it. It was a way of concretizing the forgiveness he had experienced. It was a way of looking forward to the future differently, not in *spite* of, but actually *because* of the past.

—Claypool, J.R., "Learning to Forgive Ourselves." (Adapted).

369/FORGIVENESS

An unknown Christian wrote the following poem to emphasize the overwhelming joy of forgiveness:

Not far from New York is a cemetery lone,
And all the inscription is one word alone—
FORGIVEN!
The death is unmentioned, the name is untold,
Beneath lies the body, corrupted and cold.
Above rests his spirit, at home in the fold—
FORGIVEN!
And when, from the heavens, the Lord shall descend,
Well-known and befriended, his song shall not end—
FORGIVEN!

370/FORGIVENESS

A missionary from New Zealand told the story of an old Maori woman who had won the name "Warrior Brown" because of her fighting qualities. Warrior Brown was converted to Christ and her life changed radically. On one occasion, she went into one of her old haunts of sin to talk about Jesus. As she spoke, someone in the crowd around her threw a potato which struck her on the temple. The people who had known her expected to see an explosion from "Warrior Brown." Instead, she stooped down, picked up the potato and put it in the pocket of her apron. Months later, it came time for the Fall "Thanksgiving Service." It was the custom for believers to bring some of the fruits of their labors to give to the Lord at this harvest festival. Warrior Brown brought a sack of potatoes. When asked about her offering, she explained that she had taken the potato that had been thrown at her, and had cut it up and planted it. And she was now giving the Lord the fruit of her increase that was born out of her forgiveness.

—"The Sermon on the Mount, Contemporary Insights For a Christian Life," by Pentecost, J.D. (Adapted).

371/FORGIVENESS

The story is told of a man who had been living a terrible burden of guilt for many years. He had done something reprehensible which no one else knew about and he was convinced that he was beyond all hope of forgiveness. Finally, he met a woman who was something of a mystic. She claimed to have visions in which Christ appeared and spoke to her. Seeking to test her claim, the man said to her, "You say that you are able to speak directly with *Christ* in your visions. I have a secret which no one else on earth knows. The next time you are in conversation with Christ please ask Him what sin I committed years ago that destroyed my peace of soul." The mystic said that she would gladly ask Christ the question. Several days later, the two met as agreed. Immediately the man asked:

"Did you visit with Christ in a vision?"
"Yes."
"And did you ask Him what terrible sin I committed years ago?"

"Yes."

"Tell me quickly, what did Christ *say?*"

"He said, 'I don't remember.'"

FRIENDSHIP

372

"Oh, the comfort, the inexpressible comfort of feeling *safe* with a person, having neither to weigh thoughts, nor measure words, but pouring them all out, just as they are, chaff and grain together, certain that a faithful hand will take and sift them, keep what is *worth* keeping, and with a breath of kindness blow the rest *away*."

—*Craik, D.M.*

373/FRIENDSHIP

Professional basketball coach K.C. Jones was renowned for offering his players unforgettable words of encouragement, but only when they needed it *most.* According to star forward, Kevin McHale, Jones would never congratulate a player after he had made a *great* play. McHale asked Coach Jones one night why he never complimented his players when they were turning in outstanding performances. "Kevin" he said, "after you've made the winning basket, you've got 15,000 people cheering for you, TV commentators come rushing toward you, and everybody is giving you 'high-fives.' You don't need *me* then. When you need a friend most is when *nobody* is cheering."

FUND RAISING

374

At the monastery's annual "Fish and Chips Fund Raising Festival," a visitor told the Abbot he'd like to congratulate the chef. The Abbot said, "There's your man, in the brown robe over there." The visitor approached the man in the brown robe and asked, "Are you the *fish* friar?" "No," he replied, "I'm the *chip* monk."

G

GAMBLING

375
A dejected looking man was sitting on a park bench directly across from a church. The man's clothes were in tatters and he had several days' growth of beard. Feeling sorry for the down–and–out soul, the Pastor of the nearby church presented the man with a ten–dollar bill, patted him on the shoulder and said, "*Godspeed.*" Later that evening the man ran toward the clergyman as he was crossing the street. As he approached he held out a fifty–dollar bill in his hand.

"I can't *thank* you enough," he shouted with excitement. "Godspeed *won* by four–and–a–half lengths!"

GENERATION GAP

376
The mother of a teenage boy whose musical taste was limited to heavy metal rock and roll, went with her son to a concert featuring sacred music. The mother seized the opportunity to show her son why *her* kind of music was superior to *his*. "Your music just doesn't say anything," she whispered. "It just *repeats* the same words over and over."

The boy's rebuttal came later, as both of them stood for the concert's finale from Handel's Messiah: "Hallelujah! Hallelujah! Hallelujah!"
—Seaborn, B.

GENEROSITY

377

Dr. Karl Menninger once asked a very wealthy patient, "What are you going to do with all that money?" The patient replied, "Just *worry* about it, I guess." "In that case," said the doctor, "do you experience much *pleasure* out of worrying about your money?" With a heavy sigh, the patient replied, "No, but I feel such *terror* when I think of *giving* any of it away." Commenting on his patient's money–sickness, Dr. Menninger said, "*Generous* people are *rarely* mentally ill!"

378/GENEROSITY

"You will be enriched in every way for your great generosity (II Cor. 9:11).

Have you ever seen a generous person who really lacked for anything? Perhaps that person did not have every luxury, but in all probability was content...joyous...abundantly rich in *friends* ...

> My hobby is giving something away every day—something *tangible*, so that I will be reminded to give away the vastly more important *intangibles*: a smile, a word of encouragement, a healing touch, an intercessory prayer, a telephone call or a letter to some lonely person.
>
> Every day I give something away. It may be a book, a poster, a flower, a poem, a plaque with an inspirational message—something that might enrich the life of the person receiving the gift.
>
> I may not be a person of great wisdom, but this I know:
>
> The more I give to others, the more I have. Among the rich rewards are friends who love me. I experience the

daily satisfaction that I have made life happier for at least one person. I have an inner peace that comes from the assurance that truly it is better to give than to receive. The truth is—the Gospel truth—that one cannot give without receiving in abundance...to overflowing!

—*Ward, W.A. (Adapted).*

GIVING

379

In his book, "Bus 9 To Paradise," author Leo Buscaglia recalls a letter he received from a reader:

> You are always so positive about life, so hopeful about loving and about people's behavior that it inspired me to explore the art of giving which you so often encourage. I'm young and don't really have much to give, so I decided to buy a bunch of daisies, stand at a local intersection, and hand them out with a simple "Have a beautiful day." I thought it would be fun and might help others to be a bit happier. It ended by being a very enlightening experience—not exactly what I expected, but I learned a lot about human nature.
>
> It surprised me how few people would *accept* my gift. Many just passed me by, avoiding my smile. Others actually pushed my hand away. Some simply uttered a curt "No thank you" and moved on their way. Others reluctantly took the flower and waited for some sales pitch, wondering what they had to give in return. The saddest thing I learned was that people are *suspicious* of giving. It's as if they are afraid that taking will *commit* them in some way. I wasn't even able to get rid of all the daisies. I went home with some of them drooping in my hand. What a strange world this is!

God, who gives us life and sustains our life and rules our life, God our Father, is a *Prodigal* Father, a lavish, *extravagant*

Father. Jesus tells us to look at God in just that way: a Father who never stops *giving*, a Father who never stops *pouring* out His resources, a Father who never stops lavishing His very *Self* on His children.

"All that the Father has belongs to Me and I give you My assurance, whatever you ask the Father, He will give you in My name" (Jn.16:15,23).

GOD (BELIEF IN)

380
A Sunday school teacher suddenly stopped reading a passage in the Bible and asked her pupils, "*Why* do you believe in God?" She got a variety of answers, some full of simple faith, others obviously insincere. The one that stopped her cold came from the son of one of Boston's best–known ministers. The lad frowned, then answered thoughtfully, "I guess it just runs in our *family*."

GOD (EXISTENCE OF)

381
There is a clever cartoon in which two goldfish in a bowl are arguing about the existence of *God*. One goldfish looks very exasperated as he blurts out, "If there is no God, then who changes the *water* every week?"

382/GOD (EXISTENCE OF)
Author Fulton Oursler writes of his boyhood nurse who was born a slave. It was *she*, he says, who taught him this unforgettable lesson in gratitude:

> I remember her as she sat at the kitchen table in our house—the hard, old, brown hands folded across her starched apron, the glistening eyes, and the husky old whispering voice saying, "Much obliged, Lord, for my *vittles*."

"Anna," I asked, "*what's* a vittle?" She answered, "It's what I've got to eat and drink. That's vittles." Then I said, "But you'd get your vittles whether you thanked the Lord or not." "Sure," she replied, "but, it makes everything *taste* better to be thankful."

GOD (FATHERHOOD OF)

383

"While he was yet a distance his father saw him and had compassion and ran and embraced him" (Lk, 15:20–21).

Consider this picture:

A father leaves his home to walk to work. One of his sons, hearing the door close, remembers that he has something to ask him. So he runs down the stairs, through the house, out the door, and down the street. As the father is about to turn the corner, he hears the son call out to him. The father looks back and sees the look on his son's face. It registers uncertainty, strain, *anxiety* as to whether the father has heard him and will turn to see him.

Later that day, the father is returning home from work. The son is playing in front of the house. The father sees him first and calls him by name. Hearing his name, the son turns and *runs* toward his father. It is the same boy, the same street, the same father. But one thing is vastly different: the look on the boy's face is *not* filled with uncertainty and strain and anxiety. It is a look of *certainty* and *recognition* and *response*. And one thing had made it so: the father has first called *him*.

This picture can change *our* look, so to speak, from uncertainty and strain and anxiety to clarity and recognition and response. For it is, in part, the meaning of the Biblical phrase, "He has first loved us."

—Bartlett, G.E., "The Long Way Home," Best Sermons 1962 (Adapted).

384/GOD (FATHERHOOD OF)

"The eternal God is your dwelling place, and underneath are everlasting arms" (Deut.33:27).

An eagle is teaching its young how to fly. The ceremony begins with the destruction of the nest. The old eagle tears it up and throws the pieces over the cliff. Then she takes the little eaglet on her broad back and, circling, carries him high into the sun. She tilts her wings and slides him off into space. Fluttering, screeching, screaming, he drifts down. The old eagle circles around him. Long before he reaches the sharp crags and rocks below, she glides under him and catches him on her broad wings. Two or three times she repeats this as if to say, "See, you cannot fall, for underneath are my everlasting wings."

We change the picture only slightly and make it say, "Underneath are the everlasting *arms of God*, our Father." There are times in life when life is too much for us, and we cannot keep our spirits up, and we are wounded and sick of heart. And we need desperately to experience the loving embrace of the everlasting arms of God.
—Angell, C.R., "Iron Shoes" Best Sermons 1947 (Adapted).

GOD (PRESENCE OF)

385

"There is no God! All of the wonders around us are accidental. No almighty hand made a thousand–billion starts. They made themselves. No power keeps them on their steady course. The earth spins itself to keep the oceans from falling off toward the sun. Infants teach themselves to cry when they are hungry or hurt. A small flower invented itself so that we could extract digitalis for sick hearts.

"The earth gave itself day and night, tilted itself so that we get seasons. Without the magnetic poles man would be unable to navigate the trackless oceans of water and air, but they 'just grew there.'

"How about the sugar–thermostat in the pancreas? It maintains a level of sugar in the blood without which all of us would fall into a coma and die.

"Why does snow sit on mountaintops waiting for the warm spring sun to melt it at just the right time for the young crops in farms below to drink? A very lovely accident.

"The human heart will beat for 70 or 80 years without faltering. How does it get sufficient rest between beats? A kidney will filter poison from the blood, and leave the good things alone. How does it know one from the other?

"Who gave the human tongue flexibility to form words, and a brain to understand them, but denied it to all other animals?

"Who showed a womb how to take the love of two persons and keep splitting a tiny ovum until, in time, a baby would have the proper number of fingers and eyes and ears, and hair in the right places, and come into the world when it is strong enough to sustain life?

"There is no God?"
—Bishop, J., Miami Herald (Adapted).

386/GOD (PRESENCE OF)
The believer in God must explain one thing, the existence of suffering; the non–believer, however, must explain the existence of everything else.

GOD'S LOVE

387

God has me in *His* heart,
whether I have Him in my heart or not.

I do not have to be the most willing
for Him to choose me,
or the most capable for Him to use me.

It is not only good people God
has used to do His good;
It is not only brave people God
has used to win His victories;
It is not only righteous people God
has used to establish right.

God does not help me because of what
I am. God helps me because of what He is!
—Freeman, J.D., "Because He Is Love" (Adapted).

388/GOD'S LOVE

A weathercock that once graced
A farmer's barn above,
Bore on it by its owner's will
The sentence, "God is love."

His neighbor passing questioned him.
He deemed the legend strange.
"Now, you think that, like the vane,
God's love can lightly change?"

The farmer, smiling, shook his head.
"Nay, friend, 'tis meant to show,
That 'God is love' whichever way
The wind may chance to blow."

GOD'S PLAN

389

A famous French criminologist named Emile Locard came up with a theory he called "Locard's Exchange Principle. The theory says, in effect, that any person passing through a *room* will unknowingly *deposit* something there and take something *away. Modern* technology tells us that the principle is *sound.* Yet it is but a *microcosm* of a principle the New Testament writers gave to the world *2000 years ago*:

Every human being passing through *life* will leave something and take something away. Most of this "something" cannot be catalogued or numbered or recorded with precision. This "something" doesn't lend itself to statistics. Nevertheless, in God's Plan for the *fulfillment* of all He has created—in God's Plan for the fulfillment of His *Kingdom*—this "something" is *essential.* Nothing counts *without* it.

GOD'S PRESENCE

390

A wealthy woman in New York City died and left a Last Will and Testament in which she gave her entire estate to *God.* This created legal problems which the authorities said could only be resolved in the *courts.* Consequently, a lawsuit was started in which "God" was named as a party. A summons was issued and the official process servers went through the motions of trying to *serve* it. The final report sent to the court read as follows: "After a due and diligent search, made in accordance with established procedures, God cannot be found in New York City."

In the matter of where God can be found, the search does not begin in New York City or any other city. The search begins in our *hearts!* Are you experiencing God's Presence *within* you? *That* is the question!

391/GOD'S PRESENCE

There is a story of a woman who was desperately trying to find God. She had a dream in which she was standing in front of a thick pane of glass, and she could see God standing on the other side. She pounded on the glass as hard as she could in order to attract God's attention. But her efforts ended in failure. This dream occurred many times. And each time the woman grew more and more desperate to get God to notice her. She began to cry out to Him, shrieking at the top of her voice.

Finally, in her last such dream, a gentle voice spoke to her, saying, "Why are you making such a fuss? Don't you realize there is *nothing* between us?"

GOOD FRIDAY

392

Most people in their retirement years can remember exactly what they were doing when they heard the news of the bombing of Pearl Harbor. Most people born before the late 1950's can remember exactly what they were doing when they heard the news of John F. Kennedy's assasination. And most young people remember what they were doing when they heard the news of John Lennon's death.

But *whatever* your age, on this Anniversary of the *Cross*, you must remember *this*:

"God loved the world so much that He gave His own Son, so that everyone who believes in Him may not be lost but may have eternal life" (Jn. 3:16).

GOODNESS

393

A country preacher delivered a stirring message to his people about good and evil in the world. He said: "People talk to me about the problem of evil, but I will tell you an even greater problem: the problem of goodness. How do you account for the fact that in such a world as this there should be so much self–sacrifice, so much unselfishness, so much love? By what miracle has man, who only a few thousand years ago was living on the level of beasts, risen to a point where he will literally lay down his life for his family, for a cause, for a friend?"

394/GOODNESS

In a book called "Entertaining Angels," the author cites a survey conducted by a major advertising agency. According to the report (entitled "Fears and Fantasies of the American Consumer"), about seventy–five percent of Americans have daydreamed about *saving someone else's life*, and fully one–third of the population has daydreamed about *finding a*

cure for cancer. But when it came to the question, "What is the *greatest* pleasure in life," the answer was "Watching television." *Television* topped the list. "We would love to be good, it seems, so long as it doesn't *inconvenience* us...It's one thing to dream *about* being good, another to *be* good for something."
—Church, F.F., "Entertaining Angels"

GOOD SAMARITAN

395
When you hear the story of the Good Samaritan, do you ever wonder about the *rest* of the story? What *effect* did the care and compassion of the Good Samaritan have on the man who had been robbed and beaten and thrown into the ditch? Did he remember the cruelty of the *robbers* and shape his life with *that* memory? Or did he remember the generosity of the *Samaritan* and shape his life with *that* memory? What did he pass on to the strangers in *his* life?

In *pondering* these questions, place *yourself* in the "rest of the story." Ask yourself, "What do I pass on to the strangers in *my* life? What do I do when *I* encounter a stranger in need?

GOSPEL MESSAGE

396
In the title story of his volume of short stories, "The Old Man at the Railroad Crossing," William Maxwell could be pointing to the meaning of the Gospel for the cynics of the "Me Generation."

The gatekeeper, who had faithfully tended his gate at a busy railroad crossing for many years, was growing old and nearing retirement. He developed a peculiar trait as he aged: he greeted all of the pedestrians who passed his gate with a one–word message, "Rejoice!" Some people resented his telling them how they should feel. Others believed he should tend to his own business—the gate—before someone got hurt or killed. Only a few would mutter "Thank you." Most passersby thought that he was crazy.

One day, a woman who was passing by suddenly stopped when she heard him say "Rejoice!" to her. "What do I have to rejoice about?" she asked. But the old gatekeeper merely repeated his greeting: "Rejoice!"

Some time later, when the woman again passed by, she discovered that the gatekeeper had disappeared from the crossing. She immediately sought him out and finally found him at his daughter's house where he lay dying. The woman took his hand in her's, smiled at him, and spoke the one word which seemed to have the whole Gospel Message compressed into it. "Rejoice!" She smiled, and the old gatekeeper smiled back at her and died peacefully, sustained by the hope inherent in the message–greeting that had become his mission in life.

GOSSIP

397

Winston Churchill was attending an official ceremony. Several rows behind him two gentlemen began whispering, "That's Winston Churchill." "They say he is getting senile." "They say he should step aside and leave the running of the nation to younger, more dynamic, and capable men." Churchill sat facing forward, but when the ceremony was over, he stopped by the row where the men were seated, leaned forward and said, "Gentlemen, do they also say he is *deaf?*"

—Hatcher, B.

398/GOSSIP

The United Technologies company once ran an advertisement in the "Wall Street Journal." It was entitled "THE SNAKE THAT POISONS," and it read as follows:

It topples governments, wrecks marriages, ruins careers, busts reputations, causes heartaches, nightmares, indigestion, spawns suspicion, generates grief, dispatches innocent people to cry in their pillows. Even its name hisses. It's called *gossip—office* gossip, *shop* gossip, *party gossip.* It makes headlines and headaches. Before you repeat a story, ask yourself: Is it *true?* Is it *fair?* Is it *necessary?* If not, shut up!

GRACE

399

Jerome Kern or Cole Porter could take a simple sheet of paper, write a song on it, and make it worth millions of dollars—that's creative *genius!*

John Pierpont Morgan could sign his name to a piece of paper and make it worth millions of dollars—that's *capital!*

A craftsperson can take a piece of material having little or no value and shape it into something of *great* value—that's *art!*

Almighty God can take a worthless, sinful, pride–filled life, wash it in the blood of the Savior, and make it a *blessing* to humanity—that's *Grace!*

GRANDPARENTS

400

A teacher gave her homeroom of Senior honors students a graduation gift in advance. They were permitted one unexcused absence as long as it didn't conflict with other teachers' schedules. All she asked was that they do something worthwhile and hand in a paragraph sharing that experience. Her favorite report was from a young man who wrote: "I went fish ing with my grandfather. I listened to him all day long without once saying, 'Grandpa, you already told me that.'"
—Scarpato, B.

GRATITUDE

401

If only the people who worry about their liabilities would think about the riches they do possess, they would stop worrying. Would you sell both your eyes for a million dollars...or your two legs...or your hands...or your hearing? Add up what you *do* have, and you'll find that you won't sell them for all the gold in the world. The best things in life are yours, if you can appreciate yourself. That's the way to stop worrying—and start *living!*

—Carnegie, D.

402/GRATITUDE

There is an essay about a man who had formed the habit of writing "thank you" in the lower left–hand corner of all his checks as he paid his bills. He would write a check to the electric utility or the phone company, and as he penned in the words "thank you" in the corner, he would think of all the ways in which his life was made more comfortable by the fact that the company regularly and reliably provided him with its services. He would write a check to the bank for his monthly mortgage payment and pause for a moment to reflect on the comfort of having a roof over his head. He would pay his water bill and as he wrote "thank you" in the corner, he would say to himself that the water wasn't all that great–tasting and probably had some chemicals in it that were bad for him, but how long ago was it that his forebearers had to pump water from the well in winter and worry about its going dry in summer. Even when he was not all that happy about writing a check, as when he paid his income tax in April, he disciplined himself to write "thank you" on the check, not because he believed that the IRS computer would notice it and be gratified, but because it was his way of reminding himself that he should feel grateful to be enjoying the benefits that American democracy provides.

That man's constant expressions of gratitude remind us that we cannot be *truly* grateful for the blessings that come our way without being grateful to *God.* Every *sincere* "Thank you!" is an implied "Thank you *God!*"

Thank you *God*—"who made the world and *everything* in it" (Acts 17:24).

Thank you *God*—who "gives to all men life and breath and *everything*" (Acts 17:25).

GREED

403

A man was a regular customer at a restaurant, and the management always did its best to please him. So when he complained one day that only *one* piece of bread was being given him with his meal, the waiter promptly brought him *four* slices.

"That's good," he said, "but not good enough. I like bread—*plenty* of it." So the next night he was given a *dozen* slices. "Good," he said, "But you're still being frugal, aren't you?"

Even a *basketful* of slices on the table the next day did not stop his complaints. So the manager decided to teach him a lesson. He had a colossal loaf of bread baked. It was six feet long and three feet wide. When the regular customer arrived, the manager himself, with the help of two waiters, carried it into the restaurant, laid it on the customer's table, then waited for his reaction. The man glared at the gigantic loaf, then looked at the manager and said, "So we're back to *one* piece again!"

"Because his greed knew no rest, he will not save anything in which he delights. There was nothing left after he had eaten; therefore his prosperity will not endure" (Job 20:20–21).
—deMello, A., "The Heart of the Enlightened." (Adapted).

GROWTH

404

Some say that just as hospitals minister to sick people, and schools to *ignorant* people, the Church ministers to *sinful* people. Consequently, we should not set too high a standard for our Church members. But sick people are expected to get *well*, and ignorant people are supposed to *learn*, and Christians should grow and become *better*. There is no excuse for us to stay babes on milk when we should mature and feed on the Bread of Life.

—Havner, V., "Pepper 'n' Salt" (Adapted).

405/GROWTH

The owner of a greenhouse had a gardener who was careful, methodical, and a hard worker. In spite of his diligence, the plants did not prosper under his care. The owner hired a more experienced gardener and, immediately, the plants began to thrive.

The unsuccessful gardener explained what happened: "When I transplanted flowers, I removed them carefully from their pots I disturbed them as little as possible. This new man didn't treat them that way. He was rough with them. He didn't care how much he disturbed their roots. I thought he would ruin the lot because he was so careless in his handling of them." He was silent for a moment. Then he added: "But they are growing."

He then went on to explain that the roots of the plants in the pots were packed tight, The successful gardener, by his apparent roughness, had loosened the soil and given the roots a chance to breathe and stretch, and grow stronger. By shaking them up, he actually made growing easier for them.

Are there not times when we need a little shaking up too in order to stretch our spiritual roots and grow stronger in the faith?

"...for a little while you may have to suffer various trials, so that the genuineness of your faith, more precious than gold which though perishable is tested by fire, may redound to praise and glory and honor at the revelation of Jesus Christ" (I Peter 1:6).

406/GROWTH

A man, while touring Italy, visited a cathedral that had been completed on the outside only. When the man entered the cathedral, he found an artist kneeling before an enormous wall upon which he had just begun to create a *mosaic*. On some tables nearby there were thousands of pieces of colored ceramic. Speaking in the language of the Italian artist, the visitor asked how he would ever finish such a large project.

The artist answered that he knew how much he could accomplish in one day. Therefore, each morning he marked off an area to be completed that day, and he didn't worry about what remained outside that space. He would take one day at a time. That was the *best* he could do. And if he did his best, one day the mosaic *would* be finished.

There is only so much *we* can do in one day to improve our lives and advance toward our fulfillment as human persons. To grow we need only make each day count, *one day at a time*.

—Caliandro, A., "Make Your Life Count." (Adapted).

407/GROWTH

Not long before Henry Wadsworth Longfellow's death at age seventy–five, someone asked him how he continued to write so beautifully and remain so vigorous. Longfellow pointed to an apple tree that was full of colorful bloom and said, "That is a very *old* apple tree, but the blossoms this year seem more beautiful than ever before. That old tree grows a little new wood each year, and I suppose it is out of the new wood that these blossoms come. Like the apple tree, I try to grow a little new wood each year."

GUILT

408

In one of the "Sally Forth" comic strips, Sally has had a hard day at the office. She decides to go to bed early. Before retiring, she says to her little daughter, Hillary, "I feel so guilty that I haven't spent any time with you tonight." Precocious Hillary replies, "You've got to quit this, Mom. All the time it's guilty this and guilty that! How come you're always feeling guilty?" To which Sally answers, "It's what I do best!"

Jesus came to reinforce our self–esteem; to teach us how to feel good about ourselves. If feeling guilty or laying guilt trips on other persons is what we do best, we are missing the whole point of our religion.

409/GUILT

There is an old story about the time Emperor Frederick the Great visited Potsdam Prison. He spoke with the prisoners, and each man interviewed claimed complete innocence of the crime for which he was convicted. Each claimed to be a victim of a frame–up or some other form of injustice. Someone *else* was to blame for their imprisonment. But, at last, one poor fellow, with his head hanging down, never looking up, said, "Your Majesty, I am *guilty*, and richly *deserve* my punishment." Whereupon, the Emperor shouted for the prison warden: "Come and get this man out of here before he *corrupts* all the noble, *innocent* people in this prison!"

H

HALLOWEEN

410
A little girl dressed in a "Wonder Woman" costume for her school's Halloween party was on her way out the door to catch the school bus. "I can do anything, I'm *Wonder* Woman," the little girl exclaimed as she picked up her books and lunch box and headed for the door. "Do you need any help carrying your things to the bus?" her mother asked. "Oh no," the little girl announced, "I'm *Wonder* Woman!" Her mother waited for the sound of the front door closing behind her daughter but instead heard a tiny voice cry out, "Mommy, can you come here and tie my shoe?"

HANDS OF GOD

411
In the Metropolitan Museum of Art in New York City, there is the magnificent sculpture by Rodin called "The Hand of God." Before he began sculpting the piece, Rodin sketched the hands of more than a thousand people from many walks of life: doctors, lawyers, secretaries, farmers, laborers, and others. He also sketched the hands of mothers, fathers, children, elderly persons. And from those sketches of thousands of hands, he finally sculpted "The Hand of God." In the palm of the hand, Rodin shaped a man and a woman embracing. "The Hand of God" was the artist's favorite work. And, by making it from a composite of the hands of so many people, Rodin was trying to say that we know God more intimately whenever we lovingly embrace another person. We love God

more intensely whenever we use the hands He has given us to caress, to comfort, to soothe, to heal another person. When you reach out into this needy world with love, your hands become the HANDS OF GOD!

HAPPINESS

412

In a delightful book called "To See a World in a Grain of Sand," C. L. James tells the fable of a wise old cat who notices a kitten chasing its tail. "Why are you chasing your tail so?" asked the wise old cat. The kitten replied, "I have learned that the best thing for a cat is *happiness*, and happiness is my *tail*. Therefore, I am chasing it; and when I catch it, I shall *have* happiness." To which the wise old cat responded, "My son, I too have paid attention to the problems of the universe. I too have judged that happiness is in my tail. But, I noticed that whenever I chase after it, it keeps running away from me, and when I go about my business, it just seems to come after me wherever I go."

413/HAPPINESS

Don't evaluate your life in terms of achievements, trivial or monumental, along the way. If you do, you will be destined to the frustration of always seeking out other destinations, and never allowing yourself actually to be fulfilled. Instead, wake up and appreciate everything you encounter along your path. Enjoy the flowers that are there for your pleasure. Tune in to the sunrise, the little children, the laughter, the rain and the birds. Drink it all in...There is no "way" to happiness. Happiness is the way!

—Dyer, Dr. W.W.

414/HAPPINESS

I live in the land of Disney, Hollywood and year–round sun. You may think people in such a glamorous, fun–filled place are happier than others. If so, you have some mistaken ideas about the nature of happiness.

Many intelligent people still equate happiness with fun. The truth is that fun and happiness have little or nothing in common. Fun is what we experience *during* an act. Happiness is what we experience *after* an act. It is a deeper, more *abiding* emotion.

I have often thought that if Hollywood stars have a role to play, it is to teach us that happiness has nothing to do with fun. These rich, beautiful individuals have constant access to glamorous parties, fancy cars, expensive homes, everything that spells "happiness." But in memoir after memoir, celebrities reveal the *unhappiness* hidden beneath all their fun: depression, alcoholism, drug addiction, broken marriages, troubled children, profound loneliness.

The way people cling to the belief that a fun–filled, pain–free life equals happiness actually *diminishes* their chances of ever attaining real happiness. If fun and pleasure are equated with happiness, then pain must be equated with unhappiness. But, in fact, the opposite is true: More times than not, things that lead to happiness involve some *pain*.

As a result, many people *avoid* the very endeavors that are the *source* of true happiness. They fear the pain inevitably brought by such things as marriage, raising children, professional achievement, religious commitment, civic or charitable work, self–improvement.

Of course I enjoy doing fun things. I like to play racquetball, joke with kids (and anybody else), and I probably have too many hobbies.

But these forms of fun do not contribute in any real way to my happiness. More difficult endeavors—writing, raising children, creating a deep relationship with my wife, trying to do good in the world—will bring me more happiness than can ever be found in fun, that least permanent of things.

Understanding and accepting that true happiness has nothing to do with fun is one of the most liberating realizations we can ever come to. It liberates time: now we can devote more hours to activities that can genuinely *increase* our happiness. It liberates *money*: buying that new car or those fancy clothes that will do nothing to increase our happiness now seems pointless. And it liberates us from *envy*: we now understand that all those rich and glamorous people we were so sure are happy because they are always having so much fun, actually may not be happy at all.

The moment we understand that fun does not bring happiness, we begin to lead our lives differently. The effect can be quite literally, life–transforming.
—Prager, D., "The Secret of True Happiness" (Redbook)

HEALING

415
Dr. Karl Menninger, the famous psychiatrist, once gave a lecture on mental health and was answering questions from the audience.

"What would you advise a person to do," asked one man, "if that person felt a nervous breakdown coming on?"

Most people expected him to reply: "Consult a psychiatrist." To their astonishment, he replied: "Lock up your house, go across the railway tracks, find someone in n*eed* and do something to *help* that person."

HEALTH

416

Grant me the strength that I may not fall
Into the clutches of cholesterol.
At polyunsaturates, I'll never mutter.
The road to hell is paved with butter.
And cake is cursed, and cream is awful,

Satan hides in every waffle.
Beelzebub is a chocolate drop, and Lucifer is a lollipop.
Teach me the evils of hollandaise,
or pasta with gobs of mayonnaise.
And crispy, fried chicken from the South—
If you love me, Lord, please shut my mouth.

—Belson, J., "Hilton Head Health Institute Newsletter, Spring 1988

HEAVEN

417

A young clergyman had just taken charge of his first parish. Being most anxious to please his new parishioners, he resolved to be as *tactful* as possible in his relationships with the members of his flock. Among his new parishioners was an elderly man whose sometimes irrational behavior puzzled his friends and family. And shortly after the new pastor's arrival, the eccentric man died. The pastor, hoping to offer consolation to the widow with the utmost finesse, called at her house. The bereaved woman led him into the parlor where her husband's body lay. After looking respectfully at the mortal remains for a few moments, the pastor turned to the widow and said: "This is a difficult situation for you, my dear, and I sympathize with you deeply. But remember, that this which we see here in the coffin is merely the *husk*—the outer shell. That which was *inside* the shell is all that really matters. The nut has gone to Heaven."

HELL

418

Each week, the signboard in front of a country church in Southern Florida announces the title of the next Sunday *sermon.* Once, in the midst of a particularly intense *heat*-wave, the pastor posted a title which left no doubt about the next Sunday's sermon topic:

So You Think It's Hot Here!

HOLY FAMILY

419
A Sunday–school teacher asked her class of small but eager children to draw a picture of their conception of the Biblical "Flight into Egypt." One little boy handed in his picture—it showed four people headed for Egypt in an *airplane.* Three of the passengers had haloes and the teacher asked who they were. Those with the haloes, the little boy explained, were Jesus, Mary and Joseph.

"Then," asked the teacher patiently, "who is the one *without* the halo?"

"That," said the child, "is Pontius, the *Pilot.*"

HOLY SPIRIT

420
An attending physician from Holy Spirit Hospital was seated in Church one Pentecost Sunday morning when his "beeper" sounded. An emergency at the hospital required the doctor's presence at once. However some members of the congregation were startled to hear the voice on the doctor's beeper announce loudly: "Dr. Sosebee, please call Holy Spirit."

HOME

421
Madame Ernestine Schumann–Heink, the great opera star, once was asked to give her definition of "Home." This is what she wrote:

> What is home?: A roof to keep out the rain? Four walls to keep out the wind? Floors to keep out the cold? Yes, but home is more than that. It is the laugh of a baby, the song of a mother, the strength of a father, warmth

of loving hearts, light from happy eyes, kindness, loyalty, comradeship. Home is the first school and the first church for young ones, where they learn what is right, what is good, and what is kind; where they go for comfort when they are hurt or sick; where joy is shared and sorrow eased; where fathers and mothers are respected and loved. Where children are wanted; where the simplest food is good enough for kings because it is earned; where money is not so important as loving kindness; where even the teakettle sings from happiness. That is home. God bless it!

HOPE

422

Psychologist Lee Salk feels that his job is to help people find the strength and insight to solve their problems. One of the attitudes he tries to convey came from his mother, Dora. He explains:

As a young girl in Russia, mother was driven from her home by Cossacks who burned the entire village to the ground. She fled for her life, hiding in hay wagons and huddling in ditches. Eventually, she crossed the sea to America, crowded in a ship's hold.

She was about 12 years old when she arrived in New York City in 1901, and immediately went to work 16 hours a day in a sweatshop. She tried to go to school at night—but kept falling asleep over her books. Yet she never lost *hope.*

Even after she married and her three sons were born, there were still hard times. But my mother urged us to think about what we *had*, not what we *didn't* have. She taught us that in hardship you develop a capacity to appreciate the beauty that exists in the *simplest* elements of life. The attitude that she conveyed to me was this: "When it gets *dark* enough, you can see the *stars.*"

—*Guideposts*

423/HOPE

Before the Berlin Wall was removed, "National Geographic" magazine ran a two–page aerial photograph of it. It is really a *double* wall. Between the walls there was a "no–man's land" filled with all sorts of obstacles: upturned spikes, barbed wire, electric fences, trip alarms, watch dogs, vehicle traps, flood lights, etc. In the "National Geographic" picture, one could see an abandoned Church still standing in the *middle* of the double wall. It stood empty and unused, of course. Ironically, the *name* of that Church is "The Church of *Reconciliation*."

Why the Soviets allowed the Church to remain standing has not been explained. But, for hearers and receivers of the Word, it stood as a powerful symbol of *hope* in the Resurrection Power of God. It stood as a powerful symbol of *hope* that nothing man can do will defeat God's purpose, ultimately. It stood as a powerful symbol of *hope* in the coming Kingdom of Love. As the Apostle Paul has written, "It pleased God to make absolute fullness reside in Christ and, by means of Him, to *reconcile* everything in His Person, both on earth and in the heavens, making *peace* through the blood of His Cross" (Col. 1:19).

HUBRIS

424

An egotistical supervisor, jealous of his prerogatives, called in one of his men. "Smith," he said, "it has come to my attention that you have been praying for a raise. I'll have you know that I will not tolerate anyone going over my head!"

HUMAN GROWTH

425

One of the impressive sights in the beautiful city of Florence, Italy, is a collection of huge blocks of stone with unfinished statues carved out of them by the great Michelangelo. In several instances, Michelangelo had been carving images of slaves.

The slaves are in chains, yet they seem to be coming *out* of the stone. Michelangelo had an amazing ability to make the figures he was carving appear to be literally coming out of the stone as he worked. He *thought* of his own work this way, apparently, because, on one occasion, he was seen struggling to transport a huge piece of stone, using poles and other implements to push it down the street. A bystander is reported to have asked Michelangelo why he was going to all that trouble to move that "old piece of rock." And it is said that the great artist answered in these words: "Because there is an *angel* in there that wants to come out."

Although our hearts may sometimes appear to have hardened like some "old piece of rock," nevertheless, by means of the Gift of the Holy Spirit, Jesus *can* move us and make us into effective, dedicated, devoted disciples. Jesus knows that there is a loving person in us that wants to come *out.*

HUMILITY

426

At a party given in his honor, the eminent novelist, Thomas Mann, was introduced to a man who had achieved a small degree of success as a writer. "Mr. Mann, I can't tell you how *humble* I feel in your distinguished presence," the writer groveled. "Compared to you, I don't even deserve to be called a *hack.*" Mr. Mann was courteous, but later he said to his host: "That man has no right to make himself so *small.* He is not that *big.*"

427/HUMILITY

A middle–aged woman went into an apartment building and took the elevator to the twelfth floor. When she arrived at her destination, she rang the doorbell impatiently. The door opened slowly, almost mysteriously, and she was welcomed by the smell of incense and smoke. She entered and was greeted by a young woman in a long white robe who announced her presence by striking a huge gong. With this the young woman said, "Do you wish to see the *wonderful* one—the all–knowing, all–powerful, *Maharishi Narru*?"

"Yeah," the woman said. "Tell Sheldon his *mother* is here!"

428/HUMILITY

In the summer of 1979, Boston Red Sox first baseman, Carl Yastrzemski, became the fifteenth player in baseball history to make three thousand base hits. This event drew a lot of media attention, and for about a week prior to the attainment of this goal, hundreds of reporters covered Yaz's every move. Finally, one reporter asked, "Hey Yaz, aren't you afraid all of this attention will go to your head?" Yastrzemski replied, "I look at it this way: in my career I've been at bat over ten thousand times, and I've made a base hit three thousand times. That means I've been *unsuccessful* at the plate over *seven* thousand times. That fact alone keeps me from getting a swollen head."

429/HUMILITY

Several critics have called the Japanese motion picture, "*Ikiru*," the greatest film ever made. *Ikiru* is the story of an old man's struggle to attach meaning to his life after learning that he has cancer and only six months to live. This causes him to reflect on his uneventful life as a minor city–hall bureaucrat. The realization that he has made no significant contribution to his fellow man troubles him spiritually. And, despite his weakened condition, he resolves to do something for other people before he dies. With all his remaining energy he gets behind a playground project which has had one obstacle after another thrown in its path by the local bureaucracy. Through his efforts, the playground is finally completed and the neighborhood children are presented with their new paradise. The experience transforms the stuffy, old ex–bureaucrat into a warm and compassionate human being.

The movie's touching finale illustrates with great power the depth of meaning contained in Jesus' words, "If anyone wishes to rank first, he must remain the last one of all and the *servant* of all." The old man is seen contentedly seated on one of the new playground's swings, slowly moving back and forth and softly humming a tune. There, peacefully, he dies.

The symbolism is clear. Only by rendering service to others with a warm and compassionate heart, only by assigning priority in human relations to "What can I give?" over "What can I get?" can you realize your full potential as a child of God. The childish posture of the old man on the children's swing symbolizes the child–*like* spirit which enables him to die in peace.

"If anyone wishes to rank first, he must remain the last one of all and the *servant* of all." Having said this, Jesus "took a little child...and putting His arms around him, said to them, 'Whoever welcomes a child such as this for My sake welcomes *Me*. And whoever welcomes Me welcomes, not Me but Him who sent Me'" (Mk. 9:35–37).

430/HUMILITY

A distinguished astronomer once declared at a scientific meeting: "To an astronomer, man is nothing more than an insignificant dot in an infinite universe." To which Albert Einstein replied, "I have often felt that way. But then I realize that the insignificant dot who is man is also the *astronomer*."

Einstein's observation is the flip side of Jesus' revolutionary sayings. Jesus tells us that when we humbly acknowledge ourself before God as that "insignificant dot," we simultaneously are *exalted*: we who are "the last" become "the *first*"; we who lose our life, *save* our life; we who are *insignificant* dots are transformed into *significant* dots.

431/HUMILITY

In his autobiography, "The Ragman's Son," actor Kirk Douglas wrote about how proud he felt of himself over the years when strangers would recognize him as he walked down the street and call out in adulation, "Mr. Douglas! Mr. Douglas!" Until one day, late in his career, he was walking down the street when a taxi pulled over to the curb. He heard the passenger say in a timid voice, "Mr. Douglas! Mr. Douglas!" He turned and saw a pretty girl smiling and pointing at him. "I can spare a minute of my time for her, hoping for my autograph," Douglas said to himself. Whereupon, the girl looked at him "adoringly" and said, in a velvet voice, "Wow! Michael Douglas' father!"

432/HUMILITY

A politician running for public office was talking to his wife after a hard day's campaigning. "If this race is going to run on sheer merit, I'll surely be elected," he said. "My opponent has a record of broken promises; I've never broken a promise in my life. My opponent hasn't been inside a church in years; I've never missed a Sunday in my life. My opponent bets on horse races; I've never gambled in my life. My opponent frequently goes to taverns; I've never taken a drink in my life. My opponent ..." At this point, the politician's wife suppressed a yawn and said, "My dear, I know, of course, that you are perfect. But don't worry, I'll respect your secret."

HUSBAND AND WIFE

433

A recently married man received a letter and some photographs from his best friend. The friend was very proud of a backyard deck he had just constructed and enclosed a picture of it. Impressed with his friend's skills, the man began to feel a bit inadequate since he knew he was all thumbs when it came to working with tools. When his wife returned from work that evening he showed her the photographs and asked, "But what do *I* make?"

Without a moment's hesitation she replied, "You make me *happy*."

434/HUSBAND AND WIFE

Every Sunday in Church a gray–haired couple sat holding hands just like newlyweds. One parishioner remarked to the wife how wonderful it was that they were still so much in love.

"You don't understand," she replied, "I hold Harold's hand to keep him from cracking his *knuckles*."
—Etchison, B.

435/HUSBAND AND WIFE
Just after she celebrated her twentieth wedding anniversary, Mrs. Dwight Morrow sat at a dinner next to Paderewski and was reminded of a time when she heard the great pianist from a gallery seat at college. Paderewski asked if she often went back to her Alma Mater. "Yes, I like to go back and sit in my old chapel seat, thinking how much happier I am now than I ever thought I would be," Mrs. Morrow answered. Becoming interested, Paderewski stopped eating. "You don't mean to tell me you are happier now than you thought at eighteen you would be?" "Yes, indeed!" Mrs. Morrow answered. Paderewski bowed deeply. "Mrs. Morrow," he said, "I want to meet your husband."

436/HUSBAND AND WIFE
A woman who was having a great deal of difficulty communicating with her husband finally decided to seek professional help. During her first session with a marriage counselor, it was suggested that she and her husband begin to take an active interest in each other's *hobbies*.

"That *sounds* like a great idea," the woman told the counselor, "But I *know* it will never work. You see I *know* what my husband's hobbies are. For example, his latest kick is going down to the city dump to shoot *rats* as target practice for the upcoming deer hunting season! And anyone who knows me can tell you that I haven't had *time* for hunting ever since I took up *mud wrestling* last year!"

437/HUSBAND AND WIFE
A man returned home from work one evening just moments after his wife's arrival from an obviously tough day at the office. As a result, she was short tempered and had an unpleasant attitude. Nothing her husband said improved her disposition. By 7:30 things had taken a turn for the worse so the

husband suggested that he go outside, pretend he was just returning home, and start the evening over. His wife agreed with the plan.

> The man went outside, came back in the door and cheerily announced, "Hi honey I'm home!"
>
> "And just where have you been for the last two hours, she snapped. Do you realize its 7:30!"

438/HUSBAND AND WIFE

When Elizabeth Dole, the wife of Senator Bob Dole, was appointed Secretary of Transportation some years ago, a photograph was taken of the two of them making their bed. The day after the photograph ran in the national press, Senator Dole received an irate letter from a constituent. The man complained that Senator Dole should never have allowed a picture of a man "doing such things around the house."

The Senator wrote back: "Buddy, you don't know the half of it. The only reason she was helping me was that the *photographer* was there."

—Small, M., "People Magazine" (Adapted).

439/HUSBAND AND WIFE

An elderly couple walked up to a hotel registration desk and asked for a room with a double bed. The clerk apologetically explained that only rooms with twin beds were available. Disappointed, the husband said, "I'm not sure we can stay here. We've been married for forty–five years and we've always shared the same bed." Then the wife spoke: "Could you possibly move the beds close together," she asked. Hearing this, a woman standing behind the couple, whispered, "How *romantic*!" Then the wife spoke up again: "I want to be close enough to give him a shove when he *snores*."

—Sitterly, P.

440/HUSBAND AND WIFE

It was their tenth wedding anniversary, and the married couple celebrated at a posh restaurant where the atmosphere was extremely romantic. Deeply moved by the occasion and the surroundings, the husband gently took his wife's hand and said, "My darling, this is the happiest moment of my life. And, please, don't ever leave me, because if you ever do *I'm going with you*."

441/HUSBAND AND WIFE

Years ago a husband and wife were about to celebrate their Golden Wedding anniversary. The local newspaper sent a reporter for an interview. The reporter asked the inevitable question, "What is your recipe for a long, happy marriage?"

"Mary Lou was the first one I ever kept company with," replied the husband. "When she maneuvered me into proposing, I was scared stiff. After the wedding her pa took me aside and handed me a little package. 'Here is all you need to know,' he said." Then the husband reached for a large gold watch in his pocket, opened it, and handed it to the reporter. There, across the face of the watch, where he could see it a dozen times a day, were written the words, "Say something nice to Mary Lou."

442/HUSBAND AND WIFE

A married couple in their sixties was driving down the highway. Suddenly they were passed by a young couple in their 20s. The young man was behind the wheel and the young girl was sitting right next to him with her arm around his shoulders. The older couple watched them pass when the wife, who was sitting on the passenger side to the far right observed, "Remember when *we* used to always sit close together like that?" To which her husband, who was driving the car, replied, "Well, *I* haven't moved."

443/HUSBAND AND WIFE

A man in his mid–twenties named George ran into an old school chum whom he hadn't seen in several years. "Are you married?" asked the friend. "No," sighed George, "not yet."

"Why not?" the friend wanted to know. "Well," said George, "I kept taking girls home to meet the family and my mother always *hated* them. She always found something *wrong* with them. She hated every girl I brought home, and I just stopped trying. But then I found a girl who was exactly *like* my mother. She *looked* like her, *walked* like her, *talked* like her and so I took *this* girl home." The friend said, "What happened?" George answered, "Well, my *father* hated her."

444/HUSBAND AND WIFE

A marriage counselor was asking a woman some questions about her disposition.

> "Did you sleep *fretfully* last night?" he asked.
> "No," replied the woman, "I slept *peacefully*."
> "Did you wake up *grumpy* this morning?" he asked.
> "No," replied the woman, "I just let him sleep."

445/HUSBAND AND WIFE

When Thomas Edison was inventing the electric light bulb, he spent many years trying to discover the right combination of materials to make it work: the right filament, the right container, the right gas. Finally one night, about three o'clock in the morning, it all came together. Edison actually had made the device glow. Excitedly, he ran into the bedroom where his wife was sleeping soundly. "Darling, look!" he cried out. Mrs. Edison awakened, rolled over and pleaded: "Will you shut that light off and come to bed?"

446/HUSBAND AND WIFE

Alice and Tom had been married for fifty years. Alice was in her kitchen with her sister who was visiting. As they talked, Tom walked in from the yard, wearing his work boots which left clods of dirt and grime on Alice's spotless kitchen floor. Alice's sister, who was a stickler for cleanliness, couldn't resist saying, "Those *boots* of his surely do bring in the *dirt*." Alice just smiled and, as she headed for the broom closet, said, "But I *love* those boots, because they bring *him* in also!"

447/HUSBAND AND WIFE

A salesman, calling his wife from a pay phone in a distant city, said "Goodbye" and hung up the receiver. As he walked away, the phone rang. He hesitated at first, and then answered expecting the operator to inform him of extra charges. Instead the operator surprised him when she said, "I just thought you'd like to know. As you hung up, your wife said, 'I love you.'"

448/HUSBAND AND WIFE

A customer brought an exquisite greeting card to the counter and reached for his wallet. Pushing the keys on the cash register, the clerk said, "That will be two dollars, please."

"Two dollars?" the customer bellowed. "Forget it!" He jammed his wallet back in to his pocket and stormed out of the shop. When the clerk returned the card to the rack, she noticed that it read "To my Wife, Because You Mean So Much."

449/HUSBAND AND WIFE

This true story appeared in the New York Times. At the corner of 12th Street and 6th Avenue in The Greenwich Village section of New York City, a woman pedestrian was struck by a big truck. As she was lying in the middle of the road, surrounded by several stunned onlookers, a man who identified himself as an ambulance attendant rushed over to help. The victim, about age fifty, was conscious and alert. She said to the ambulance attendant, "My left *hip* is numb. I thing it's *broken*. But, please, the most *important* think is for somebody to call my husband and give him this message. Tell him I got knocked down by a big truck, but *it wasn't my fault.*"

450/HUSBAND AND WIFE

A woman was looking through a photo album of her grandparents' marriage ceremony fifty years ago. "Grandma," she said, "so many of these clothing styles have come *back* over the years." Grandma replied, "That's why I've kept *Grandpa* all this time, I just *know* he'll be back in style one of these days."

HYPOCRISY

451
A man was on a business trip and stayed in a hotel that had a bug problem. He complained about this to the management, and later received a letter of response to his complaint. Signed by the President of the hotel chain, it said,

> We are humiliated that a man of *your* integrity, a man of *your* reputation, a man of *your* importance in the community should have had this experience in one of our hotels.

This made the man feel somewhat better about the situation but, as he was folding the letter to put it away he noticed a little piece of paper at the bottom of the envelope. It read, "Send this guy the '*Bug* Letter'."

I

IDENTITY

452
The uniqueness of living things is one of life's most awesome wonders. No two blades of grass, no two roses, no two insects or birds or dogs or cats are precisely alike. Each human creature of God is different from all the rest—each a unique creation of God. Geneticists tell us that prior to birth each person has an array of genes unlike that of any other person, living or dead. Each set of fingerprints, footprints and voiceprints is unique, individual, unmatched. Heart specialists tell us that no two cardiograms are alike. Neurologists tell us that no two brain–wave tests produce the same results. Over seventy–seven billion persons have lived on the planet earth, which means that each of us is a seventy–seven billionth wonder of the world––each a unique marvel.

Not only is each human being uniquely different from every other human being, but also the entire species—the entire community of man—is uniquely different from every other species. And this is true precisely because we are members of the only species capable of asking, "Who am I?" The question is built into our very beings. "Who am I?" is the name of the game of life.

IDENTITY CRISIS

453

Modern computer technology has the capacity to record a variety of the distinguishing marks of every living person, as well as all those yet to come. We have reached the point where it is relatively easy to establish one's identity and virtually impossible to conceal it. Yet, fingerprints, footprints, cardiograms, voiceprints and brainwaves to the contrary notwithstanding, we never cease to ask ourselves and each other, "Who am I?" "Who do you say I am?" All of us are caught up in the relentless search for identity. We all want to be somebody.

Each in his or her own way is like the billionaire whose final, bizarre request was to be buried in his gold-plated Rolls Royce, sitting in the driver's seat with his hands on the wheel, a $20.00 cigar in his mouth, state–of–the–art stereo playing, and the air–conditioning running. After his request was fulfilled, and as relatives and friends left the graveside, one of the grave diggers looked down at the spectacle and exclaimed, "Man, that's really living!".

However misguided his attitude and approach to life (and death), it can at least be said of the deceased man that he was acutely conscious of the nagging question, "Who am I?" Not only had he spent a lifetime trying to prove that he indeed was somebody, but in his own pitiful way he seemed to be expressing the hope that not even death could destroy his unique identity.

IGNORANCE

454

In a place known as "The Town of Fools," a man asked, "In our world, which is more important: the sun or the moon?"

A wise man answered, "Of course it is the *moon*. The moon casts its light at night when it is *needed* most. The sun shines only during the day when we already *have* all of the light we need."

INDIVIDUALITY

455
Here are some mind-boggling figures:

> If human population growth continues at its present rate, by the year 3530 the total mass of human flesh and blood will be equal to the total mass of the earth itself. And by the year 6826, the total mass of human flesh and blood will be equal to the total mass of the *Universe.*
>
> The total human population in the time of Julius Caesar was 150 million. Today, the human population increases by 150 million in just two years.
>
> In the next two minutes 200 human beings will *die,* but 480 will be *born.*
>
> Statisticians inform us that about 60 *billion* human beings have been born thus far.

But *given* all these big, impressive numbers, perhaps the *most* mind-boggling statistic of all concerns our *uniqueness* as human beings—our *individuality*:

If you were to line up every single human being who ever lived or ever will live, and you took a good look at everyone in that mind-boggling crowd, you wouldn't find a single person quite like you!

INGENUITY

456

A truck driver was making his way across town, faithfully following the designated truck route. But something was strange about this driver. Every time he came to a stop light or stop sign, he jumped out and repeatedly beat the truck with a baseball bat.

A curious observer followed this unusual driver until he saw him maneuver his truck into a diner parking lot. As soon as the truck stopped, the driver again jumped out and proceeded to beat on the truck. The observer asked the obvious question, "Why do you beat your truck with a bat every time you stop?"

The driver said, "Well, it's like this. I have a two-ton truck and four tons of canaries. So I have to keep two tons in the *air* all the time!"

—Timmons, T., "Hooked On Life."

INNOCENCE

457

"Do all that has to be done without complaining or arguing, and then you will be blameless and genuine" (Phil. 2:15).

A man was struck by a car as he walked across the street. Ultimately, the matter came to court. In his argument to the jury, the attorney for the driver of the car said: "My client has been driving for forty years and his record is *blameless.* Never before was he in an accident." Whereupon the attorney for the pedestrian rose and said, "It appears that my learned colleague would like to resolve this matter on the basis of *experience.* In that case, I can tell you that my client has been walking for *sixty* years and that *his* record is blameless. Never before has he been struck down by a car."

INSPIRATION

458

How far-reaching the singlehanded acts of anyone may extend can never be foreseen. In 1848 the United States was at war with Mexico. Henry Thoreau, author, naturalist, and hermit philosopher at Concord, Massachusetts, was opposed to war. In protest he wrote an essay entitled "On the Duty of Civil Disobedience."

In 1928—eighty years later—Webb Miller, a United Press correspondent, interviewed Mahatma Gandhi. Miller asked Gandhi: "Did you ever read an American writer named Henry Thoreau?"

"Why, of course," replied Gandhi. "I read his 'Walden' first in Johannesburg, South Africa, in 1906, and his ideas influenced me greatly. I adopted some of them and recommended the study of Thoreau to some of my friends. Why, I actually took the name of my Movement from Thoreau's essay 'On the Duty of Civil Disobedience.'"

Several years later Webb Miller stood beside Thoreau's grave at Concord and asked himself:

What would Thoreau think if he could know that his ideas had directly influenced the current of history and the lives of millions of Indians three generations later?

Ask yourself:

What would Jesus think if He could know that through my efforts and through my example, His ideas had directly influenced and inspired the lives of even a handful of people?

459/INSPIRATION

Lou Little was a very successful football coach at Columbia University in the thirties. One year, there was a youngster on the squad who was no great shakes as a football player but whose personality served as a morale booster for the whole team.

Coach Little was fond of the boy. He liked the proud way he walked arm-in-arm with his father on campus. And whenever the team was far enough ahead, Little would let him into the game for the last few minutes of play.

A week before the final game of the boy's senior year, his mother called Coach Little and said, "My husband died this morning of a heart attack. Will you break the news to my boy?
He'll take it better from you." Lou Little did what the mother asked, and the boy went home. Three days later he was back, and he went straight to Lou Little. "Coach," he said, "I want to ask something of you that means an awful lot to me. I want to be in the starting lineup in the final game. It's what my father would have liked the most." Little granted the request and the boy played inspired football—running, blocking, and tackling like an All-American and leading the team to victory.

After the game, Lou Little threw his arms around the boy. "Son, you were terrific," he said, "you never played like that in your life." The boy replied, "Remember how my father and I used to walk on campus arm-in-arm? There was something about him few people knew. My dad was blind. And I knew that today would be the first time ever he could see me play."

460/INSPIRATION

"Inspiration" was the title given to a seminar sponsored by a large insurance company. In one of the sessions, the speaker was trying to inspire the company's agents to sell more policies. He began to tell the "success story" of a man whom he would later identify as the president of their company. "I know of a man," he shouted, "who drove straight to his goal. He looked neither left nor right. He pressed forward with only one purpose in mind. Neither friend nor foe could delay or divert him from his course. All who stood in his path did so at their own risk. What, my friends, would you call such a man?" From the rear of the hall, an obviously *non*-inspired veteran agent called out, "A cab driver!"

The contagious joy of the Apostle Paul and the small band of early Christians who were able to turn the world upside down, were not inspired by corny speeches. The source of their inspiration was the *Holy Spirit of God*, breathed into their inmost being by The Risen Lord.

INTERDEPENDENCE

461

While on a tour of California's giant sequoias, the guide pointed out that the sequoia tree has roots just barely below the surface.

"That's impossible!" a man exclaimed. "I'm a country boy, and I know that if the roots don't grow deep into the earth, strong winds will blow the trees over."

"Not sequoia trees," said the guide. "They grow only in groves and their roots *intertwine* under the surface of the earth. So, when the strong winds come, *they hold each other up.*"

There's a *lesson* here. We human beings are like those giant sequoias. We need to *hold each other up* against the strong winds—destructive forces of evil that threaten over humanity. We need to *reinforce* each other in times suffering and deprivation and loneliness. Beginning with Church and family and then reaching out to the larger communities, we need to *intertwine* with each other to keep from being blown over, so to speak, by the winds of despair and disbelief.

J

JEALOUSY

462

When he started out as a county music singer, Conway Twitty occasionally resented other performers who were suddenly recognized while he remained obscure. He says: "I'd think, 'Man, why doesn't something like that happen to me?' Then one day somebody told me a story":

> A missionary who had been in China for many years and a famous entertainer who had been there for two weeks were traveling back to the United States on the same boat. When they docked in New York, the missionary saw a crowd of the entertainer's fans waiting at the pier. "Lord, I don't understand," the missionary said. "I gave 42 years of my life to China, and he gave only two weeks, yet there are thousands welcoming *him* home and nobody here to welcome *me*." And the Lord replied, "Son, you're not home yet."

"I'll never forget that story," said Conrad Twitty. "From then on, I never felt pangs of jealousy about some other guy's success."

—*Cross W. and Kosser, M., "The Conrad Twitty Story" (Doubleday)*

JESUS CHRIST: PRESENCE OF

463

"Would Jesus Wear a Rolex on His Television Show?" is the title of a song that appeared on the country music scene several years ago. An enterprising journalist put that question to several of the best-known TV Evangelists. One responded by saying that he did not subscribe to the "theology of prosperity" being broadcast by the "health and wealth" preachers. "God is not a holy slot machine," he said. "I wear an *inexpensive* watch. I think *Jesus* would."

A member of a famous evangelical TV family said: "Jesus was not afraid to wear nice things. To maximize His ministry He would need television. For television programs he would need to tell time. Would Jesus wear a Rolex? Why not?"

Another of the best-known television preachers had no doubt that Jesus would be on *TV.* But to the question of His wearing the super-expensive Rolex watch, he answered, "The deepest human problem is the *ego* problem. It is our effort to prove that we have value and worth that motivates us to identify with fancy cars and fancy watches. So, would Jesus wear a Rolex? I think *not.*"

The question, of course, is totally irrelevant! The truth is that not only is God not a "holy slot machine" but also that Jesus is not a "holy game-show subject." Jesus Christ is Lord. Jesus Christ is Risen. And whether you wear a Rolex watch or a Mickey Mouse watch, you'll never know what time it is, in the spiritual sense, unless you have opened the channels of your heart to the voice of Jesus. And when you hear him speaking to your heart, you will simultaneously see him, not on TV, but in the faces of your brothers and sisters everywhere.

JOURNALISM

464

While planning a trip to Washington, D.C., a foreign emmissary was warned by his colleagues to beware of American journalists who might "misquote" him. With that warning in mind, he braced himself as he stepped off the plane to be greeted by several newspaper reporters. "Are you going to visit any night clubs during your stay here in Washington?" was the first question asked. "*Are* there any night clubs in Washington?" was the diplomat's reply. During breakfast the next day he opened his morning paper and turned to a story about his mission in Washington. According to the report, the first thing he asked upon his arrival was, "Are there any night clubs in Washington?"

JOY

465

Mark Twain had a bad habit of spicing his conversation with profanity. Twain's wife, a delicate, refined woman, often became very upset by his rough language. She tried, in many ways, to cure him of the habit—always unsuccessfully, of course. On one occasion she tried a shock technique. When Twain arrived home from a trip, he was greeted at the door with a string of profanity from his wife. From the lips of that delicate, refined woman, he heard everything he had ever said, and more. Twain stood quietly, listening, until she had finished. Then he said, "My dear, you have the words, but not the music."

This, I fear, is what often happens to us in our worship and prayer experience. We have the words, but not the music: not enough soul; not enough enthusiasm flowing into it. Consequently, not enough joy—contagious j-oy—flowing out of it.

JUDGMENT

466

Piaget, the eminent child psychologist, tells a story in his book, "The Moral Judgment of the Child," pertaining to lying behavior. He gave children the following proposition: Two children break cups. Their mother asked them who did it. The first child said it wasn't he, and the mother believed him. The second child said it wasn't he, and his mother didn't believe him, and punished him severely. Piaget then asked, "Are both lies equally naughty?" The children answered without hesitation, "No." "Which, then, was the naughtiest?"' the psychologist asked. The children answered, "The one who was punished."

—Buscaglia, L., "Loving Each Other."

K

KINDNESS

467
At a family reunion the discussion turned to the subject of "Living each day as though it were *your* last." "Well," said grandmother, "that's a fine idea, but I have always lived by one that is slightly different. It's this: Treat all the people you meet each day as though it were *their* last day on earth."

You can preach a better sermon with your life than you can with your lips. The best way to ease your troubles is to ease the troubles of others.

468/KINDNESS
A guide in the Swiss Alps always demonstrated the wonder of the echoes that resound in certain areas. Instead of giving the visitors a technical explanation of how echoes are caused by reflected sounds, the guide would offer them a bit of his own attitude toward life. "When you speak kind words," he said, "you will be answered by kind echoes."

KINGDOM

469
A woman who had recently moved to the United States from her home in England was hired as secretary to the president of a major corporation. While the executive was away on a business trip in London, the secretary received a call from a salesman who had never before spoken to her.

"Mr. Johnson is in the United *Kingdom*," the secretary informed him.

The caller seemed *shocked* to hear this. "I'm terribly sorry," he stammered. "Is it too late to send *flowers*?"

KINGDOM OF HEAVEN

470
There was a long line of travelers waiting for immigration clearance at a Florida airport. The immigration officers seemed to be exercising more than usual care in inspecting baggage and credentials. After waiting in line for almost an hour, one man finally said in a loud voice, "Entering the *United States* is harder than entering the Kingdom of *Heaven*." Whereupon, one of the immigration officers shot back, "My friend, there's a whole lot more folks *tryin*!"

KNOWLEDGE

471
Most of us consider an ordinary flea nothing more than a nuisance to ourselves and to our pets. But few of us consider the awesome feats these tiny creatures can perform.

For example, a flea can jump a distance 150 times its own length (equivalent to a man jumping 1,000 feet). Entomologists have clocked a "rat flea" jumping 30,000 times without stopping. Other flea species can accelerate 50 times faster than the *space shuttle*. Fleas have even been known to go months without a meal, and survive after being frozen for a year.

Consider the *grim* side. As carriers of *plague*, fleas have caused more *deaths* than all the wars ever fought.

The Apostle Paul wrote that now we see things as "a *dim* reflection in a mirror." The knowledge we have now is "*imperfect*," he said, but in the day of fulfillment we will "know *fully*." In the day of fulfillment we will no longer see the wonder of God's creation dimly as in a mirror. On that great day we may even know why God made *fleas!*

—*The National Geographic Society (Adapted).*

L

LAST DAYS

472
A fire and brimstone preacher was delivering his usual doomsday sermon about the end of the world. "Reform!" he boomed. "Reform your lives because sooner or later the signs of the end time will appear in the sun, the moon and the stars. On the earth nations will be in anguish, distraught at the roaring of the sea and waves. Men will die of fright in anticipation of what is coming upon the earth. The powers in the heavens will be shaken" (Lk. 21:25-26). Then, lowering his voice, the preacher said, "God hasn't told us when He would bring the world to an end. That's not for us to know. It could be a billion years from now." Whereupon a worried voice from the back of the Church rang out, "How long did you say?" "It could be a billion years," the preacher repeated. To which the much relieved voice replied, "Thank God! I thought you said a million years."

LAST RITES

473
George lay on his deathbed. He was eighty-eight-years-old. His children and grandchildren and great grandchildren were gathered around the old man, and they listened respectfully and lovingly as he spoke a special word to each of them. Finally, George took his wife's hand, stroked it endearingly, and said to the others: "My children, I want you to remember always what a wonderful marriage this has been. For sixty years I've had the world's best wife. She has been my best friend and companion

for all those years, and what a *cook!* Always the family meals were delicious, but best of all were her great *desserts*. At this very moment I can smell her freshly baked chocolate cake." Then he said to his wife, "Molly, would you bring me one last piece of your chocolate cake?" "I'm sorry, George," Molly replied, "I'm saving it for the *funeral*."

LEADERSHIP

474

During a sales meeting, the manager was berating the sales staff for the dismally low sales figures they had turned in. "I've had just about enough of poor performance and excuses," he began. "If you can't do the job," he added, "perhaps there are other sales people out there who would jump at a chance to sell the worthy products that each of you has the privilege to represent." Then, pointing to the newly recruited, retired pro-football player, he said, "If a football team isn't winning, what happens? The players are *replaced*—right?"

The question hung heavy for a few seconds, but then the ex-football player answered, "Actually, sir, if the whole team was having trouble we usually got a new *coach*."

—Lysen, D. (Adapted).

LENT

475

On the dashboards of those small "Volkswagon"-type airplanes, there is a safety device usually referred to as a "Stall Warning Indicator." The owner of such a plane has described the "Stall Warning" as follows:

> The Stall Warning Indicator is there to help the pilot avoid big trouble. In a light plane, if you get below a certain speed you'll fall right out of the sky. On my particular plane the stall speed is 55 miles per hour. If you

get below 55, say your prayers. If your airspeed drops to around 60 miles an hour, you begin to hear a buzzer--the Stall Warning Indicator is doing its thing. When that buzzer begins to squawk and the corresponding red light begins to flash, you know you're close to losing control...thank God for that Stall Warning Indicator. It's a built-in device to help you avoid tragedy.

For the Christian Community, the Season of Lent is like a Stall Warning Indicator. It is here to help us avoid big trouble in our life. In Biblical language, it is a season of *repentance*:

A time in which to heed the warning that since we are all sinners to one degree or another, we are always subject to the danger of our life getting out of control; a time to check the progress of our journey to the Promised Land; a time to take stock of anything in our life that is stalling our efforts to follow Jesus.
—Hybels, B., "Christians Under Construction"

LIFE

476
The path of life which Jesus trod was one of service. If you will walk this same pathway of service, you will find that life holds blessings for you beyond any you have ever dreamed of having.

If you want to know whether or not you are really walking the path of service, ask yourself this question, "Is my life like a brush pile or a tree?" In contrasting your life in this way, remember, first, that the brush pile is a heap of cut and broken branches. From a distance it may look like a tree, but its branches have no communion with a living stem, and they are in a process of decay. The tree, however, is still alive, and its branches are vitally related to one another. Jesus said, "I am the vine, you are the branches..." (Jn. 15:5) Give your life the purpose of service, and you will have communion with the living stem of Christ. You will walk the path He walked.
—Fischer, W.L., "The Nature of Our Creation" (Adapted).

477/LIFE

Author Robert Fulghum has calculated (with some notable exaggeration) that in his life so far he has spent 35,000 hours eating, 30,000 hours in traffic getting from one place to another, 2508 hours brushing his teeth, 870,000 hours just coping with odds and ends, filling out forms, repairing things, paying bills, getting dressed and undressed, and 217,000 hours at work. "There's not a whole lot left over when you get finished adding and subtracting," he says. "The good stuff has to fit in *somewhere*. Which is why I often say, 'It's not the meaning *of* life, it's the meaning *in* life.'"

All of us have attended lectures which end with the speaker asking, "Are there any questions?" On such occasions, Fulghum says he usually asks the most important question of all: "What is the meaning of life?" He says that the question is never taken seriously—people laugh and nod and gather up their stuff and the meeting ends on that ridiculous note. But once when he asked that question, to his surprise, he got a serious *answer*. It came from Doctor Alexander Papaderos, a Greek philosopher and teacher and founder of an Institute on the Isle of Crete dedicated to human understanding and peace. One summer, Fulghum attended a two week seminar at the Institute. At the conclusion of the final session, Doctor Papaderos asked: "Are there any questions?" There was only quiet. So Fulghum asked, "Doctor Papaderos, what is the meaning of life?" ...

> The usual laughter followed, and people stirred to go. Papaderos held up his hand and stilled the room and looked at me for a long time, asking with his eyes if I was serious and seeing from my eyes that I was. "I will answer your question," he said. Then, taking his wallet out of his hip pocket, he fished into a leather billfold and brought out a very small round mirror, about the size of a quarter. Then he said: "When I was a small child, during the war, we were very poor and we lived in a remote village. One day, on the road, I found several broken pieces of a mirror. A German soldier's motorcycle had been wrecked in that place. I tried to

find all the pieces and put them together, but it was not possible, so I kept only the largest piece. *This* one. And by scratching it on a stone I made it round. I began to play with it as a toy and became fascinated by the fact that I could reflect light into dark places where the sun would never shine—in deep holes and crevices and dark closets. It became a game for me to get light into the most inaccessible places I could find. I kept the little mirror, and as I went about my growing up, I would take it out in idle moments and continue the challenge of the game. As I became a man, I grew to understand that this was not just a *child's* game but a metaphor for what I might do with my *life.* I came to understand that I am not the light or the source of light. But light—truth, understanding, knowledge—is there, and it will only shine in many dark places if I *reflect* it.

I am a fragment of a mirror whose whole design and shape I do not know. Nevertheless, with what I have I can reflect light into the dark places of this world—into the black places in the hearts of men—and change some things in some people. Perhaps others may see and do likewise. This is what I am *about.* This is the meaning of *my* life.

And then he took his small mirror and, holding it carefully, caught the bright rays of daylight streaming through the window and reflected them onto my face and onto my hands folded on the desk.

—Fulghum, R., "It was On Fire When I Lay Down On It." (Adapted).

LIFESTYLE

478

A confident applicant for a job as office boy presented his credentials to a personnel manager. The manager looked them over and said, "I see you've got recommendations from your pastor and your Sunday School teacher. That's good. And I must say, you *look* honest and *appear* to be of good character. Nevertheless, I'd like to see a recommendation from someone who knows you on *weekdays.*"

479/LIFESTYLE

"... He turned and said to Peter, 'Get behind Me, Satan! You are an obstacle in My path because the way you think is not God's way but man's'" (Mt. 16:23).

The story is told of a man who, resisting the cost of the *oats* he fed his mule, began gradually to change over to *sawdust* in its diet. Day by day, the animal was fed less oats and more sawdust until, finally, it was *all* sawdust. Everything went fine for a while—but by the time the mule became *satisfied* with sawdust, he died of malnutrition.

Our constant temptation is to change our spiritual diet from the ways of God to the ways of man. Often the changeover is a *slow* process. And if we're not *careful,* we may get to the point where we don't recognize the *difference.* We become *satisfied* with the ways of man and, *when* this happens, we are spiritually *dead.*

LISTENING

480

An eighty-year-old grandfather went to his daughter's house for Sunday dinner. When the meal was over he announced that he was going to take a walk through the neighborhood. "I'll be back in twenty minutes," he said. But two hours had passed before he finally returned. "Sorry I'm late," he said, "but I stopped to talk to an old friend and he just wouldn't stop *listening.*"

481/LISTENING

At the annual meeting of the National Hospice Association, one of the speakers gave an illustration that generated a great deal of discussion among the doctors and the nurses present. The speaker told the story of a young nurse who was ministering to a young man her own age. The patient had terminal cancer. The nurse knew that the young man wanted to talk with her but because she was afraid that she wouldn't have "the right answers," she decided to back off. In her own words:

> I *know* he wanted to talk to me, but I always turned it into something *light*: a little joke or some evasive reassurance, which *had* to fail. The *patient* knew, and *I* knew, but as he saw my desperate attempt to *escape*, and as he felt my *anxiety*, he took pity on me by keeping to *himself* what he wanted to share with another human being. And so he died, and did not bother me.

In the discussion that followed, the more *experienced* nurses and doctors pointed out that when you are with a terminal patient you don't *need* to worry about having "the right answers." If you have an answer in the situation, that is *good*. *Share* it. But, just letting the person *talk*, just being *present* to him and really *listening* to him, releases tremendous forces of reassurance within him. Listening, in a *caring* way, can be the greatest gift you can give in that situation. The nurses' and doctors' discussion was limited to the rather restricted area of terminal illness. But it applies to *all* of life. *Listening* is a way of *loving*.

482/LISTENING

The famous longshoreman-philosopher-author, Eric Hofer, was cared for as a child by a Bavarian peasant woman, after his mother had died. For about eight years during this period of his life, Eric Hofer was *blind*. Years later, he had this to say about the woman who cared for him:

> This woman, Martha was her name, took loving care of me. I remember she was a big woman, and she must have *really* loved me because I remember those eight years of blindness in my childhood as essentially a *happy* time of my life. I remember a lot of *talk* and a lot

> of *laughter*. I must have talked a great deal as a child because Martha used to say to me again-and-again, "Do you remember when you said this? Do you remember when you said that?" And I realized that she had been *listening* to me and *remembered* what I said. And all my life I have had this feeling about myself: that what I think and what I say are *worth* listening to and remembering. This is the *gift* she gave me!"

When we give to those who are *close* to us the feeling that what they think and what they say are *worth* listening to, we are offering them one of the *priceless* gifts—of *love*.

483/LISTENING

A quiet little woman was surrounded by seven big strapping sons and a husband. When asked how she ever made her soft voice heard above the boisterous males in her family she replied: "That's very simple. I *whisper*. In my family a whisper is so unusual that everyone listens to it with *profound* attention."

"The words of a whisper are like delicious morsels" (Prov. 18:8). "What you hear whispered, proclaim upon the housetops" (Mt.10:27).

484/LISTENING

The noted Harvard scholar, Charles T. Copeland, was once approached by a student who asked: "Why are there no courses in *conversation?* Is there anything I can do to learn the art of conversation?"

"Of course there is," answered Copeland, "and if you'll just listen, I'll tell you what it is."

There ensued a long and awkward silence, which the student finally interrupted: "Well, I'm *listening*," he said.

"You *see*," said Copeland, "you're learning *already!*"

485/LISTENING

There are times when we yearn for peace and quiet—away from honking horns, screeching brakes, blaring transistors, throbbing washing machines and jarring jets. We treasure such periods of rest for our sensitive ears. But do you know how difficult it would be to find a moment of peace and quiet if our ears were only a *bit* more sensitive? If they were but *slightly* more powerful, we would be tuned into the chatter of rats. Were our ears *three* times more powerful, we would be tuned into our own heart beats and digestive processes. Were they *five* times more powerful, we would hear what field mice were saying. If they were *seven* times as powerful, we would hear what bats were saying. And as the din grew louder, as more of nature's secret sounds assaulted our sense of hearing, the possibilities for peace and quiet would decrease proportionately. If our ears were exposed to *all* sound, the roar would be intolerable; deafening. In nature's grand design, there are sounds which are not intended to be heard with the naked ear.

Scientists tell us that the deaf person who *suddenly* recovers his hearing is likely to find exposure to the world of sound a frightening experience. During the adjustment period it is not uncommon for the cured person to seek to return to the world of silence. It takes time and conditioning to learn how to interpret sounds, how to distinguish between those that threaten and those which do not—in other words, to learn how to *listen*. Being born with the ability to *hear* is not of our own doing, but the ability to *listen* is an art that we must develop ourselves.

LIVING WATER

486

There is the story of a spring with waters that had certain *medicinal* properties. Many who drank from it were healed of various infirmities. In the course of time, homes sprang up around the spring. Then came a hotel, stores, and eventually a town that grew into a big city. But there came a day when visitors would ask, "Where is the *spring* from which this grew?" And the residents would say, with embarrassment, "We are sorry, but somehow in the midst of all our progress and improvement, we *lost* the spring."

Institutional Christianity's biggest problem today is to find its lost "*spring*." We need to *rediscover* the Wellspring of God's Love that is still in our midst, waiting to overflow into the world around us. We need to *drink* of that Living Water!

LOAVES AND FISHES

487

A British columnist expressed his displeasure with the attitudes of two drama critics as follows:

> If this pair had been present at the miracle of the loaves and fishes, one of them would have complained that there was no *lemon* to go with the fish, and the other would have demanded *butter* for the bread.

LONELINESS

488

Several years ago, a New York City man was quoted as follows in a New York Times newspaper column:

> I live on a high floor of a building facing a busy avenue on the West Side of Manhattan. Across the street from me, a few floors down, at a window with a rather large sill, sits an elderly woman. She is playing cards by herself. She sits there all day long, from morning till evening, stopping only for brief moments during the day. Once I saw someone else moving about in the room behind her, but she seemed to pay no attention to whoever it was, and went on playing.

This has been going on for at least six years. The other day I finally found myself satisfying my intense curiosity. I took a pair of binoculars over to the window, to see just what kind of game of solitaire she was so engrossed in. When her window came into focus, I saw that what she was shuffling and laying out was not a deck of *cards*, but a stack of *photographs*; they were the faded photographs of *children*.

LORD'S PRAYER

489
One Saturday morning, little Dennis's daddy went to pick him up at Catechism Class.

Dennis came skipping down the church steps. "Daddy," he said proudly, "I learned something *new* today!"

"You did?" said his father. "Tell me what it was."

At that the boy began to recite the Lord's Payer. After the first slow careful phrases, his father joined in.

Suddenly Dennis stopped reciting and looked up at his father. "Aw!" he said, "somebody *told* you!"

LOSS

490
Snoopy, the wise, modern philosopher, once said, "It doesn't make any difference whether you win or lose—*until* you lose!" Then it makes a *big* difference!

What a great observation concerning human nature! For most people, *real* motivation to change and *genuine* appreciation for life don't occur until they experience *loss*. The principle is absolute: only when you come to the *end* of yourself does life truly *begin*.
—Timmons, T., "Hooked On Life."

LOVE

491
A proud mother wrote:

> My daughter Francesca was about four years old when she first became aware that numbers were not just new words in her vocabulary or names of digits, but that they can be useful to express *quantity*. This step, as all parents learn, follows the "so big" stage.
>
> One memorable day, Francesca turned to me to express her *love* with the help of her new-found knowledge. She said, "Mummy, I love you *ten* times," followed by deep thought and "I love you *twenty* times." After another short pause, she reached a breathless pinnacle with "I love you *six hundred* times."
>
> A grateful hug and kiss from me produced a tiny frown and more concentrated thought which disappeared in a sigh of relief in her final outburst, "Mummy, I love you more than *all* the numbers."

—Hughes, M. ed., "We Cannot Measure Love." (Adapted).

492/LOVE
In a story called "Caught In That Music," a young woman named Debbie is about to marry a young man named Norman. Debbie's brother objects to the marriage because he thinks Norman is dull and disagreeable. Debbie asks her brother to be more tolerant. She says: "Nothing is ever *completely* the way you think it is, or would *like* it to be. I didn't love Norman right away. He loved me—so much, that I wished I could love him in return. Some people have to *see* love before they themselves can love." "Is that the way it works?" Debbie's brother asks. "Because he loves *you*, you love *him*?" To which Debbie replies, "Because he *loves* me, *I* see what you *don't* see!"
—Epstein, S.

493/LOVE

A Riddle:

> What is everlasting and our most precious gift in life?
>
> Money cannot buy it, yet we often abuse this greatest of life's treasures.
>
> From the moment we are given life, we seek it, but when we find it we often disregard it.
>
> But when we embrace it for own, we discover that the more we share it the more we have left.
>
> What is it?
>
> "Love" is the answer!

494/LOVE

Pop singer Cliff Richard visited a Bihari refugee camp in Bangladesh. When he returned home, he described this moving incident:

> The first morning I was there I must have washed my hands a dozen times. I didn't want to touch anything, least of all the people. Everyone in those camps was covered in sores and scabs.
>
> I was bending down to one little girl, mainly for the photographer's benefit, and trying hard not to have too close a contact. Just then someone accidentally stood on the child's fingers. She screamed and, as a reflex, I grabbed her, forgetting her dirt and her sores. I remember that warm little body clinging to me and the crying instantly stopping. In that moment I knew I had much to learn about practical Christian loving, but that at least I'd started.

—*"Which One's Cliff?" Hodder & Stoughton, London (Adapted).*

495/LOVE

The teacher in an adult-education creative-writing class told the students to write "I love you" in 25 words or less, without using the words "I love you." The assignment was to be completed in fifteen minutes. A woman in the class spent about ten minutes looking at the ceiling and wriggling in her seat. Then she began to write frantically. Later she read the results to the rest of the class, in the form of three illustrations of how to say "I love you" without using the words "I love you":

1) "Why, I've seen lots worse hairdos than that, honey."

2) "These cookies are hardly burned at all."

3) "Cuddle up - I'll get your feet warm."

—*Mortimer, C., "Let Me Grant the Ways."*

496/LOVE

Infantile love follows the principle:
"I love because I am loved."

Mature love follows the principle:
"I am loved because I love."

Immature love says:
"I love you because I need you."

Mature love says:
"I need you because I love you."

—*Fromm, E.*

497/LOVE

What is love? ...
It's silence when your words would hurt.
It's patience when your neighbor's curt.
It's deafness when the scandal flows.
It's thoughtfulness for another's woes.
It's promptness when stern duty calls.
It's courage when misfortune falls.

498/LOVE

Where there is love
the *heart* is light,
Where there is love
the *day* is bright.

Where there is love
There is a *song*
To help when things
are going *wrong.*

Where there is love
there is a *smile*
To make all things
seem more *worthwhile.*

Where there is love
there's quiet *peace,*
A tranquil place
where turmoils *cease.*

Love changes darkness
into *light*
And makes the heart
take "wingless *flight.*"

Oh, *blest* are they
who walk in love,
They also walk
with *God* above!
And *when* man walks
with God again,
There shall be *peace*
on earth for men!

499/LOVE

Human love can be compared to the sunshine which shines brightly on the trees of the forest. The trees sink into the earth and finally are dug up as coal. When the coal burns, it returns the light and heat that came from the sun. Like the trees which receive *sunlight*, the human heart receives the capacity to *love* from God. Then, in union with another heart, love *burns* and returns again to God the love that came from Him.

500/LOVE

In a delightful "Peanuts" cartoon strip, Lucy says, "Guess what...If you don't tell me that you love me, you know what I'm going to do? I'm going to hold my breath until I pass out!" Looking up from his piano, Shroeder says, "Breath-holding in children is an interesting phenomenon...It could indicate a metabolic disorder...A forty-milligram dose of Vitamin B6 twice a day might be helpful...I think that's probably it...You need Vitamin B6...you might also consider eating more bananas, avocados, and beef liver..." As he goes back to his piano, Lucy sighs,"I ask for *love*, and all I get is *beef liver!*"

501/LOVE

From her remarkable true story, ANGELS WITHOUT WINGS, Jane Vonnegut Yarmolinsky writes about the tragic death of her brother-in-law who perished in a freak train accident. Just thirty-six hours after his own death, his wife would die of cancer leaving three small children without parents. In the following passage from ANGELS WITHOUT WINGS, Jane writes of her quiet moments of reflection following the double tragedy, and the new responsibility she and her husband Carl were facing:

> During the hour I sat by the pond, my thoughts slowly evolved, changing from a confrontation with death to a confrontation with the lives ahead...Young lives had been broken. They needed to be mended. I would do what I could.
>
> I had no idea where the energy was going to come from to do all the things that needed to be done, to meet the gaping emotional needs created by the double tragedy. But suddenly I did have the energy, and I

found myself doing those things without even questioning the rightness of it. Many years went by before I could identify the source of the energy, could put a name to it. I had simply come face to face with *agape*—ultimate, unconditional *love*...

You can't just love in the abstract, any more than you can paint a picture in the air. No, you need five boys and two girls and one husband, three dogs, two cats, two birds, lots and lots of friends, and much, much more...

LOVE OF GOD

502
If you are a person who travels a lot, you are familiar with the sinking feeling that comes when you land at an airport and no one is there to greet you—you look all around, searching the crowd in the hope of finding someone to say "Welcome!"

If you are a travelling person, you are also familiar with the sinking feeling that comes when you try to show people pictures of the places you've been. "Who would like to see my slides?" you ask. And there is silence. All travelers have that problem with their family and friends. But take heart! Not only is God at the airport saying "Welcome! How was your trip?" God is also saying, "I would like to see your slides."

503/LOVE OF GOD
The campus newspaper ran a photograph of a piece of graffiti someone had painted on the "Department of Sciences" building of a large University. It read, "Where will you spend eternity?" Immediately below, someone else had written, "As far as I can see, it looks like Biology 201!" Perhaps to some of you it seems that we are eternally preaching about the love of God. But, if we believe Jesus who tells us that everything in our faith and life depends on experiencing God's love, then how can we not preach this reality, in season and out?

504/LOVE OF GOD

A little girl wrote a letter to God about something that apparently was bothering her a great deal:

> Dear God,
> Instead of letting people die and having to make new ones, why don't you just keep the ones you've got now?
> Alice

Well, Alice, there is Good News for you today from God Himself: "Because I *love* them so much, I *do* keep the ones I've got now. Because I love *you* so much, Alice, I want to keep *you* for my own, *always!*"

M

MARRIAGE

505
A man went to his lawyer for advice about a divorce. The lawyer asked him what had gone wrong with the marriage. "It was great in the early years," the man said. "But then we began more and more to notice things about each other that we didn't like. Somehow we grew more and more intolerant of each other's little faults." Whereupon, the lawyer told his client the story of a man he knew who took great pride in his lush, green lawn until gradually it became studded with an irksome crop of dandelions. After trying every known device to get rid of the dandelions, the man wrote to the Department of Agriculture in Washington, D.C. In his letter he listed all the things he had tried, then ended with the question, "What shall I do now?" In due course the man received the following reply: "We suggest that you learn to love them!"

506/MARRIAGE
When the knot is tied, men sometimes don't get all the support they might like from their spouses.

Governor James Hunt of North Carolina recalled that a few years ago his wife got a call from a local civic leader for some biographical information. It seems that Governor Hunt had been selected as the organization's Man of the Year.

"Well," Mrs. Hunt told him over the phone, "that just shows what kind of year it's been."
—Scott, W., "Down Home Stories."

507/MARRIAGE
When Mr. and Mrs. Henry Ford celebrated their golden wedding anniversary, a reporter asked them, "To what do you attribute your fifty years of successful married life?"

"The formula," said Ford, "is the same formula I have always used in making cars: Just stick to one model."

508/MARRIAGE
Over breakfast one morning, a woman said to her husband, "I bet you don't know what day this is."

"Of course I do," he indignantly answered. Then he went out the door on his way to the office.

At 10 a.m., the doorbell rang, and when the woman opened the door, she was handed a box containing a dozen long-stemmed red roses. At 1 p.m., a foil-wrapped, two-pound box of her favorite chocolates arrived. Later, a boutique delivered a designer dress.

The woman couldn't wait for her husband to come home. "First the flowers then the candy and then the dress!" she exclaimed. "I've never spent a more wonderful 'Groundhog Day' in my whole life!"
—Bosa, E.C.,

509/MARRIAGE
Perhaps you have seen or read the best-seller entitled "Looking Out For Number One." But did you know that after the book was *published*, the author's wife divorced him and is now receiving thousands of dollars in *alimony*. When asked about this, she is reported to have said, "I read the *book!*"

510/MARRIAGE
A woman came into the post office and asked to see a selection of 29-cents stamps. She wanted to choose a stamp design and theme appropriate for the *wedding* invitations she was mailing. After careful consideration, she happily announced

she'd found exactly the right one: the John Paul Jones commemorative stamp that bears his rallying cry, "I have not yet begun to fight."
—Brayton, T.

511/MARRIAGE
Three little sisters had just returned home from a wedding. They decided to play their own game of "Wedding." Each child had a role to play: bride, groom, and minister. As the game began, the "bride" and "groom" stood next to each other and the minister asked, "Do you take this man for richer or poorer?" The little "bride" replied, "For *richer!*"

512/MARRIAGE
Late night television advertising is no longer limited to selling kitchen gadgets, real estate seminars or miracle car waxes. According to one commercial, you can pick up the phone, dial a "900" number and speak to "someone who shares your interests" and would "love to meet you." While most people probably don't really believe that a "900" number service is a good way to meet their future spouse, some *have* turned to computer dating services in an attempt to find a compatible mate. Computer dating services around the country claim to have arranged thousands of introductions that have resulted in marriage.

One recently divorced thirty-five-year-old man decided to use a dating service in search of a new mate. After completing a detailed questionnaire and a one hour personal interview, the computer presented him with five names selected from a data base of tens-of-thousands of potential candidates. Much to his surprise, the first name on the list belonged to his *former wife!*

513/MARRIAGE
According to band leader Maynard Ferguson...

> Some guys change their wives every few years, and their music remains the *same.* But I've been married to the same woman for over twenty years, and my music keeps *changing.* I *like* it that way!

514/MARRIAGE
A husband and wife, both golf addicts, decided to celebrate their eighteenth wedding anniversary on the golf course. After playing a full round, they went to their favorite restaurant for dinner. Looking into her husband's eyes over the candlelit table, the wife said, earnestly, "Would you like to go for another eighteen?" "No," the husband answered, "it's getting dark. We wouldn't get past the fourth hole."

515/MARRIAGE
Building a good marriage and building a good log fire are similar in many ways. You build a fire with paper and kindling, and all at once it goes up in a brilliantly burning *blaze.* Then the primary blaze burns down and you wonder if the fire will fizzle out and leave you in the dark. You blow on it and fan it for all you are worth. Sometimes smoke billows out and almost chokes you, but if the *materials* are good and if you invest enough *energy* and *interest* in maintaining it, soon the big solid logs catch, and your fire takes on *new* qualities.
—Lowman, J.

516/MARRIAGE
First-grader Melanie had announced that she was engaged to marry the young gentleman next door, but the engagement was broken abruptly.

"Why aren't you going to *marry* Danny? asked Melanie's mother, with a twinkle in her eye.

"Well," replied the child loftily, "he just isn't ready for marriage yet. And besides that, he scribbled in my *coloring* book."

517/MARRIAGE
A widower of many years, with marriage on his mind, began courting a woman he admired very much. And the day came when he called his daughter to announce his *engagement.* The daughter wanted to know all the details. "How did you propose?" she asked. "Did you get down on one knee, dad?" "No," he replied. "You see, it was *she* who proposed to *me.* I first

asked her to marry me a year ago. She said that she would never marry a man who wasn't thrifty. Then she told me that if I could save $5,000 in one year she would say 'Yes!' On our last date, the year was up but I didn't even mention marriage. However, she asked me how much I had managed to *save* during the year. I told her, $22.86. And she replied, 'That's close enough!'"

518/MARRIAGE

A young bride-to-be learned, to her dismay, that some of her fiance's religious beliefs were less than orthodox. "What shall I do?" she asked her mother anxiously, "Harold doesn't even believe in *hell!*" "Don't worry dear," her mother replied, "between the two of us we'll show him how *wrong* he is."

Later, during the wedding rehearsal, the bride-to-be grew nervous about her walk down the Church's extremely long aisle. "Don't worry dear," her mother said, "you can get rid of any last minute jitters if you concentrate on three words. First, think of the *aisle.* It's the same aisle you've walked down every Sunday since you were a little girl. Second, focus on the *altar.* You were baptized at that same altar and have knelt before it every Sunday for years. Third, think about *him*—your loving groom, waiting to begin your new life together. On the wedding day, mother's advice worked like a charm. The bride focused hard on the first word, as she began her wedding march: "Aisle!...Aisle!...Aisle!," she repeated over and over again. Then the second word: "Altar!...Altar!...Altar!..." Then the third word, "Him!...Him!...Him!..." Finally, when the march ended and she took the groom's arm, she looked into his eyes and said, *"I'll alter him!"*

519/MARRIAGE

A young man and woman, soon to be married, were walking along the seashore. It was such a moment of bliss for the young man that, in his excitement, he looked out over the sea and cried out, "Roll mighty ocean, *roll!*" Whereupon, the starry-eyed young woman looked at him lovingly and said, "Oh you wonderful man, it's *doing* it."

When two people are in that kind of blissful state, it's easy to pledge a lasting union. It's not difficult for them to say that they will love each other and remain faithful "until death do us part." But as time goes by, and the daily pressures build and close in on them, the blissful episodes seem to grow further and further apart. Actress Joanne Woodward once said that she could not understand how her husband, Paul Newman, could still be a teenage sex-symbol because "He's forty-five years old, he has six children and he *snores*." One of the beautiful things about a *good* marriage relationship is that, *after* the honeymoon is over—even after twenty-five or thirty years of all that *snoring*—the union still *endures*.

MEANING OF LIFE

520
A newly-hired assistant bookkeeper was being briefed by his employer. He said to him, "These accounts are especially important. Therefore, I want you to add each column of figures at least three times before you give me the result." Later, the employee laid a piece of paper on the employer's desk and said, "I have added this column of figures ten times..." The employer broke in, intending to compliment him for his thoroughness, until he heard the assistant bookkeeper say, "...and here are my ten different answers."

When we raise the question of life's meaning these days, we are likely to receive ten, or even one-hundred and ten different answers.

"Yes, God loved the world so much, that He gave His only Son, so that everyone who believes in Him may not be lost but may have eternal life" (Jn. 3:16).

"...the usefulness of spirituality is unlimited, since it holds out the reward of life, here and now and of the future life as well" (I Tim. 4:8).

521/MEANING OF LIFE

The "Detroit Free Press" ran an interesting feature article on the subject of why a pigeon walks so *funny*. In case you didn't know, a pigeon walks the way it does in order to see where it is going. While it is in motion, a pigeon is unable to adjust its focus to see clearly. It literally must bring its head to a complete stop between steps in order to refocus. And that is why a pigeon walks as follows: head forward, stop; head backward, stop. Because we live in such a fast-moving world, we might do well to take a *lesson* from the pigeon: learn how to do a *pigeon*-walk. In terms of what we're *doing* with our lives, where we're *going* with our lives, we need to *pull up* from the often maddening pace. We need to stop and *refocus* on the true meaning of our life. We need to reset our sights on where we are in relation to the Will of *God*. We need to have a clearer view of the *Christ* Presence in our midst.

MERCY

522

According to an ancient legend, four angels approached God when He was about to create man. "Create him not," advised the Angel of Justice, "For he will commit all kinds of wickedness against his fellow men; he will be hard and cruel and dishonest and unrighteous." "Create him not," said the Angel of Truth, "For he will be false and deceitful to his brothers, and even to Thee." "Create him not," urged the Angel of Holiness, "For he will follow that which is impure in Thy sight, and dishonor Thee to Thy face." Then the Angel of Mercy stepped forward and said: "Create him, our heavenly Father, for when he sins and turns from the path of right and truth and holiness, Thou canst take him tenderly by the hand, and speak loving words to him, and lead him back to Thee."

MIRACLES

523

In a New York court room, a man, bandaged from his toes to his chin was suing for $4 million for injuries allegedly sustained in an accident. He won the suit. The lawyers for the insurance company went over to him and said, "You're never going to enjoy a penny of this. We're going to follow you twenty-four hours a day. We know you're faking and the first time you move, we'll have you." The plaintiff said, "Will you now? Well, let me tell you what's going to happen to me. They're coming in here with a stretcher. They're taking me out and they're putting me in an ambulance. They're driving me straight to Kennedy Airport and they're putting me on an airplane in that stretcher. We're flying direct to Paris, France, and there they're taking me on the stretcher off the plane and putting me in another ambulance. We're going direct to the Shrine of Lourdes and there you're going to see the greatest miracle you've ever seen."

—As told by Ronald Reagan

524/MIRACLES

From Walt Whitman's poem, "Miracles":

> To me every hour of the light and dark is a miracle,
> Every cubic inch of space is a miracle…
> To me the sea is a continual miracle,
> The fishes that swim, the rocks,
> the motion of the waves,
> The ships with men in them…
>
> As to me, I know of nothing else *but* miracles,
> Whether I walk the streets of Manhattan…
> Or talk by day with any one I love,
> Or sit at table at dinner with the rest,
> Or look at strangers, opposite me riding in the car…
> What strange *miracles* are these?

525/MIRACLES

At the conclusion of a week-long prayer and meditation retreat, the participants were asked to write their impressions. One man wrote:

> My ambition to succeed had taken over my life to such an extent that I was feeling out of touch with reality. I

was missing out on *life.* So I came here looking for an answer. I came here looking for some sign or *miracle.* And what I've discovered is that the real miracle is the miracle of the *people:* the way they *greet* each other, the way they open up their *hearts* to each other. Here everything is so simple and basic you can *read* the signs that are written everywhere in life. When you're moving too fast, you *can't* read the signs. When you're moving too fast you miss the miracle of *life.*

—State Times, Baton Rouge, La. (Adapted).

MONEY

526/MONEY

Comedian Richard Pryor, critically burned in an accident, told Johnny Carson that when you're seriously ill, suddenly money isn't that important anymore. He said: "All I could think of was to call on God. I didn't call the Bank of America once."

527/MONEY

The great composer Rachmaninoff was unhappy at being labeled a genius. It was his desire to at all times appear perfectly normal. Once, a stage-struck listener asked, "What ever inspired you to compose such a wonderfully marvelous piece as you 'C-Sharp Minor Prelude'?" The master made a deep bow and, with a perfectly composed face, replied, "Because, madam, I needed the dough."

528/MONEY

"Talk shows" are among the most popular features on American radio stations. Listeners are invited to call the station and, via telephone, talk "live" on the air with the program host. Some shows allow the caller to comment or ask questions on any subject. Others limit the talk to specific topics. Perhaps the most popular of all are the "money" talk shows hosted by investment counselors who advise callers about their finances. Each week, from coast to coast, thousands of questions are put to these radio hosts by callers looking for free advice on what to do with their excess money. Without exception, they not only want to hold onto it, they want it to grow as fast as possible. On the other hand, callers never ask for advice on how to give away some of their excess.

I think most of us would have to admit that this is our attitude toward money. If we don't have enough money, or if we think we don't, we take the matter up with God. We pray for it. We ask God to show us how to get it. But when is the last time any of us asked God to show us how to give some of it away?

529/MONEY

Some years ago, a testimonial dinner was given in honor of John B. Fulton, one of Arizona's most famous citizens. Speaker after speaker rose to pay tribute to Fulton's achievements as a banker, rancher, manufacturer and real estate man. All of them recalled how Fulton had arrived in Phoenix at age twenty, bare-footed, clothes in tatters and nothing but a pack on his back. After the ceremonies, former United States Senator Abraham Ribicoff approached Fulton and asked, "Sir, what did you have in the pack on your back?" Fulton took a puff of his cigar, blew some smoke in Ribicoff's face and replied, "Two million dollars cash."

530/MONEY

A Minneapolis newspaper conducted a readers' poll in which a wide range of questions was asked. The readers' answers to one of the questions revealed that only four percent of them believed *they* deserved to go to hell. But *twenty* percent of them said they knew *other* folks who deserved to go to hell.

Our attitude toward money is much the same. Do most Christians *really* believe that the Biblical warning, "You cannot serve God and money," applies to *them*? To *others*, perhaps, but not to *them*; to *others*, perhaps, but not to *us*.

531/MONEY

A prominent psychiatrist has written a book called "For the Love of Money" which really unmasks us all. He helps us to understand how *important* money has become to us and how we are greatly *motivated* by it. And he makes a case for us to be *honest* about it and just come right out and *say* that money is our god.

Many of us build a wall around the "money" part of our lives. As Church people we try to get our lives lined up and in harmony with our religious beliefs, but we say to God, "Stay out of my stocks and bonds, stay out of my savings account, stay out of my vacation nest-egg, stay out of my children's education money." "For the Love of Money," reminds us that the rest of life isn't going to fit into place until we break down that wall and say to God, "Okay Lord, even our *money*."

532/MONEY

One prominent psychiatrist has called our preoccupation with money the number one crippling disease in this country. He credits our "money sickness" as the source of much frustration and anxiety. The love of money can cripple us, diminish us, and even destroy us, more effectively than any other form of illness. It can cause physical illness, demolish marriages, break up families, even drive persons to murder and suicide. Doctors now tell us that often they are able to trace internal medical problems directly to patients' attitudes toward money and possessions—the *economic* aspects of their lives. As the man said to his psychiatrist: "By the time I discovered that money doesn't buy happiness, I had already earned five million dollars."

Several years ago there appeared an amusing cartoon that perfectly illustrates our "money sickness." Two well dressed businessmen are seated at the bar in a posh restaurant. With a terrified look on his face, one man turns to the other and says, "I had the most awful dream last night. I dreamed the value of the dollar had slipped so low that it was no longer worth *worshipping*!"

533/MONEY

Stage director Moss Hart had a beautiful house in the country that he enjoyed re-decorating and landscaping. On his weekend

visits, he would have his landscape designer move large trees about the property, design streams, gardens and elaborate rock formations. Once he even had the landscaper move a small "*mountain*" several hundred feet! Playwright George S. Kaufman once remarked after visiting the director's home, "This is how God would do it if only He had the money."
—Roger, J., McWilliams, P., "Life 101." (Adapted).

534/MONEY
"The love of money is the root of all evils and there are some who, pursuing it, have wandered away from the faith, and so given their souls any number of fatal wounds" (I Tim. 4:10).

There is an old legend about a rich, but selfish old man who kept all of his money hidden in a secret chest in the darkest corner of his attic. Each night, when he was sure he would not be seen, he stole up into the attic, quietly opened his treasure chest and gazed lovingly at his money. He did this for years until, one night, his hiding place having been discovered, the money was stolen. When the miser found out what had happened, he ran into the street and began to moan and groan so loudly that all his neighbors came out to see what had happened. When they heard about the robbery, one of the neighbors said to the victim, "You say that each night you opened the chest and looked at all your money. But did you ever take any of it *out?*" "No," said the old man, "I just opened up the chest and *looked* at the money." To which the neighbor replied, "In that case, the money wasn't doing a thing for you or anyone else, so you might just as well look into an *empty* chest every night."

535/MONEY
The dying request of an eccentric old man was that his body be *frozen* in the hope that one day, as the result of scientific advances, he would be *rejuvenated.* Fifty years later, through a miracle of science, he was *defrosted.* Immediately, he phoned his stock broker. "What's the stock market done in the last fifty years?" he asked. His broker reported that his 100 shares of IBM were now worth $10 million; his 100 shares of General

Motors were worth $8 million and his real estate holdings had increased to $22 million. "Great!" exclaimed the rejuvenated man. "I'm *rich*!" At which point, the telephone operator interrupted and said, "Your three minutes are up, sir. Please deposit three-hundred thousand dollars for the next two minutes."

536/MONEY

After giving the new patient a thorough diagnostic examination and prescribing vitamin supplements, exercise therapy and a specialized diet, the Park Avenue sports medicine doctor announced that his fee would be $500. The patient balked, "That's more than I make in a week." The doctor offered to reduce the bill to $400. Still the man protested. After much haggling, the physician reluctantly accepted $100. "But why," he asked, "did you come to a specialist like me? Why not a general practitioner in your local clinic? That would have cost you far less."

"Oh, no" replied the patient, "when it comes to my *health*, money is *no object!*"

537/MONEY

A mother of a little girl named Christine said that one of the aspects of child rearing she enjoyed most was sharing her interest in books and reading with her little girl. Actually, she took this role very seriously and, therefore, was truly proud when, at the age of 4, Christine applied for and received her first library card. But her parental pride was quickly shattered when she accompanied Christine on her first visit to the local library. The child handed the librarian her carefully chosen books with the new card on top and said, '*Charge* it , please.'"

MOTHER

538

On a dismal, stormy, winter's night, the owner of a neighborhood bakery decided to close his shop early. "There won't be any customers on a night like this," he reasoned. As he was about to lock the bakery door, a man rushed in, shivering and wet from head to toe. "I would like two sweet rolls," he said. The baker was amazed that anyone would brave such bad weather for just two sweet rolls. "Are you married?" he asked the customer. "Of course I'm married," the man replied. "Do you suppose my *mother* would send me out on a night like this?"

539/MOTHER

I had the meanest mother in the whole world. While other kids ate candy for breakfast, I had to have cereal, eggs or toast. When others had cokes and candy for lunch, I had to eat a sandwich. As you can guess my supper was different from the other kids, too. But at least I wasn't alone in my sufferings. My sister and two brothers had the same mean mother I did.

My mother insisted upon knowing where we were at all times. She had to know who our friends were and what we were doing. She insisted if we said we'd be gone an hour that we be gone an hour or less—not one hour and one minute.

The worst is yet to come. We had to be in bed by ten each night and up early the next morning. We couldn't sleep till noon like our friends. While they slept my mother actually had the nerve to break the child labor law. She made us work. We had to wash dishes, make beds, learn to cook and all sorts of cruel things. I believe she laid awake at night thinking up mean things to do to us.

She always insisted upon our telling the truth, the whole truth, and nothing but the truth, even if it killed us—and it nearly did.

By the time we were teenagers she was much wiser, and our life became even more unbearable. While my friends were dating at the mature age of 12 and 13, my old-fashioned mother refused to let me date until the age of 16, and that was only to go to school functions three or four times a year.

Now I am trying to raise my own children. I stand a little taller and I am filled with pride when *my* children call me "mean." Because, you see, I thank God. He gave *me* the meanest mother in the whole world.
—*Anonymous*

540/MOTHER
A drill sergeant was frustrated in his efforts to make a soldier out of a certain recruit. The trainee lagged behind on marches, used any excuse to go on sick call, grumbled constantly about the food, and never made his cot up properly. But one day, a noticeable change took place in the young man's attitude. When asked to what he attributed the soldier's change in attitude the drill sergeant explained, "Threats and punishment didn't work, so I had to resort to the ultimate weapon. I wrote his mother!"

541/MOTHER

> She is pitied, old dear,
> For she had no career.
> She was merely a wife and a *mother.*
> Ego structure unborn,
> Id fulfillment forlorn,
> Her poor soul was permitted to *smother.*
>
> But she's happy! She glows!
> Ah...perhaps what she chose
> Was to love, not herself, but *another!*

542/MOTHER
In a letter to the Wall Street Journal, author Charles McCarry tells the story of how he almost wasn't born:

> My mother became pregnant with me at the age of 39. She had nearly died while giving birth to my only sibling. Her doctor, who believed the second pregnancy was a serious threat to her life, advised an abortion. The advice made sense, but my mother refused to accept it.

Just before she died at age 97, I asked her why she had refused to accept the advice. She replied, "I wanted to see who you were going to turn out to be."

543/MOTHER

During World War II, a chaplain was talking to a soldier—a tough, hard-drinking type who didn't wear his heart on his sleeve, yet whom the chaplain suspected came from a good, Christian family. The soldier asked, "Can you tell me how it is that sometimes when my nerves are all a-twitter, I suddenly feel calm and ready for anything?"

The chaplain paused for a moment and then said, "Might it not be that at such times your mother is praying for you?"

544/MOTHER

What is a mother? Two enterprising reporters, Joan Scobey and Lee Parr McGrath, decided to ask the experts: *children*. In their book, "What Is a Mother?", they report:

> A mother is the only one, if she sings your favorite song, it stops thundering—Louise.
>
> Mothers are wonderful! She spends all her time on you. A mother is just like God, except God is better—Laura.
>
> It is lucky that we have a mother because if we did not have a mother everything would be in a big big mess— Fred.
>
> What is a mother? When I have something to tell somebody I can tell my mother sometimes but not all the times—Betsy.
>
> A mother is a person too—David

—Hughes, M. ed., "A Mother Is Love"

545/MOTHER

Out of the French Revolution came the story of a mother who had wandered through the woods for three days with her two children, trying to survive on roots and leaves. On the third day, she heard some soldiers approaching and quickly hid herself and the children behind some bushes. The sergeant in charge prodded the bushes to see what was stirring behind them. When he saw the starving woman and children he immediately gave them a loaf of brown bread. The mother took it eagerly, broke it into two pieces and gave one piece to each of the children. "She has kept none for *herself*," the sergeant said. "Because she is not *hungry?"* a soldier asked. "Because she is a *mother*," the sergeant replied.

MOTHER-IN-LAW'S PRAYER

546

Teach me to speak—or hold my tongue.
Silence is divine.
Help me, I pray, to understand
This new-found child of mine.

Keep me from taking bitter sides,
Or feeding angry flames.
Help me to let them both alone,
Like children at their games.

Counsel me when to call on them
And when to say "Good-bye."
Instruct my heart to love them both,
And not ask the reason why.

Teach me to be a friend in need,
Whose smile they're glad to share.
Never too near, yet never too far,
This is my humble prayer.

—Kenny, N.

MOTIVES

547
A cartoon which appeared in "The New Yorker" magazine shows a group of hogs eagerly assembled for feeding as a farmer is filling their trough to the brim. One pig suspiciously asks the others in the group, "Have you ever wondered *why* he's being so good to us?"

MUSIC

548
Two men were quietly fishing on a river bank one evening, content to just listen to the sound of the crickets. One man offered, "Gee, those crickets sure do sing." The other man answered, "Sure do." Just as he spoke he heard the sounds of a choir rehearsing in a nearby church. "That sure is beautiful music," he said. The first man, now lost in thought replied, "And to think they do it by rubbing their legs together."

549/MUSIC
The program of an elementary school graduation exercise concluded with a rendering of the hymn "Amazing Grace" by one of the graduates, accompanied by the seven-piece school orchestra. The singer had a passable voice, but the young musicians played terribly off-key and the result was a musical "train wreck." During the rendition, one of the teachers noticed that a distinguished looking, white haired guest had bowed his head and was weeping quietly. The teacher touched his arm and said softly, "Are you a Christian?" "No, ma'am," the elderly guest replied, "I'm a musician."

MYSTERY

550

> "You're out of date, God. You were all right in the Middle Ages, God, when people were superstitious, but You just don't fit in now!"

Voice: What do you mean?

"Well, people in the Middle Ages didn't understand things like disease. They thought sickness was caused by demons."

Voice: Yes.

"And they didn't understand comets or eclipses—they were frightened by these things."

Voice: Right.

"And they were afraid of plagues and pestilences."

Voice: I know.

"But now we understand all these phenomena and know that diseases are caused by germs, that comets and eclipses are just part of the natural order of the universe, and that plagues can be averted by proper sanitation and preventive medicine."

Voice: Right.

"We understand these things and aren't frightened by them, so we don't need to come running to You any more."

Voice: You think this was the only reason people of the Middle Ages needed Me—because they were afraid?

"People turned to You when they couldn't understand things. But today the mystery is gone."

Voice: The mystery is gone! Would you care to explain human life to Me?

"Well...uh..."

Voice: Or perhaps the mystery of a flower's petals? In the Middle Ages many people turned to Me not because they were afraid, but because they realized My love for them ... because they found in Me the meaning of life.

551/MYSTERY

We often hear protests against our preoccupation with "*things.*" But it is well to remember that things are a part of life and partake of life's infinite character. There is nothing wrong with a thing per se. It is only when we see the thing in a very limited way (as just *this*, or merely *that*) and not in terms of infinite *mystery.*

A *flower* is a thing. But *what* a thing! Even if you have studied botany, do you know all about that flower? You can give botanical names to all its parts. You can tell your neighbors what kind of fertilizer you used in the growing of it, and precisely how you tended it. But have you told the *whole* story of how it came to be? It is, after all, a *long* story, and a very *wonderful* one. And we do *not* know the whole of it. It extends back, as *all* things do, into *mystery.*

Alfred Tennyson once plucked a flower and held it in his hand and thought about it. This thought carried him into the infinite character of life of which that flower partook, and he said that if ever he *knew* that little flower, "all, and all in all," he would know "what God and man is." If he felt that way about a flower, about *plant* life, whatever must he have felt about human life, about a human being!

—Fletcher, N.D., "Don't Resign From Life" Best Sermons 1962 (Adapted).

N

NEGATIVISM

552

Charles Darwin, a chronic complainer, was at his happiest when he had something to gripe about. One night, he and his wife were guests at a banquet at which everything went wrong. The speeches were dry, the champagne was not. The food was inferior, the service even more so. Worst of all, Darwin was sitting in a draft, about which he had a phobia.

All through the evening, he grumbled and complained. When the banquet was over, the sponsor of the affair came over to Mrs. Darwin and said apologetically:

> "I couldn't help noticing that your husband was terribly upset. I do hope he will forgive us. We wanted so much for him to have a good time."
>
> "He had a wonderful time," Mrs. Darwin assured him. "He was able to find fault with everything."

553/NEGATIVISM

A New Yorker of Italian ancestry hoped for years that he would someday be able to go to Rome and see the Pope. He saved his money and finally had enough to make the trip. On the day before his departure he went to the barbershop for a haircut. The barber asked him about his trip. "Which airline are you going on?" "I'm traveling on Air Italia," the man replied. "You'll be sorry," said the barber. "That airline never arrives on time.

It's always late. And when you get to Rome, where will you stay?" "At the Hilton Hotel," the man replied. "You'll be sorry," said the barber, "their reputation for service is terrible. And what are you going to do when you are in Rome?" "I'm going to see the Pope," the man replied. "Forget it," said the barber, "you'll never get to see the Pope. You're just a nobody!" A few weeks later, the man again went into the barbershop. The barber said, "I suppose you never got to Rome!" "Oh, yes I did," the man replied. "I flew on Air Italia and not only was the plane on time, it arrived thirty minutes early. I stayed at the Hilton Hotel and the service was great. They treated me like a king. And what's more I had a private audience with the Pope." "What did you do when you saw the Pope?" the amazed barber asked. "I bent down to kiss his ring. And when I did that, the Pope said to me, "My son, where did you get that terrible haircut?"

NEIGHBOR

554

A newspaper cartoon shows a rather testy-looking woman greeting her minister on the way out of church. The caption reads, "I'd like to see you love my neighbors!"

NEWNESS

555

Guess what? This new day, beginning with your next heartbeat, has never been lived in before ...

loved in before,
believed in before,
thought in before,
felt in before,
spoken in before,
prayed in before,
worked in before,
played in before,
laughed in before.
And what's more,

It's up to you—
what you do
with this newness.

NEW LIFE

556
The Scotch Minister, George Matheson, was known far and wide for his eloquent preaching. A poor Scotch woman who lived in a tiny basement began attending services in George Matheson's Church. Sunday after Sunday she was deeply moved by his eloquent sermons. After several months of this, and at great financial sacrifice, she moved from her windowless basement apartment into a sunny upstairs apartment with windows all around. When she was asked why she had done this she replied, "Oh, you can't hear George Matheson preach week after week and go on living in a basement." Of course it wasn't George Matheson, it was George Matheson's Lord who began to shine in her life.

Yes, the dawn comes! Yes, God is offering us the light! The question is "Will you come up out of the basement of your life, throw open the windows of your heart, and let the sun shine in?" Will you make the decision to say "Yes!" to God in Jesus Christ? It is sad but true that there are many people who have been coming to Church for years, have been involved in Church activities for years, but have never really said "Yes!" to Christ's offer of new life.

NEW YEAR

557
Halfway through January, most people will already have forgotten their "New Year's Resolutions." Perhaps they should try again by following this "recipe" for a happy new year, prepared by an unknown author:

> Take twelve full-grown months, free from old memories of bitterness, hate and jealousy. Cleanse them completely from every clinging spite. Pick off the little specks of pettiness. See that these months are free and

clean as when they came from the storehouse of time. Cut these months into thirty or thirty-one equal parts; the whole batch equals one year. If you try to make up the whole batch at once you may spoil the whole lot. Prepare one day at a time according to this pattern: into each day put 12 parts of faith, 11 parts of hope, 10 parts of prayer, 9 parts of kindness, 8 parts of patience, 7 parts of work, 6 parts of fidelity, 5 parts of courage, 4 parts of generosity, 3 parts of quiet meditation, 2 parts of good humor, and a dash or two or three of fun and play. Put love into the whole batch and mix with enthusiasm. Garnish with smiles and a sprig of cheer. Follow these directions and a happy new year is guaranteed!

NEW YEAR RESOLUTIONS

558

There appeared a cartoon in which a grisly looking character, filing out of Church on Sunday, reaches out to shake the preacher's hand. "You really inspired me with your sermon on how to start off the New Year. I've already made my Resolution. Starting today I'm going to keep one commandment a week until I get through all ten."

559/NEW YEAR RESOLUTIONS

WHEREAS, the key words of our Age are speed, automation and electronics, and

WHEREAS, the key words of our Age are also violence and moral chaos, and

WHEREAS, man is apparently willing to abide by the absolute judgment of the computer,

NOW THEREFORE, BE IT RESOLVED, that there be fed into the computer the Ten Commandments and the Sermon on the Mount, and

> BE IT ALSO RESOLVED, that when in doubt about the just application of human knowledge, private or public, man be required to press a button marked MORAL DECISION, and
>
> BE IT ALSO RESOLVED, that the decision of the computer be irrevocable and binding upon all men.

—Levenson, S., "You Can Say That Again, Sam!" (Adapted).

NICENESS

560

Actress Pat Carroll rediscovered the experience of "being nice" on a visit to Oregon:

> Four of us went to Ashland, Oregon, to attend a Shakespeare festival. I had never been there before. We saw six shows in five days. Beautiful! There's an outdoor Shakespearean stage and an indoor seven-hundred-seat theater. It was wonderful. Everyplace we walked, in every store, every Bed and Breakfast Inn, every restaurant, people looked at us and smiled and said, "How are you?"
>
> We walked out of the Elizabethan theater one night. The costuming, the lighting, the acting, had been wonderful. I suddenly became very aware of something. I thought, "What is this?" There was no shoving. There was no pushing. There was no yelling. There were no high-pitched voices. People were simply talking. Very pleasant. There were no policemen. We were all walking out like human beings who respected each other. I realized, "We're acting civilized. We're acting as if we have regard for each other. We aren't pushing our bodies. We aren't offending our sense of hearing. We aren't taking advantage of one another's spaces. We are respecting each other." I thought, "I like this place. Why can't we act like this in New York and Chicago? Why can't we do that?"

It made things so pleasant for each of us. It was the marvelous thing of being nice to one another. Nice is a dull word, you may say. I say we could use a bit more of it. I want a dollop of nice every hour. It's so easy to make life more pleasant for one another. We don't have to take out our credit cards for a smile.

—(Adapted).

NOAH'S ARK

561

Little Dorothy was still small enough to imagine that her grandfather had lived through all the events she had ever heard of. One day, at the dinner table, she looked at grandfather very intently. Finally, she asked, "Grandpa, were you in Noah's Ark?" "Certainly not," grandpa replied. "Then why weren't you drowned?" Dorothy asked.

NOBILITY

562

"In the city of Stockholm stands its town hall which is the most gracious and spectacular I have ever seen...There, great public events like the "Nobel Prize" dinners are held. There, great sculptures and tapestries surround the viewer. But the greatest of all was a decision made by the planners. In a niche over the entrance to every office is a bust of one of the ordinary laborers who participated in that noble project."

—Polish, D., "The Humble Shall Inherit the Earth"

O

OBEDIENCE

563

The "Fable of the Birds" is a story about Creation. All the newly-made animals were walking around discovering what it was like to be alive. All except the birds! They were doing nothing but complaining because God had given them a heavy burden that He'd given no other animal: those awkward appendages on their shoulders. God must be punishing them somehow. Why did they have to carry these things around, making it hard to walk? "Why?" they asked. "Why us?" Finally, two or three of the more adventurous birds began to move their appendages. They began to flutter them, and soon they discovered that the very thing they had regarded as a burden actually made it possible for them to fly. And no other animals could fly. The "heavy burden" turned out to be a beautiful gift.

Many of us act like those silly birds. We regard God's call to obedience as an awkward appendage to our lives—weighing us down. Thou shalt not! Thou shalt! Heavy burden it is until we discover that God's Law is really the wind of the Spirit, enabling us to fly as no other creature can fly.

564/OBEDIENCE

There is a story about a little boy whose mother, when disciplining him, used to say, "God would not like that." And when the little boy really got out of hand, the mother would say, "God will be angry."

Usually these reminders were sufficient. But one evening at supper the youngster rebelled. He would not eat the prunes provided for desert. He would yield neither to persuasion nor warnings. Finally he was sent to bed with the reminder that "God will be angry."

Soon after the child had gone to bed, a violent thunderstorm arose and the mother went to her son's room to quiet him, expecting that he would be in terror at God's anger. But to her surprise she found him at the window, looking out on the terrible storm. "It's an awful fuss to making over a few prunes," the boy said to his mother.

OPPORTUNITY

565
Have you heard the story of the three negative–thinking women who lived in the bayou? They complained everyday, "We've got it bad living in this bayou. No opportunity here. Others are living in the city where they have unlimited opportunities. Us, we've got nothing." This is the complaint they lived their lives by, until one day a positive-thinking woman came along. After listening to the complaints, she said, "Nonsense! You want opportunity? You've got opportunity. You live on the bayou. The bayou leads to the river. The river leads to the gulf. The gulf leads to the ocean. You can go anywhere you want from where you are!"
—Schuller, R.

P

PARENTING

566

A wife and mother was preparing the usual Saturday hamburgers for supper. Her husband said that he had to run an errand and asked her if she would like to ride along. She grabbed her jacket and noticed an elegant scent of perfume still clinging to the sleeves. As she slid into the front seat of the car next to her nine-year-old son, he sniffed and exclaimed, "Boy, you smell good, Mom!"

"Yes, I know," she replied. "That's the perfume I sprayed on my wrists while I was shopping today."

"No, it isn't," he answered. "That's hamburgers!"
—Reintz, M., "Young America." (Adapted).

567/PARENTING

A little girl was sitting on her father's lap, listening, with obvious delight, to bedtime stories. At the conclusion of each story, she would say, "Tell me another one Daddy, tell me another one!" After the fifth story, Daddy was getting bored. "Now we'll play one of your bedtime story records," he said. "No, Daddy," the little girl pleaded, "I want you to tell me the stories." "But I bought you that nice new record player," he said. "I know," said the little girl, "but it doesn't have a lap."

568/PARENTING

There were four little children in the family, and all of them wanted a puppy. Mother protested because she knew that she would end up having to take care of the dog. But the children promised that they would do all the work. And so the children got their puppy. His name was "Danny." At first, the children kept their promises to care for the puppy. But after a month or so, mother found herself being more and more responsible for cleaning and brushing and feeding the animal. Finally, she had enough. She told the children that a new home would have to be found for Danny. Surprisingly, the children's reactions were mild. Only in a matter-of-fact manner did they indicate that they would "miss him." Mom agreed that they would all "miss him," but she explained that "he was too much work for one person." One of the children asked, "If he wouldn't eat so much and wouldn't be so messy, could we keep him?" But mom stood firm: "It's time for Danny to go to his new home." To which the oldest child responded, "DANNY? ... We thought you said Daddy!"

569/PARENTING

When singer John Davidson was learning to drive, his father—a Baptist minister—told him he could have a car if he got at least straight "B's" on his report card, if he read the Bible more, and if he got a haircut.

"On my next report card, I got all 'B's,' and I told my dad I had been reading the Bible," said Davidson. He said, 'That's fine, but how about the haircut?' I told him the Bible I read had pictures of Jesus with long hair. My father replied, 'Yes, but Jesus also walked most everywhere.'"

570/PARENTING

Jerome, a hyperactive nine-year-old, was asleep one night in his room downstairs. His mother was sleeping in her upstairs bedroom. Suddenly she was awakened by a thunderous crash. A panel truck had veered off the road, crashed into the side of the house and come to a stop in the dining room. Mother's terrified first thought was for her son. "Jerome," she cried out. Whereupon, from his room downstairs, Jerome hollered, "I didn't do it, mama!"

571/PARENTING

A seven-year-old girl asked her mother why her grandfather walked with a limp. Believing honesty to be the best policy, the child's mother gave her a lengthy account of her grandfather's bout with polio. She went into great detail about all the suffering he had endured and the long struggle to rebuild his withered limbs. She explained that the doctors had once said that he would never walk again. Then she added, "Even though he has a very difficult time, and still struggles with a limp, he is at least able to walk." This upset the little girl very much, and she lay awake most of the night, sobbing because "grandpa is so sick." Fearing that she had placed too much of a burden on the child with her detailed explanation of grandpa's hardships, the mother asked her husband how he would have handled the situation. "What would you have said?" she asked. Peeping over his newspaper at breakfast, he answered, "Bad leg," and continued reading the sports page.

572/PARENTING

Your children are not your children …
They come through you but not from you,
And though they are with you yet they belong
not to you.

You may give them your love but not your thoughts,
they have their own thoughts.

You may house their bodies but not their souls,
their souls dwell in the house of tomorrow,
which you cannot visit, not even in your dreams.

You may strive to be like them, but seek not to make them
like you. For life goes not backward nor tarries with yesterday.

You are the bows from which your children as living
arrows are sent forth.

> The Archer sees the mark upon the path of the infinite, and He bends you with His might that His arrows may go swift and far.
>
> Let your bending in the Archer's hand be for gladness; For even as He loves the arrow that flies, so He loves also the bow that is stable.

—*Kahlil Gibran*

573/PARENTING

The "Journal of the American Medical Association" published an article by Dr. Paul Ruskin in which the author demonstrated how one's perspective can be immediately changed by a bit of humor. To illustrate, Dr. Ruskin described a case study he had presented when teaching a class on the "Psychological Aspects of Growing Old." It went as follows:

> The patient neither speaks nor comprehends the spoken word. Sometimes she babbles incoherently for hours on end. She is disoriented about person, place, and time.
>
> She does, however, respond to her name. I have worked with her for the past six months, but she still shows complete disregard for her physical appearance and makes no effort to assist her own care. She must be fed, bathed, and clothed by others. Because she has no teeth, her food must be pureed. Her shirt is usually soiled from almost incessant drooling. She does not walk. Her sleep pattern is erratic. Often she wakes in the middle of the night, and her screaming awakens others. Most of the time she is friendly and happy, but several times a day she gets quite agitated without apparent cause. Then she wails until someone comes to comfort her.

After presenting the class with this case, the doctor then asked his students whether or not they would like to volunteer to take care of this person. No one offered. And when he insisted that he himself derived much pleasure from taking care of that person, the class seemed puzzled. Whereupon, Dr. Ruskin then passed around a photo of the "patient." It was his six-month-old daughter.

574/PARENTING

If you wander into one of those discount toy stores these days, you'll find a bewildering array of playthings. You can spend a lot of money in such places and often, whatever you buy is soon discarded.

Parents who want to give their children—or anyone—something lasting should consider this story by a successful attorney:

> The greatest gift I ever received was a gift I got one Christmas when my dad gave me a small box. Inside was a note saying, "Son, this year I will give you 365 hours, an hour a day every day after dinner. It's yours. We'll talk about what you want to talk about. We'll go where you want to go. We'll play what you want to play. It will be your hour."
>
> "My dad not only kept his promise," the attorney said, "but every year he renewed it. Whatever good I may do or achieve is the result of his time."

—*"Moody Monthly" (Adapted).*

575/PARENTING

A father had given his son a globe of the world. One night he slipped into the boy's room to look up a spot on the globe. The little fellow woke up and asked, "What are you doing with my world?"

Plenty of youngsters might well ask us adults what we have done with their world. Teenagers did not create our world situation today—they inherited it. What have we oldsters done with their world?

—*Havner, V., "Pepper 'n' Salt"*

576/PARENTING

In a "Doonesbury" comic strip, Mike Doonesbury is in the park with his little boy, Christopher. There he meets Joan who is accompanied by her little son, Jeffrey. "... it looks like Christopher is quite taken by your little Jeffrey," Mike says. Joan replies, "Yes, they seem to get along"...

Mike says: "Listen, why don't you bring him by for Christopher's birthday party next week? Here's the address. It's casual. We're trying to keep the birthday simple. Some parents just overdo it, don't you think?"

> "You're so right!" answers Joan.
> Then Mike adds, "Oh, he's not scared of elephants, is he?"

577/PARENTING

When God wants a great work done in the world or a great wrong righted, He goes about it in a very unusual way. He doesn't stir up His earthquakes or send forth His thunderbolts. Instead, He has a helpless baby born, perhaps in a simple home and of some obscure mother. And then God puts the idea into the mother's heart and she puts it into the baby's mind. And then God waits. The greatest forces in the world are not the earthquakes and the thunderbolts. The greatest forces in the world are babies.

—Kennedy, G., "A Second Reader's Notebook,"

578/PARENTING

In Thomas Wolfe's "Look Homeward Angel," there is a scene in which Eliza Gant, the mother, is saying goodbye to her son who is going away to school. It will be his first lengthy time away from home. Mother and son have had a very difficult love/hate relationship. He says, "Goodbye," and as he walks away from her he is carrying strong feelings of "unfinished business" with his mother. Suddenly, he turns and comes back to her. They embrace each other. He starts to say, "Goodbye, goodbye, goodbye..." and his thoughts almost instantaneously take him back over the years to his earliest childhood. But he cannot communicate what he feels. Thomas Wolfe says the cry that crosses his lips is like the cry of an animal in pain. His mother understands, partly. She is feeling much of what her son is feeling, but from the parent's side. All she can say is, "My child…my child…my child!" Both are crying now. Finally, she is able to say, "My son, we must try to love one another."

"My son, we must try to love one another." Thomas Wolfe says that this is a "terrible and beautiful sentence"—and he is right! "Terrible" because of the pain! "Beautiful" because of the potential, in every parent/child relationship.

PARISH LIFE

579

A certain long-winded pastor went into the pulpit one Sunday morning and said to the congregation: "I have been informed that I am to become the pastor of another congregation. The same Jesus who led me to this Church is now leading me to another." Whereupon the choir rose and began singing, "What a friend we have in Jesus..."

580/PARISH LIFE

A fellow moved into a strange city and began to look around for a Church where, in his words, "I can feel comfortable." One Sunday morning he dropped into a Church just as the sermon began. "Today I am going to give you some straight talk," he heard the preacher say. "This congregation before me has left many things undone! This congregation before me has done many things it ought not to have done!" Hearing this, the newcomer in town slipped into a pew and, with a sigh of relief, said to himself, "Thank goodness! I've found my crowd at last!"

581/PARISH LIFE

The following notice appeared in the bulletin of a midwestern Lutheran Church:

> The eighth-graders will be presenting Shakespeare's "Hamlet" in the church basement on Friday at 7:00pm. The congregation is invited to attend this tragedy.

PATIENCE

582
A salesman called on Steinway & Sons to show them a new piano-key pin. "My company believes this aluminum pin is greatly superior to the pin you have been using," he said to the elder Steinway. Mr. Steinway deliberated for some moments. "Well, young man," he said at last, "we are an old firm, slow and cautious about making changes. But we will install your pins in one of our pianos and give them a trial." The salesman was delighted. "That's good enough for me," he said. "How long a trial will you need?" "Oh," said Mr. Steinway thoughtfully, "I'd say about 50 years."

583/PATIENCE
As a young Frenchman pushed his son's carriage down the street, the youngster howled with rage. "Please, Bernard, control yourself...Easy there, Bernard, keep calm!" the father said quietly.

"Congratulations, Monsieur," said a woman who had been watching. "You know just how to speak to infants —calmly and gently, and with great patience." Then she said, "So the little fellow is named Bernard?"

"No, madame," corrected the father. "His name is Andre. I'm Bernard."

584/PATIENCE
Two big turtles and one little turtle decided to have a picnic on the river bank. They packed a lunch basket with sandwiches and headed for the river. When they arrived, it began to rain, and the two big turtles ordered the little turtle to return home for an umbrella. The little turtle agreed, on the condition that the others should not begin eating the sandwiches until he returned. Then the little turtle left and the big turtles began to wait patiently for his return. A day passed, then a week, then a month, then a year. Still there was no sign of the little one. So one of the big turtles said to the other, "He's not coming back.

I think we should start eating without him." Whereupon, the little turtle stuck his head out from a nearby rock and said, "If you do, I won't go any further."

PEACE

585

A wife had provided a tombstone for her husband's grave. On it she had inscribed two sentences: "Rest In Peace" ... "Until Wc Meet Again." Individually, those are two good statements, but together they don't come out quite right. That's the problem with our using the word "peace" in the limited sense that we do so often. We say "peace," meaning "the cessation of hostilities" (until we meet again, perhaps).

In Scripture, the word for the peace of Christ is "shalom." The peace of Christ is not just the absence of discord. It is the presence of harmony and wholeness. This is what Jesus means when He comes into the midst of the disciples, saying, "Peace be with you." Jesus is not just resolving the disharmony in their lives. He is bringing them the gift of wholeness of life. Deep inside, we crave to become the full and complete person God created us to be. Deep inside, we want shalom!

586/PEACE

On December 10th, 1980, a small, stooped woman wearing a faded blue sari and well-worn sandals received an award from the hand of the King of Norway. Surrounded by famous people dressed in formal black suits and elegant gowns—a select group of the rich, the powerful, the brilliant and the talented of the world—the little old lady in sari and sandals, Mother Teresa of India, received the Nobel Peace Prize.

Mother Teresa "is a person who has profoundly disturbed my peace of mind for a long time," author Robert Fulghum has written. "She doesn't even know me, but she continually goes around minding my business. She drives me crazy ... Alongside my mirror is a photograph of this troublesome woman. Each time I look in the mirror at myself, I also look at her face. In it

I have seen more than I can tell; and from what I see, I understand more than I can say ... Mother Teresa, of India, servant of the poor and the sick and the dying. Yet no Shah or President or King or Prime Minister holds the key to as much power as she possesses. None is as rich. For hers is the invincible weapon against the evils of this earth: the caring heart. And hers are the everlasting riches of this life: the compassionate spirit. 'We can do no great things; only small things with great love,' she once said. And while I wrestle with frustration over the impotence of the individual, she goes right on changing the world. While I wish for more power and resources, she uses her power and resources to do what she can at the moment. She upsets me, disturbs me, shames me.

"If ever there is truly peace on earth, goodwill to men, it will be because of women like Mother Teresa. Peace is not something you wish for; it's something you make, something you do, something you are, and something you give away!"

587/PEACE

A tourist bought a peace pipe from an Indian display. Looking it over, he saw some very small print on the bottom. He took it to the chief and asked him to read it. The chief looked carefully at the inscription, then read it aloud: 'Smoking is hazardous to your health.'"

588/PEACE

An ancient Oriental maxim:

> If there is righteousness in the heart, there will be
> beauty in the character.
> If there is beauty in the character, there will be
> harmony in the family.
> If there is harmony in the family, there will be
> order in the nation.
> When there is order in the nation, there will be
> peace in the world!

PEACE OF MIND

589
When he was a young man, Joshua Liebman made a list of the things he would like to have. The list was long and included such things as health, love, talent, power, wealth, and fame. He showed the list around, asking others for their opinion. A wise, old friend of the young man's family looked the list over and said, "Joshua, this is an excellent list. It is well-digested in content. It is set down in a reasonable order. But it appears, my young friend, that you have omitted the most important element of all. You have forgotten one ingredient, lacking which, each possession becomes a hideous torment, and your list as a whole, an intolerable burden." "And what is that missing ingredient?" Joshua asked. The wise old friend replied by taking a pencil and crossing out Joshua's entire list. Then he wrote down three words: "Peace of mind." That young man, Joshua Liebman, later became the author of the inspiring book called "Peace of Mind" which has sold millions of copies.

PERFECTION

590
Have you heard about the young man who spent a long time searching for the perfect wife? Eventually he found her. But unfortunately it didn't lead to anything. The trouble was that she was looking for the perfect husband!

And isn't it the case that "perfect" people would be rather boring and extremely difficult to live with!

PERSPECTIVE

591
An old hunter took his new retriever out early one morning to test him out. The old man shot a bird and it fell into the water. The dog immediately darted after it, walked on top of the water, picked up the dead bird, returned on top of the water,

and dropped the bird at his master's feet. The old hunter rubbed his eyes in disbelief, but decided it really didn't happen. Then he set himself up to shoot again. He shot a second bird, and again the dog retrieved the bird by walking on top of the water.

Amazed by his dog's behavior, the old hunter decided to show off the animal to his best friend. So he invited him to go out hunting early the next morning. His friend got the first shot and hit a bird. The dog walked on top of the water, picked up the dead bird, and returned on top of the water. The old hunter said, "Do you notice anything different about my new dog?" His friend nonchalantly replied, "No, looks like just another bird dog to me."

The old hunter then shot a second bird out of the sky. Again his remarkable dog walked on top of the water and retrieved the bird. The old hunter asked again, "Are you sure you don't see anything different about my new dog?" His friend thought a moment and said, "I sure do, that dog can't swim!"
—Timmons, T., "Hooked On Life." (Adapted).

POSSESSIONS

592
A yuppie was driving his new BMW convertible. He had the top down, his right hand on the wheel and his left arm hanging over the door. With the tape deck going full blast, he didn't notice th rusty old pickup truck that pulled around to pass until it sideswiped him. The yuppie pulled to a stop.

"My car!" He cried. "My beautiful car!"

When a policeman came by, the yuppie told him about the accident. His car was a wreck, and it didn't even have 50 miles on it.

"You've got more to worry about than your car," the officer replied. "You need an ambulance. Your arm is badly injured."

The young man looked down at his arm and cried, "My Rolex watch—my beautiful Rolex!"
—Thien, A. Milwaukee Sentinel (Adapted).

593/POSSESSIONS
After meeting the King of England, a reporter commented to Gandhi on how scantily dressed he had been in the presence of the King. Gandhi replied, "It's okay. The King had on enough for both of us."
—Fields, R. "Chop Wood, Carry Water."

594/POSSESSIONS
A popular preacher delivered a Sunday sermon entitled "God's Ownership." Later that day he was invited to the home of a wealthy parishioner. The rich woman conducted the preacher over her vast estate. Looking over her broad acres and recalling the morning's sermon, the woman said, "Do you mean to tell me that this land does not belong to me?" To which the preacher replied, "Ask me that question one hundred years from now!"

595/POSSESSIONS
The "Wall Street Journal" published a special supplement entitled, "The Gimme Generation." One of the articles recalled an advertisement published in 1986 in "Time" magazine by Pioneer Electronics (manufacturers of the Pioneer SX–V500 Audio/Video Quartz–Synthesizer Non–Switching Receiver). The ad displayed a photograph of an obviously rich and self-satisfied young man standing in front of a priceless painting and apparently listening, on the Pioneer SX–V500, to a Mozart piano concerto. Echoing the words of the Eucharist, the copy read: "Mozart died to bring me pleasure." The "Wall Street Journal" writer commented: "Perceived as sacraments, the acts of consumption acquire a quasi–spiritual meaning in our society. The advertising business tells us that consumer products bestow health, long life, status, sexual prowess, intelligence, national security, happiness and peace of mind—all the blessings that devout Christians expect from the hand of God. Moreover we are being brainwashed into believing that to

admit being satisfied is to confess a crime against the State and to risk alliance with the Evil One—that is, with anybody who knows, or has, what he or she wants."
—Lapham, L.H., "An American Feast" (Adapted).

PRACTICALITY

596
The great English writer, G. K. Chesterton, once was playing a little quiz game with some friends. One of the questions was, "If you were shipwrecked and alone on a deserted island what one book, above all others, would you wish to have with you?" One of the players immediately said "The Bible," and gave a very pious reason for his selection. Another said "A volume of Shakespeare," and gave a very learned reason for wanting Shakespeare. Chesterton said, "Well, if I were allowed just one book on that deserted island, I would choose a one-volume manual of instruction for amateur boat-builders." Chesterton was a very practical person.

PRAISE

597
According to one educator, teaching a third-grade Bible-study class often affords an opportunity to test one's sense of humor. "One morning as I was listening to prayers and awarding gold stars for each one said correctly, the box of stars slipped out of my hand. Gold stars descended like confetti all over the floor. I got down on my hands and knees and attempted to insert my fingernails under the tiny gold stickers, conscious all the while of what an undignified picture I must be presenting.

"Finally I looked up and said sharply, 'Isn't anyone going to give me a hand?' Immediately all twenty-four of my pupils began to applaud enthusiastically."
—Sexton, B.J.

PRAYER

598
When life knocks you to your knees, and it will, well, get up! If it knocks you to your knees again, as it will, well, isn't that the best position from which to pray?
—*Ethel Barrymore*

599/PRAYER
Bill Moyers was asked to say grace before the meal at a private gathering at the White House. He began praying softly when Lyndon Johnson interrupted him with, "Speak up, Bill, speak up." Moyers, a former Baptist minister stopped in mid-sentence, raised his bowed head and replied, "I wasn't addressing you, Mr. President."

600/PRAYER
A grandmother was sitting on the beach with her young grandson. He had on his little hat, his little sunsuit, and was playing with his little bucket and shovel. Suddenly a big wave came and swept the child out to sea. The grandmother fell to her knees and prayed, "Oh, God, please return my grandchild. He is such a sweet boy, such a good boy, such a wonderful child." Miraculously another big wave returned the child exactly to the spot where he had been before, unhurt, wearing his little sunsuit, carrying his little bucket and shovel. The grandmother looked to the heavens, threw up her arms, and cried out, "He had a hat!"

601/PRAYER
HIS ANSWER COMES

Know this, my heart, that when you pray,
before you find the words to say,
your Father hears. Without delay
His answer comes.

In simple ways, in varied forms,
like morning sun that heals and warms,

like sudden rainbows after storms,
His answer comes.

Like gentle tappings on the door,
or friendly footsteps on the floor
to bring you joy unknown before,
His answer comes.

Have you not felt upon your brow
His calming touch? Then feel it now,
And ask now longer when or how
His answer comes.

—Stanley, I.

602/PRAYER

Hope to pray? Here is one man's good advice:

> Instead of affirming anything about physical circumstances, affirm your complete trust in God. Get your heart into the state where you don't care which way He works out the problem, literally do not care (this is important). Then ask Him to work His perfect and loving will in the situation—His will. You are not asking for the good; you are asking for His great love and His infinite intelligence working for the greatest good. Then just stand back and watch the miracles fall neatly into place.
>
> Sound simple? It isn't. But if you have faith enough to take the first step of not caring which way He works out the problem, the rest is easy. You will be releasing the problem to His loving will. And what you turn loose on earth is loosened in heaven.

603/PRAYER

How many of us pray for the wrong reasons! We have a "slot machine" approach to prayer. All we have to do is insert a prayer and out will come instant fulfillment, immediate gratification, regardless of whether what we are asking for is moral, ethical, or possible; regardless of whether or not is clashes with the needs and hopes of others.

When what we ask for is denied us, we often abandon prayer as an exercise in futility. We forget that prayer at its highest involves praise and thanksgiving and that its primary concern is not getting but becoming. Our prayers are answered when they enable us to grow toward the person we are capable of being, and live as God would have us live.

How many of us perform our small acts of charity and goodness for the wrong reasons? We expect a kind deed to be rewarded by a kind fate, to preserve us from trouble and misfortune. More than once have I heard this melancholy verdict: "When my mother died, I stopped believing in God. She was such a good person, how could God let this happen to her?"

Goodness does not confer immunity to disease, disaster, or death. It does not guarantee a life without trouble or tragedy. These are the common lot of all of us.

—Greenburg, S., "Say Yes To Life."

604/PRAYER

A little five-year old was saying his bedtime prayers. Halfway through, he looked up at his mother and said, "Mom, would it be all right if I put in a commercial bout a new baseball mitt?"

605/PRAYER

An alcoholic who was fighting to stay away from drink made a daily visit to Church. "Jesus, this is Jim," he'd say, as he fixed his eyes on the Cross.

A woman in utter despair, unfamiliar with God or prayer, knelt, clasped her hands and cried, "Somebody ... something!"

A simple French peasant, seen going into the cathedral day after day, was asked what happened to him when he went there. "Oh," he replied, "I just look up at Him and He looks down at me."

These may seem almost childish prayers in their simplicity. But any of us who has learned even a little about prayer knows that we are "not heard for our eloquent speaking." There is great power in utterly simple words that come straight from the heart.
—Shoemaker, Dr. S., "Beautiful Prayers."

606/PRAYER

In her book, "The Scent of Roses," The famous harpist, Mary O'Hara, describes a lesson in how to pray she learned through her music:

> One summer, after I'd been working on some songs, I left my harp before the open window. Suddenly I heard the sound of distant and very lovely music. It lasted only a few seconds and left me very puzzled. When it happened again I noticed that the sound came from the instrument, and was caused by the gentle breeze from the open window playing on the harp strings.
>
> At times of prayer we can be like that harp, by allowing sufficient calm to gather 'round us so that the Holy Spirit, the Breath of God, may play His music on us. But remember, it was a very gentle breeze and the music could be heard only because of the surrounding stillness.

607/PRAYER

> Q.What counsel do you give to the young men who are fighting a losing battle with their lower selves and come to you for advice?

A.Simply, prayer. One must humble oneself utterly and look beyond oneself for strength.

Q.But what if young men complain that their prayer is not heard?

A.To want an answer to one's prayer is to tempt God. If prayer fails to bring relief, it is only lip-prayer. If prayer does not help, nothing else will. One must go on ceaselessly. This, then, is my message to the youth. In spite of themselves, the youth must believe in the all-conquering power of Love and Truth.
—*Mohandas K. Gandhi*

608/PRAYER

When Brother Bruno was at prayer one night he was disturbed by the croaking of a bullfrog. All his attempts to disregard the
sound were unsuccessful, so he shouted from his window, "Quiet! I'm at my prayers."

Now Brother Bruno was a saint, so his command was instantly obeyed. Every living creature held its voice so as to create a silence that would be favorable to prayer.

But now another sound intruded on Bruno's worship—an inner voice that said, "Maybe God is as pleased with the croaking of that frog as with the chanting of your Psalms." "What can please the ears of God in the croak of a frog?" Bruno asked. But the voice refused to give up: "Why would you think God invented that sound?"

Bruno decided to find out "Why?" He leaned out of his window and gave the order, "Sing!" The bullfrog's measured croaking filled the air to the ludicrous accompaniment of all the frogs in the vicinity. And as Bruno listened to the sound, their voices ceased to jar for he discovered that, if he stopped resisting them, they actually enriched the silence of the night.

With that discovery Bruno's heart became harmonious with the Universe and, for the first time in his life, he understood what it means to pray.
—deMello, A. "Taking Flight." (Adapted).

609/PRAYER
Two men on a bird–watching safari were leisurely approaching a rope bridge when all of a sudden a lion began to charge. Each man immediately took off, heading for the entrance of the bridge. When it became apparent that they weren't going to make it, one of the men turned to the other and said, "You better start saying your prayers!"

Panic–stricken, the man began to recite the first prayer that came to mind. "Dear Lord, we are truly thankful for what we are about to receive."

610/PRAYER
People who pray for miracles usually don't get miracles ... But people who pray for courage, for strength to bear the unbearable, for the grace to remember what they have left instead of what they have lost, very often find their prayers answered...Their prayers helped them tap hidden reserves of faith and courage which were not available to them before.
—Kushner, H.S.

611/PRAYER
Once, in a corner of the State of Iowa, the countryside was severely parched by a record drought. One Sunday, the local pastor exhorted his congregation to stay with him in Church, praying for relief, until the drought ended. They knelt together in prayer until Monday morning when, suddenly, the heavens opened and the rain fell in torrents. The downpour continued for days. By Thursday, the tiny community was all but wiped out as flood waters rose from the nearby stream. A rescue party spied the pastor sitting on the roof of his house. Pointing below to the swirling waters, the pastor cried out joyfully, "Not bad for a little Church like ours!"

612/PRAYER

During his many appearances in Summer Stock in the role of Tevye in "Fiddler On the Roof," Robert Merrill had learned to expect the unexpected. "One night on stage," he says, "as I implored God to give me a replacement for my horse (which had lost its shoe), suddenly, a small, spotted dog walked onto the stage. I looked up again and added fervently: 'Oh God, please try again.'"

613/PRAYER

A little girl was travelling with her family on a long sleeper train. When night came, she was put in the upper bunk and told that God would look after her. As everyone began to doze off the little girl became a bit frightened and called out, "Mummy, are you there?"

"Yes dear," replied her mother.

A little later she called, "Daddy, are you there?"

"Yes, dear," came the reply.

This was repeated several times, until at last another passenger lost patience, and said: "We're all here! Your father, your mother, your brothers and sisters. now go to sleep!"

Silence ruled for several minutes. Then the child was heard to whisper, "Mummy, was that God?"

614/PRAYER

From a young mother in Scotland, comes these lines which she calls "A Mother's Prayer:

> "Oh, God, you know I'm busy each moment of the day.
> Please help me to remember that I still have time to pray...
> While I'm washing up the dishes,
> or working at the sink,
> when I give my babe his bottle,
> let me use the time to think.

Grant me patience and good humour,
contentment with my lot.
Help me show by my example
what I'd like my children taught.

Help me make a happy home,
the way a home should be,
wherein the trust of all of us
remains secure in Thee."

615/PRAYER

A young man was taking his first flying lesson. After showing him some of the basics, the instructor said to the student, "Now, I'm going to show you how to go in for a landing." Whereupon, the instructor suddenly blacked out. The student immediately called the tower, and while he was receiving instructions on how to land the craft, the engine went dead. Whereupon, a voice from the control tower said: "Repeat after me…'Our Father, who art in heaven…'"

616/PRAYER

One of the great "Musical" successes of all time is "The Sound of Music." In a recollection about the production of the original Broadway version, composer Richard Rodgers said:

> One musical problem confronting me in The Sound of Music was the opening piece in which nuns are heard chanting a Catholic prayer. I had to make sure that what I wrote would sound authentic. Through friends, I got in touch with Mother Morgan, head of the music department at Manhattanville College in Purchase, N.Y. She invited me to a specially arranged concert at which the nuns and seminarians sang and performed many different kinds of religious music. An unexpected moment came when Mother Morgan, waving her arms like a cheerleader at a football game, was vigorously conducting a particularly dramatic passage. As the music built to its peak, Mother Morgan's booming command could be clearly heard: "Pray it!"

617/PRAYER

There is an amusing story about a group of men in a congregation who formed a Bible Study and Prayer Group. They met every two weeks to study the Scriptures and pray together. When they came to the Sermon on the Mount, they agreed that each would do his utmost to discipline his life accordingly, verse-by-verse. It proved to be a very helpful exercise, actually—until they came upon the verse that reads, "...anyone who looks lustfully at a woman has already committed adultery in his thoughts" (Mt. 5:28). This is a very difficult passage and they thought about it very seriously. Finally, they decided that whenever one of them was faced with this problem he would immediately begin to pray for the woman. The next morning, one of the men was walking down the street and along came a very beautiful woman. As she passed by, the man immediately began to pray, "Lord bless her! Lord bless her!" And he heard a voice from above say, "I already have!"

618/PRAYER

In a little book about children and religion, actor Dick Van Dyke tells the story of a little girl who is asked by her mother if she had said her night-prayers. "Yes, mother," she replies, "but when I got down on my knees I began thinking that God hears the same old stuff every night. So I told Him the story of 'The Three Bears' instead."

Dick Van Dyke tells of another little girl who was asked to suggest a prayer for her Sunday School class. She said, "I think we should pray for all the people with the blahs!"

619/PRAYER

A family's pet dog gave birth to a litter of five puppies. The parents told the children that they would keep one and give away the others. The youngest child was an enterprising lad. He decided to try to sell the extra pups. That night, his father overheard him end his night prayers saying, "Dear God, tomorrow I want to sell the puppies. Please God, I want to get $10,000 each for them." The next evening, when the father returned home from work, he asked the youngster if his prayer had been answered. "I sold one," the boy said. "And did you get your price?" the father asked. "Yes," the boy replied, "a little girl gave me two $5,000 kittens."

"Please God, I want to get $10,000...please, God I want..., please God, I want...please God, I want!" If "I want" is the central theme of your prayer experience, you are likely to discover that instead of communicating with God, you've been talking to yourself. When you position yourself before God in an attitude of prayer, you are on holy ground; you are on God's turf; you are in Love's domain. Consequently, you must endeavor to approach God with an open heart rather than open hands. Instead of "Please God, I want," the central theme of your every prayer should be, "I want to please God!"

620/PRAYER

From his book, "The Road To Daybreak," author/teacher Henri Nouwen writes of his frustrations on a day seemingly without any accomplishment—a day that might have been wasted if not for his quiet hour of prayer:

> Not much to report today except for many little frustrations, interruptions, and distractions. One of those days that pass without having felt like a real day. Many letters, telephone calls, short visits, little talks, but no real work, no sense of moving, no sense of direction. A day that is so fragmented that it does not seem to come together at all—except perhaps by writing about it!
>
> One of the great gifts of the spiritual life is to know that even days like this are not a total waste. There was still an hour of prayer. There was still the Eucharist. There were still moments of gratitude for the gifts of life. And there is the opportunity to realize that a day like this unites me with thousands, even millions of people for whom many days are like this, yet who are in no position to do anything about it. So many men, women, and children dream about creative lives; yet because they are not free to shape their own lives, they cannot realize their dreams. I had better pray for them tonight!

621/PRAYER

There is an old missionary story in which a clergyman is making his way through a thick jungle when, suddenly he is face-to-face with a ferocious lion. "I'm going to have you for lunch," the lion roars, "so you had better prepare for your death." Hearing this, the missionary immediately assumes the kneeling position, covers his eyes with his hands and begins to pray with great intensity. Hearing nothing further from the lion, however, he opens his eyes and takes a quick peep through his fingers. He is amazed to see that the lion also is kneeling, with his front paws over his eyes. The missionary breathes a deep sigh of relief, then raises his eyes to the heavens, saying, "Thank you, Lord, for letting my words of prayer melt this wild beast's heart and cause him to repent." Whereupon, the lion dropped his paws and said, "Quiet please! I'm saying 'Grace'."

622/PRAYER

A recent college campus survey revealed that a majority of students believe that "The Church is losing its influence." In the survey, they charged that this loss of influence results from "watering down" Christian teachings. And with watered–down teachings, they said, religion gets "flabby and out of shape." One student prescribed "Sanctified Calisthenics" as the way to get Christian people back in good spiritual shape. Number one on the student's list of exercises was the "Deep Knee Bend."

"Pray without ceasing!" (I Thessalonians 5:17)

623/PRAYER

A troubled man visited a psychiatrist. "I think I'm going mad," he said. "When I go to bed and try to sleep I keep hearing voices." After much discussion the doctor said, "You are under a lot of stress. You must learn to relax. I had a patient a few months ago with your exact symptoms. He took up fishing and the voices have gone away. Why not try taking long walks or do some bicycle riding?" Although it was mid-winter and the weather was freezing, the man decided to follow the other patient's example and go fishing. He cut a hole in the ice, lowered his line, and said a silent prayer. "Please Lord, I need a good night's sleep. Please take the voices away!" Whereupon, he heard a loud voice say, "There are no fish there." Startled, the man moved to another spot, cut a hole in the ice and lowered his line. "Please Lord," he prayed, "take the voices away!" Again, he heard a loud voice say, "There are no fish there." The bewildered man then moved to another spot, cut a hole in the ice and lowered his line, and prayed, "Please Lord, take the voices away!" And again he heard a loud voice say emphatically, "I told you there are no fish there." Now trembling with fear, the troubled man cried out, "Is that the voice of God?" To which the voice replied, "I am the ice-skating rink manager."

624/PRAYER

A CBS news team was taping at Jerusalem's Wailing Wall. Every day they saw the same elderly man praying, morning, noon, and night.

On their last day they got curious and asked him, "What is it you pray for so fervently?"

The old man thought for a moment and said, "I pray for health, for happiness, and for peace in my land."

"I see," said the reporter. "You don't look that healthy. Are you happy?"

"Not really," said the man.

"And your homeland is in turmoil. Do you really believe your prayers are heard?"

The man replies, "Sometimes it's like talking to a wall."

625/PRAYER

The root word for both "miracle" and "mirror" is the Latin, "Mirari"—meaning "to wonder at." Long ago, before the age of glass mirrors, to see an image of oneself in a piece of polished metal was indeed a cause of great wonder. Such mirrors were filled with wonder for ancient peoples who could not otherwise see their own reflections except in pools of still water. But who among us today is caught up in wonder when looking into the bathroom mirror while combing his or her hair? We usually regard mirrors as practical aids to being well-groomed and neat. But mirrors may also be regarded as instruments for learning how to perform miraculous deeds. Recall the famous scene with the evil queen in the fairy tale, "Snow White." She stands in front of her mirror and asks, "Mirror, mirror on the wall, who's the fairest of them all?" Someone has described a wonderful prayer exercise that playfully parallels those words from "Snow White"... daily, after you have finished with the practical use of your mirror, stand for a moment in silence. Then look directly into your mirror and with great devotion pronounce this short prayer:

MIRROR, MIRROR ON THE WALL,

MAY I LOOK WITH LOVE ON ALL.

Then, consciously, as your day begins, look with eyes of love upon every tree, bird, animal, person and task of your day. And each time you find yourself tempted to think a careless thought of anger, resentment or indifference, remember your mirror-prayer and open yourself to see the miraculous flashing out from all creation.

This prayer exercise is reminiscent of words dating back to the 4th century: "The face is the mirror of the mind, and eyes without speaking confess the secrets of the heart." Praying with your mirror can not only keep you aware of all that is in your heart, it also can help you change anything in your heart that is unworthy of a follower of the Lord of Love.

626/PRAYER

We mutter and sputter,
We fume and we spurt.
We mumble and grumble,

Our feelings are hurt.
We can't understand things,
Our vision grows dim.
But all that we need,
Is a moment with Him!

PRAYER OF PEACE

627

Our Father, up in heaven,
hear this fervent prayer:
May the people of all nations
be united in Thy care,

For earth's peace and man's salvation
can come only by Thy Grace
And not through bombs and missiles
and our quest for outer space ...

For until all men recognize
that "the battle is the Lord's"
Peace on earth cannot be won
with strategy and swords.
We will go on vainly fighting,
as we have in Ages past,
Finding only empty victories
and a peace that cannot last ...

But we've grown so rich and mighty
and so arrogantly strong,
We no longer ask in humbleness,
"God, show us where we're wrong" ...

We have turned our eyes away from Him
to go our selfish way,

Money, power and pleasure
    are the gods we serve today...
And the good green earth God gave us
    to peacefully enjoy,
Through greed and fear and hatred
    we are seeking to destroy...

Oh, Father, up in heaven,
    stir and wake our sleeping souls,
Renew our faith and lift us up
    and give us higher goals,

And grant us heavenly guidance
    as war threatens us again
For, more than guided missiles,
the world needs guided men.

—Rice, H.S., "Just For You,"

PREACHING

628

A newly appointed bishop delivered a sermon at an evening Sunday service celebrating his arrival. Because he wanted to repeat some of his stories at meetings the next day, he requested reporters to omit them from their accounts of his sermon. A rookie journalist reporting on the speech, finished his story with the line: "And the bishop told a number of stories that cannot be published."

629/PREACHING

While preaching his Sunday Sermon, a pastor was distracted by a man who rose from his pew, walked slowly down the aisle and out of the Church. Later, the man's wife called the pastor and apologized for her husband's behavior in Church. "Well, it did throw me off the track a bit," the pastor said. "But please don't take it personally," the woman replied. "You see, my husband has been walking in his sleep since childhood."

630/PREACHING

Deaf ears can't be reached,
lectures go unheard;
Words that are lived,
not preached,
Outtalks the spoken word.

—*Maerz, F.S.*

631/PREACHING

Cartoonist Leo Garel depicts a Sunday morning scene in front of Church. The pastor is standing at the door, waiting to greet the congregation as it makes its way out. It seems clear from the people's faces that they have just listened to a fiery sermon. A distinguished looking, middle-aged man seems particularly upset and, as he files past the pastor, he looks him in the eye and says, disapprovingly, "Sticks and stones may break my bones, but words can never hurt me."

632/PREACHING

A newly ordained clergyman was preparing to preach his first sermon which he had scrupulously memorized. Filled with enthusiasm, he bounced into the Church's very high pulpit, looked out at the congregation and began to speak: "Behold I come . . ." Then he froze. He forget what he was supposed to say next. Trying not to panic, he told himself that if he just sat down for a moment the words would come back to him. So he sat down for a moment, then bounced up, rushed back into the pulpit and said, "Behold I come . . ." And again nothing came. He sat down again, then bounced up, rushed back into the pulpit crying out, "Behold I come . . ." This time he had bounced so hard that the pulpit broke loose from the floor and the preacher went tumbling out and into the lap of a woman sitting in the front pew. He got up, apologizing profusely. The woman said, "Oh don't apologize, young man. You warned me three times you were coming."

633/PREACHING

"This morning," said the preacher, "I'm going to speak on the relationship between fact and faith. It is a fact that you are sitting here in the sanctuary. It is also a fact that I am standing here speaking. But it is faith that makes me believe that you might be listening to what I have to say."

634/PREACHING

A preacher well known for his long-winded talks, accepted an invitation to speak at a "Fourth of July" exercise. When the chairman of the event received his acceptance, he wrote to the preacher and said, "We are delighted that you are going to speak to us at our 'Fourth of July' celebration. The program will start with the mayor giving a word of welcome, then the American Legion drum and bugle corps will perform, then a high school student will read the Declaration of Independence, then your message, and then the firing squad."

635/PREACHING

The minister was sick, and a pastor noted for his never-ending sermons agreed to fill in. When he stood up in the pulpit, he was annoyed to find only ten worshippers present, including the choir. Afterward, he complained to the sexton.

> "That was a very small turnout. Were they informed that I was coming?"
>
> "No," replied the sexton, "but word must have leaked out!"

636/PREACHING

The new pastor of a small Church in the Tennessee hills was a dedicated teetotaler. Consequently, he was deeply disturbed to learn that several men in the congregation were operating illegal stills. He tried to persuade them to mend their ways and close down the stills, but without success. Finally, with the entire congregation assembled for the New Year's Day service, he announced his intention to take decisive action. "I have made the following New Year's resolution," he said:

> Be it resolved that tomorrow I shall journey to

> Washington, D.C. There the Attorney General of the United States will deputize me as a special Federal Marshal, authorizing me to put an end to the illegal production of alcohol in these parts. I will then return here with a truck loaded with empty jugs, go to each still in these hills, and drain every last drop of alcohol into those jugs. Then I will go down into the valley and empty them into the river. Amen! Please stand now for the singing of Hymn Number fifty-two.

Whereupon, the congregation rose and sang with gusto, "Shall We Gather By the River?"

637/PREACHING

A woman was listening to her pastor preach a Sunday morning sermon about Simon Peter's wife's mother who was ill with a fever. Not only was it an obscure text but also it was an insignificant sermon. The woman lasted through the experience, but left the Church feeling somewhat unfulfilled. Consequently, she decided to go to Church again that day, out in the country where she had grown up. When she arrived, she discovered to her dismay that her pastor had been invited to be guest preacher and again he had chosen to preach the sermon about Peter's mother-in-law being ill with a fever. (Obviously, he was getting a lot of mileage out of that sermon.) Believing that there was still time to redeem the day, the woman decided to go to the hospital chapel. As you may have guessed, the same preacher was there doing hospital duty, and he was preaching the same sermon on Peter's wife's mother who was ill with a fever. Next morning, the woman was on a bus riding downtown and, believe it or not, the same clergyman boarded that bus and sat down beside her. An ambulance raced by with sirens roaring. In order to make conversation, the pastor said, "Well, I wonder who it is?" "Surely it must be Peter's mother-in-law," she replied. "She was sick all day yesterday."

638/PREACHING

The story is told of a clergyman and an ordinary working man: a bus driver. They arrived together at the gates of heaven. An angel gave the clergyman a plain cotton gown, a wooden halo and modest living quarters containing only the bare necessities of eternal life. To the bus driver, the angel presented a complete wardrobe of the finest materials, a golden halo and lavish living–quarters containing every imaginable luxury and convenience. When he saw this, the clergyman protested: "Why does he get so much and I so little?" The angel checked the records and said, "It seems that when you were preaching, your congregation slept; when he was driving, his passengers prayed.

639/PREACHING

A preacher was asked to prepare the opening remarks at a convention. As was his custom, he greatly exceeded the time allotted him. Afterwards a woman came up to the speaker's table to shake his hand. "How did you like my speech?" he asked.

She answered, "I liked it fine. But it seems to me you missed several excellent opportunities."

The clergyman was puzzled. "Several excellent opportunities to do what?"

"To quit," she replied.

PRESENCE OF GOD

640

Calvin Coolidge, 30th President of the U.S., once found himself addressing a tribe of American Indians on a reservation where there had been no rainfall for months. Native medicine men and professional "rain-makers" had practiced their art in vain. The skies were cloudless and crops were going to ruin. Coolidge was looking into the faces of a depressed group of Indians as he began to speak. "Do not think," he said, "that in Washington I have not been aware of your situation. Do not think that I have not been wondering what I could do to help you. Do not think that I have not been praying to the Almighty for guidance." Whereupon, a veritable cloudburst descended upon the astonished but delighted gathering. The President was soaked before he got under shelter. As he watched the rain pouring down he was heard to say to himself, half-aloud, "Gosh! I didn't know I had it in me!"

Only the experience of God's love can satisfy your longing for a more fulfilling life. Open yourself up to God's loving presence at the deepest level of your being and you will hear yourself saying, "Gosh. I didn't know I had it in me!"

641/PRESENCE OF GOD

Sister Joselma, first-grade teacher in the laboratory school at Alverno College, Milwaukee, Wisconsin, wrote and published a children's book called "The Littlest Brother."

Her pupils, who watched the book grow from stories told in class to a printed volume, were fascinated by the project. They began writing books of their own.

One student wrote what was, perhaps, the shortest book you could find anywhere. It was composed of a sheet of paper, folded into four pages. On the front was the title "Swift Things." Inside was a crude but lively sketch of a deer.

And beneath the deer was this penciled text: "A deer is very swift, but God is already there."
—Milwaukee Journal

642/PRESENCE OF GOD

A man who lived in one of the poorer sections of town was known for his perfect Church attendance. Each morning on his way to worship he was barraged with requests for a little help by the homeless people in the neighborhood. However the man was so focused on getting to Church that he would pass them by, oblivious to their cries.

One morning, when the man arrived at the Church, he found that the normally wide open door was shut tight. Worried that he might be unable to visit in God's House that day, he looked heavenward. To his complete surprise he saw a sign posted above the door. It read:

> "If you don't find Me in the neighborhood
> you won't find Me in here."

643/PRESENCE OF GOD

"One day, when I was a child, an old man took me to his knee and placed his hand on my head as though he were giving me his blessing. 'Alexis,' he said, 'I'm going to tell you a secret. You're too small to understand now, but you'll understand when you are bigger. Listen, little one: neither the seven stories of heaven nor the seven stories of earth are enough to contain God; but a man's heart can contain Him. So be very careful, Alexis—and may my blessing go with you—NEVER TO WOUND A MAN'S HEART.'"

—*Zorba the Greek*

644/PRESENCE OF GOD

The greatest computer that had ever been built up to that moment was ready to be put into action. From all over the world, scientists gathered for its unveiling. Far more complex than anything that had gone before, the new computer was capable of solving intricate problems that previously had defied analysis. But those present couldn't agree on what the first question to be asked of the machine should be. While they argued the matter, the janitor suddenly pushed himself forward. Still holding his broom, he called out, "Is there a God?" An eerie silence fell over the room as all waited for the answer. Slowly, the vast machine began to go into action. Lights flashed, and a solemn whirring sound could be heard. Then, a deep voice rang out from the depths of the computer: "Now there is."

645/PRESENCE OF GOD

In the film "Oh God!" John Denver plays the role of a grocery store manager. He encounters God (played by George Burns) in the frozen food aisle. The store manager wants to know why God would choose to appear on earth as a man and walk among the people. He asks, "What good could that possibly do?" God replies: "You never know: a seed here, a seed there, something is bound to take hold and grow."

646/PRESENCE OF GOD

A first–time airline passenger was petrified during a mildly turbulent flight. The traveller was in such a state that the co-pilot personally walked back to the passenger's seat in an attempt to calm him.

"Are you a religious man?" the aviator asked. "Yes," was the man's reply. "Well then, don't you believe that when it's your time to go, you will, and not before then?" "Of course I do," he said. "Then what are you so nervous about?" the pilot inquired. The man said solemnly, "I'm afraid your time might come before mine."

647/PRESENCE OF GOD

Helen Keller, early in her life, lost the ability to see, to hear or to speak. She was less than two–years–old when she began to live in this disabled condition. Yet, through the help of Anne Sullivan, her teacher, and the Perkins Institute for the Blind (where she lived and studied for a time), she became one of the most sensitive, most alert, most aware persons in contemporary life.

Because of her handicap, Helen Keller developed a remarkably keen sense of the reality of life around her. On one occasion, she was walking in the woods with a friend. It was Springtime and she was using her fingers constantly to read the signs of new life bursting out in that forest. She felt a slender birch tree and the vibrations of a bird singing in its limbs. She felt flowers and leaves beginning to sprout. She felt stones in a cool brook. And when she returned home, she had the memory of many things that she had seen on the walk, even though she was blind. She asked her friend (who had perfectly good eyes) what she had seen. The friend said, "Nothing in particular." Helen Keller was astounded: to walk through the woods in the Springtime and see "nothing in particular." She began to ask other people, and she discovered that there were persons all around her who had eyes to see but were more blind than she was with her sightless eyes.

People at the Highway Department in New England apparently realize what a problem this is. When you drive through the New England mountains, every now and then you will come to a breathtaking vista of beauty, complete with a highway department sign that reads, "Scenic Area"—as if in recognition that people need to be informed, in writing, about the beauty that is surrounding them.

This is an important observation for us, because we have this problem not only with our physical eyes but also with our eyes of Faith. God is continually giving us signs of His Presence. He is constantly showing us, in hundreds of ways, that He is present, that He loves us, that He wants us to move into union with Him, that this union with Him is the only thing that can give genuine meaning to everything else in life. But we need to develop an alertness, a sensitivity to these signs as we move through our day's activities.

648/PRESENCE OF GOD

In a book called "Reaching Out," the distinguished religious educator and author, Henri Nouwen, describes a beautiful occasion in which he experienced a deep sense of the union with fellow human beings and God that Jesus is directing us toward:

> I vividly remember the day on which a man who had been a student in one of my courses came back to the school and entered my room with the disarming remark: "I have no problems this time, no questions to ask you. I do not need counsel or advice, but I simply want to celebrate some time with you." We sat on the ground facing each other and talked a little about what life had been for us in the last year, about our work, our common friends, and about the restlessness of our hearts. Then slowly as the minutes passed by we

became silent. Not an embarrassing silence but a silence that could bring us closer together than the many small and big events of the last year. We could hear a few cars and the noise of someone who was emptying a trash can somewhere. But that did not hurt. The silence which grew between us was warm, gentle and vibrant. Once in a while we looked at each other with the beginning of a smile pushing away the last remnants of fear and suspicion. It seemed that while the silence grew deeper around us we became more and more aware of a Presence embracing both of us. Then he said, "It is good to be here" and I said, "Yes, it is good to be together again," and after that we were silent again for a long period. And as a deep peace filled the empty space between us he said hesitantly, "When I look at you it is as if I am in the Presence of Christ." I did not feel startled, surprised or in need of protesting, but I could only say, "It is the Christ in you, who recognizes the Christ in me." "Yes," he said, "He indeed is in our midst," and then he spoke the words which entered into my soul as the most healing words I had heard in many years. "From now on, wherever you go, or wherever I go, all the ground between us will be holy ground."

Through our obedience and our discipleship, God's sheer gift of Grace will become real to us and, from then on, wherever we go, we will be on the holy ground of oneness with our fellow human beings and oneness with our God.

649/PRESENCE OF GOD

A man landed a job painting the yellow line down the center of the highway. This he had to do by hand. After three days the foreman said to him: "Your first day out, you did great. You painted that line for three miles. Your second day wasn't bad. You painted two miles. But today you only painted one mile, so it looks as though I'll have to fire you." On his way out of the office the employee looked back and said, "It's not my fault. Every day I got further away from the paint can."

Some people feel that as they journey though each day they are moving further and further away from God. And life gets increasingly more difficult as they wander from their Source of peace.

If you are not experiencing God's Presence in your life, if you find yourself getting further and further away from God—who moved?

PRESTIGE

650

A businessman invited one of his biggest customers to a posh New York restaurant for lunch. Before his customer arrived, the man went to the rest room where, to his great delight, he saw Lee Iacocca, the famous President of the Chrysler Corporation. "Mr. Iacocca," he gushed, "I've been a great admirer of yours for years. I've read all your books and I'm trying to do all the things you've done in order to be successful." "Thank you very much," Iacocca replied politely. "Sir," the man continued, "I wonder if you would do me a small favor. The man I am having lunch with is trying to decide whether to place a big order with me or with one of my competitors. I need to do everything I can to impress him. Would you please stop at our table and say 'Hello Fred,' to me? Then I'll introduce you to my customer and he'll be terribly impressed." Mr. Iacocca reluctantly agreed. Then, a bit later, as he walked toward Fred's table, the customer said, "Holy smoke! Look who's coming over to our table. It's Lee Iacocca!" "Hello Fred," Iacocca said. "Won't you introduce me to your friend?" Whereupon, Fred nonchalantly replied, "Come back later, Lee, can't you see we're trying to have lunch?"

PRIDE

651

In a New England seminary, a brilliant student, not known for his humility, became extremely puffed up when informed that he had received perfect grades in all his theology subjects. Because of his superior academic standing, he was chosen to be the guest preacher one Sunday at a large New York City church.

Early that Sunday morning, he found himself running late, and he almost missed his train. With his suitcase of books clutched to his chest, he ran down the platform and jumped on board, only to discover that all the seats were taken. He began to walk from one car to the next until, at last, he reached an empty car. With a sigh of relief he sat down, spread his books out and began putting the finishing touches on his sermon. At that moment, the porter came through and said, "I'm sorry, sir, but this car has been reserved for a group of mental patients we're picking up at the next stop." The student replied, "That's all right. I'll take full responsibility. I'm on my way to preach in one of the biggest churches in New York."

When the train stomped at the next station, the mental patients boarded the car and began milling around the student. They were escorted by an attendant wearing a white jacket and holding a clipboard in his hand. The attendant said in a loud voice, "All right, everyone sit down and be quiet while I make my count." After they had settled down, the man with the clipboard began to count the occupants in the car, pointing his finger at each person: "One, two, three, four, five, six..." until he came to the seminary student. "Who are you?" the man asked. The student replied, "I'm a divinity student and I'm being rewarded for my theological expertise. I suppose one could say that I'm a Neo-Kierkegaardian existentialist. Actually, I'm just now preparing an address on 'The eschatological implications and general efficacy of the Redemption as expressed in the Atonement.'" Whereupon, the man in the white jacket pointed his finger directly at the young man and continued: "...seven, eight, nine, ten..."

"For everyone who humbles himself will be exalted, and he who exalts himself will be humbled" (Lk. 14:11).

R

RE-BIRTH

652
Approximately 80 years ago, Thomas Edison's factory in West Orange, NJ was virtually destroyed by fire. Although the damage exceeded two million dollars, the buildings were only insured for $238,000 because they were made of concrete and were thought to be fireproof. Much of Edison's life's work went up in smoke and flames that December night.

At the height of the fire, Edison's 24-year-old son, Charles, searched frantically for his father. He finally found him, calmly watching the fire, his face glowing in the reflection, his white hair blowing in the wind.

"My heart ached for him," said Charles. "He was 67—no longer a young man—and everything was going up in flames. When he saw me, he shouted, 'Charles, where's your mother?' When I told him I didn't know, he said, 'Find her. Bring her here. She will never see anything like this as long as she lives.'"

The next morning, Edison looked at the ruins and said, "There is great value in disaster. All our mistakes are burned up. Thank God we can start anew."

Three weeks after the fire, Edison managed to deliver the first phonograph.

RECOGNITION

653
Sir Arthur Conan Doyle, author of the famous Sherlock Holmes stories, once hailed a cab in Paris. He threw his handbag inside and climbed in after it, but before he could say a word, the driver said, "Where to, Mr. Conan Doyle?"

"You recognize me?" said the author in surprise.

"Not really. I've never seen you or a picture of you."

"Then how do you know I am Conan Doyle?"

"Well," said the driver, "I had read in the newspapers that you were on vacation in the south of France; I noticed you getting off a train that came from Marseille; I see you have the kind of tan that bespeaks a week or more in the sun; from the ink spot on your right middle finger, I deduce you are a writer; you have the keen look of a medical man, and the cut of clothes of an Englishman. Putting it all together, I felt you must surely be Conan Doyle, the creator of the great detective, Sherlock Holmes."

Conan Doyle replied excitedly, "But you are yourself the equal of Sherlock Holmes since you recognized me from all these small observations."

"There is," said the driver, "one additional fact."

"And that is?" Doyle asked.

"Your name is lettered on your suitcase," said the cab driver.

"...and whoever sees Me, sees the One who sent Me
(Jn. 12:45).

654/RECOGNITION

A rich banker died, and his family met in the lawyer's office for the reading of the Last Will and Testament. The lawyer began: "I hereby give, devise and bequeath to my wife all of my real estate holdings and $1 million in cash. To each of my three brothers and two sisters I give $100,000 in cash. To each of my five first cousins I give $25,000. And to my nephew, Billy, who always wanted to be remembered in my will, I say, 'Hello Billy!'"

655/RECOGNITION

Christine Spark's inspiring biography, "The Elephant Man," tells the story of John Merrick, a victim of neurofibromatosis, an incurable disease which causes hideous disfigurement, great pain and premature death. Adding to John Merrick's misery was the popular belief, in late eighteenth-century London, that the disease was caused by some lapse of morality on the part of the victim.

Dr. Frederich Treves, a senior surgeon at the prestigious London Hospital, discovered the terribly mistreated Merrick in a circus freak show. Dr. Treves took John Merrick into his personal care and began to work with him. Merrick's sensitive and caring personality began to shine through and, in time, the Elephant Man gained notoriety. Even the Prince and Princess of Wales paid him a visit. Money was raised on Merrick's behalf to provide him with books, a teacher and craft lessons.

One day the beautiful actress Madge Kendall discovered the Elephant Man through friends. Kendall was deeply moved by Merrick's condition and was determined to help. At their first meeting, Madge Kendall presented him with the complete works of William Shakespeare. Tears welled up in his eyes as he began reading aloud from "Romeo and Juliet":

> See how she leans her cheek upon her hand: O' that I were a glove upon that hand, that I might touch that cheek.

Madge Kendall responded with Juliet's lines, and they continued page-after-page until they had completed the entire second act of "Romeo and Juliet." Then, Madge leaned over, kissed the Elephant Man on the cheek and said, "Why Mr. Merrick, you're not an Elephant Man at all. Oh no! You are Romeo!"

REDEMPTION

656

A group of Christians once met with the atheist philosopher, Friedrich Nietzche, in an effort to convert Him to Christ. After listening for a while, Nietzche is reported to have said to the group: "Show me first that you are redeemed, and then I will listen further to your talk about a Redeemer."

Has your faith in the Risen Christ made such a difference in your life that it "shows"?

657/REDEMPTION

The story is told of a saintly old man who had endured almost every misfortune imaginable. His beloved wife died. His children never contacted him. His house burned to the ground. He lost his job. Everything he touched turned into a disaster—or so it seemed. Yet, through it all, he always remained a cheerful person. He always returned good for evil. Then the old man died. When he arrived at the heavenly gate, the angels had already gathered to greet him. Even the Lord was there, so great was this good man's fame in heavenly circles. Then the ritual of his final judgement began. The Prosecuting Angel announced: "For the first time in the memory of my office there are no serious charges to be made." Then the Angel For the Defense rose and said: "This saintly man has endured extreme hardship on earth but has ever remained cheerful. All his life was spent in returning good for evil." Then the Lord spoke: "Not since Job have we heard of a life such as this one." Whereupon, the Lord turned to the man and said, "Ask, and it shall be given unto you." The old man looked up and said, "If I could start every day with a hot buttered roll ... "And, at that, all the angels wept.

In a beautiful commentary on this story, the former pastor of the Riverside Church in New York City (Rev. William Sloane Coffin) wrote: "It wasn't so much the modesty of the request as the understanding of the preciousness of what he was asking for that caused the angels to weep with joy. Sunshine should always be more important to us than another acquisition. We don't need all things to enjoy life; we have been given life to enjoy all things. Happiness lies in discerning the value of all the things we have. And if we have only fish and bread—and JESUS—any routine is redeemed. So 'Bless the Lord, O my soul, and forget not all His benefits.'"

RELATIONSHIPS

658

Relationships seldom die because they suddenly have no life left in them. They wither slowly, either because people do not understand how much or what kind of upkeep, time, work, love and caring they require, or because people are too lazy or afraid to try. A relationship is a living thing. It needs and benefits from the same attention to detail that an artist lavishes on his art.

—*Viscott, D.*

RELIGION

659

"You are the light of the world. A city on a hill cannot be hid. Nor do men light a lamp and put it under a bushel" (Mt. 5:14-15).

A distinguished anthropologist visited a Bantu village in South Africa to make certain surveys of the customs and habits of the people. They were a primitive people without any semblance of Western culture, but they welcomed and received him most cordially. When the anthropologist returned to the United States, he sent the people a sun dial, as an expression of his gratitude and appreciation, so that they might have some way of telling time. They were so grateful that they thought they could preserve the gift for a long time by completely covering it with a thatched roof to keep it from wind and weather.

Many treat their religion that way. They hide it under a thatched roof, so to speak. When there is a divorce between what you say and what you do, when words do not match deeds, religion is a hollow and empty thing.
—Sizoo, J.R., "The Tyranny of Words" (Adapted).

RELIGIOUS EDUCATION

660
In religion classes, among the first lessons taught to children are the Ten Commandments. Some teachers require that they be memorized. Others prefer to stress the underlying principles of the Commandments. One teacher, who combined both approaches, would relate an incident to illustrate one of the Commandments and then ask the children which Commandment applied. The dialogue went something like this:

Teacher: John's parents went shopping at 9 a.m. Before leaving the house, they told John to get out of bed and wash the breakfast dishes before they returned. The parents returned at noon. John was still in bed and the dirty breakfast dishes were still on the table.

Student: Honor your father and mother.

Teacher: Helen was with her mother in a supermarket. While mother was busy unloading her basket at the checkout counter, Helen took a candy bar from the shelf and slipped it into her pocket.

Student: You shall not steal.

The young students did very well on the simple illustrations. But they could be stumped by more complex examples. For instance:

> Teacher: George sometimes had a nasty temper. One day he got into an argument with his sister. When it seemed that George was losing the argument, he grabbed his sister's pet kitten and tried to pull its tail off.

The children were puzzled. There was a long pause. Then a student raised his hand triumphantly and blurted out:

> What God has joined together, let no man put asunder!

661/RELIGIOUS EDUCATION

Samuel Taylor Coleridge and a friend were discussing religion. Coleridge's friend believed that children should not be given formal religious education of any kind. They would then be free to select their own religion when they were old enough to decide. Coleridge did not bother to debate the point, but invited the man to see his rather neglected garden.

"Do you call this a garden?" asked his visitor. "There are nothing but weeds here."

"Well, you see," said Coleridge, "I did not wish to infringe on the liberty of the garden in any way. I wanted the garden to be free to express itself."

RENEWAL

662

We cleaned our little church today—
Wiped all the dust and dirt away.
We straightened papers, washed the floors;
Wiped off the lamp and painted doors.

We brushed the dirt stains from the books
And whisked the cobwebs from the nooks.
We polished windows so we'd see

The newly greening shrub and tree.
The menfolk, too, raked up the yard—
They laughed and said it wasn't hard,
And, oh, it felt so very good
To have the place look as it should.

We said, "How wonderful 'twould be
If we cleaned out what we cannot see—
Such things as grudges, hates and lies,
And musty thoughts much worse than flies.

REPENTANCE

663

We may be a little fuzzy on the meaning of repentance, but we can be sure that it involves much more than several small adjustments in our lives:

Repentance penetrates the crusts of piety we wrap around ourselves to keep us from it.

Repentance begins inside the heart and turns life upside down for us and right side up for God.

Repentance reverses our priorities, upsets our values, turns our pockets inside out.

Repentance shatters our systems of security and hangs us on the thin thread we call the "Will of God."

Repentance revolts against the sin we have loved and reconciles us to God whom we have not loved.

—*Wedel, A.F., "Prepare the Way" (Adapted).*

RESPONSIBILITY

664

I have only just a minute.
Only sixty seconds in it.
Didn't seek it, didn't choose it.

But it's up to me to use it.
I must suffer if I lose it.
Give account if I abuse it.
Just a tiny little minute.
But Eternity is in it.

665/RESPONSIBILITY

There is a story about the philosopher, John Dewey, walking with his little boy on a wet, cold, windy day. The youngster wasn't wearing any shoes and he was splashing around in a puddle. A friend coming by said, "You had better get that boy out of the water. He will get pneumonia." "I know it," the philosopher replied, "but I am trying to find a way to make him want to get out of the water."
—Kennedy, G. "A Man With Two Sons."

666/RESPONSIBILITY

Three workmen fashioning a cross
On which the fourth must die!
And no one ever thought to ask
"And why? And why? And why?"
Said they: "This is our business,
Our living we must earn;
What happens to the other man
Is none of our concern!"

RESTITUTION

667

Early in his career, Jackie Gleason was hired one summer to perform at a seaside resort in New Jersey. He rented a room in a boarding house that was run by an aged woman who sat behind a desk at the foot of the stairs. She saw to it that no one left without paying.

When the engagement ended, Gleason was told that his paycheck would be mailed to him the following week. But, he needed $35 to pay for his room and he had no money. How was he going to get past the old woman without paying?

Gleason was determined. He phoned a couple of his friends in New York City and asked them to drive down and help him. When they arrived, he lowered his suitcases out the back window to the waiting car. Then he squeezed into a striped bathing suit that was all the rage and went down the front staircase. The woman nodded. Gleason gave her one of his biggest smiles. "Nice day for a dip in the ocean," he said. Then he walked out, he turned the corner, climbed into the waiting car and sped toward New York City with his friends.

Two weeks later, he was working at a club and making good money. He thought of the old woman who ran the boarding house. He began to feel guilty because he still owed her $35. He felt as if he had stolen the money from her and his conscience told him that he must make restitution. The next day he drove to the Jersey shore and strode into the boarding house, $35 in hand. Sure enough, the old woman was behind the desk. He gave her the money, and she burst into tears. "We thought you had drowned," she cried.

RESURRECTION

668

Someone designed an unusual Easter card which portrayed the Nativity scene—twice. In both renditions there are Mary, Joseph, the newborn Babe, the shepherds, and some others. Actually, both scenes are the same, but with one notable exception. Those who are young in the first scene are middle–aged in the second scene. Those who were middle–aged in the first scene are old in the second scene. In the background of the Nativity scenes is an outline of the "empty tomb." The message to us is clear: our Christian Faith takes us

> . . . from the place of Jesus' birth to the place where the stone is rolled away from His burial place;
> . . . From the place of worship of the newborn Babe to the place of worship of the Risen Savior;

. . . from standing in awe before the revelation of God's infinite Love to going forth as living witnesses to His Resurrection Power.

669/RESURRECTION

It was a beautiful Spring day, and a sense of peace stayed with me as I left the Cathedral on Easter Monday morning. I paused for a moment on top of the steps leading to the Avenue, now crowded with people rushing to their jobs. Sitting in her usual place inside a small archway was the old flower lady. At her feet, corsages and boutonnieres were parading on top of a spread-open newspaper.

The flower lady was smiling, her wrinkled old face alive with some inner joy. I started down the stairs. Then, on an impulse, turned and picked out a flower.

As I put it in my lapel, I said, "You look happy this morning."

"Why not? Everything is good."

The flower lady was dressed so shabbily and seemed so very old that her reply startled me.

"You've been sitting here for many years now, haven't you? And always smiling. You wear your troubles well."

"You can't reach my age and not have troubles," she replied. "Only it's like Jesus and Good Friday ..." She paused for a moment ...

"Yes?" I prompted.

"Well, when Jesus was crucified on Good Friday, that was the worst day for the world. And when I get troubles I remember that, and then I think of what happened only three days later—Easter and Our Lord arising. So when I get troubles, I've learned to wait three days ... somehow everything gets all right again."

And she smiled goodbye. Her words still follow me whenever I think I have troubles ... "Give God a chance to help! ... Wait three days."

—Barnes, P., "The Magic of Three Days" (Adapted).

REVELATION

670

A man was plagued with worry over a recurring dream. He explained his problem to a psychiatrist: "Every night I dream that I am standing before a huge door, trying to push it open. There is a sign on the door, and I push and push against it with all my strength but nothing happens and the door will not budge. Then I awaken in a cold sweat and I cannot get back to sleep. I keep worrying about the door that will not open. Please, you must help me! This thing is driving me crazy." To which the psychiatrist replied, "I'll try to help you. But tell me first: What does the sign on the door say?" The anxious man thought for a moment, trying to recall his dream, then answered, "Pull!"

671/REVELATION

A little girl sat at her grandmother's feet to listen to the creation story from the Book of Genesis. As the wondrous tale unfolded, the grandmother noticed that the child was unusually quiet. "Well, what do you think of it, dear?" she asked. "Oh, I love it," the child answered, "You never know what God is going to do next."

That little girl was making a profound distinction between our preconceived notions of who God is and what He does, and who He really is and what He is really doing. It is the difference between being a passive listener to the revealed Word and an actual hearer of the revealed Word. It is the difference between some vague, general understanding that God has spoken, and an abiding conviction that God is speaking—right now, and to me!

REVERENCE

672

Edgar Bergen of the "Edgar Bergen/Charlie McCarthy" comedy team was fond of telling this story of a visit to Mexico City:

> It has always been a favorite entertainment of mine to stand on a busy corner and watch the people go by. Once when I was doing a broadcast down in Mexico City, I jumped at the opportunity to play my old game. I walked across the street from the place where I had lunched and stood there studying the people. A Mexican walked past, looked toward me, and tipped his hat. I thought at first it might be a mistake. But I realized that he must have seen me in the movies.
>
> Then a second and a third man walked past and tipped their hats. It suddenly dawned on me that I was better known in Mexico than I had imagined. It was a great feeling of satisfaction to be so internationally known and loved.
>
> However, when nearly every man tipped his hat, and I had tipped mine in return, it occurred to me that it was almost impossible that I was that well known in Mexico. I looked around.
>
> I was standing before a Catholic Church.

S

SACRIFICE

673
The pastor of a small church was walking home one day when he was summoned by an old woman who called him from her front yard. The woman was bad tempered and unkempt, and the minister generally tried to avoid her. On this day, however, she extended an offer of afternoon tea. The pastor hesitated. "Is it because I'm old and dirty that you never come to visit me?" the old woman asked. Again he hesitated, but then informed the old woman that he was expected by his wife for afternoon tea. The old woman repeated, "Is it because I'm old and dirty that you won't come into my house?" This time he followed her in.

The house was filthy and bug–infested. The old woman led him into the kitchen where the dishes were piled to the ceiling. "Will you drink a cup of tea with me?" she asked. Once again, the pastor hesitated. And once again the old lady moaned, "Is it because I'm old and dirty?" "All right!" he said. "I'll drink your tea."

She removed a cup from the dirty stack of dishes, filled it with tea and handed it to the man. As he looked into the dirty contents of his cup, he could still hear the woman's nagging words in his ears. Then suddenly, his mind took him back two thousand years to a lonely garden spot and to another cup and to a Savior who said, "Not My will but Thine be done," and a Savior who drank that cup to its bitter end.

That cup was filled with your sins and mine. It was the cup of suffering and shame and bitter death; yet Jesus drank it to the very last drop. And the pastor drank too. Because of Him, because of the Lord, he was able to drink from that dirty cup.
—Ravenhill, L. (Adapted).

674/SACRIFICE

Sever me from myself that I may be grateful unto Thee;
May I perish to myself that I may be safe in Thee;
May I die to myself that I may live in Thee;
May I wither to myself that I may blossom in Thee;
May I be emptied of myself that I may abound in Thee;
May I be nothing to myself that I may be all to Thee.
—Desiderius Erasmus (1466-1536)

SALVATION

675

It was the start of a holiday weekend, and the service station was crowded. Finally, an attendant hustled up to the local minister who had been waiting in line for some time. "I'm sorry about the delay, Pastor," the attendant apologized, "but it seems like everybody waits until the last minute to get ready for a trip which they knew they were going on all along." The pastor smiled and said, "I know what you mean. I've got the same problem in my business."

676/SALVATION

That great philosopher, Charlie Brown of the "Peanuts" cartoons, once made a profound observation that touches on the way we feel about this thing we call "salvation." Charlie is leaning against a tree talking to Lucy. She asks, "What do you think security is Charlie Brown?" He says, "Security is sleeping in the back seat of a car when you're a little kid and you've been somewhere with your mom and dad and it's night. You don't have to worry about anything. Your mom and dad are in the front seat and they're doing all the worrying. They take care of everything." Lucy smiles and says, "That's real neat." Charlie Brown, who never seems to know when to stop, gets a serious look on his face and says, "But it doesn't last. Suddenly you're grown up and it can never be that way again. Suddenly it's all over and you'll never get to sleep in the back seat again. Never!" Lucy gets a frightened look on her face and asks, "Never?" And Charlie Brown replies, "Never!" As they stand there, sensing the terrible loneliness that goes with being an adult, Lucy reaches over and says, "Hold my hand, Charlie Brown."

677/SALVATION
If we could carry human goodness to infinity, we could not earn one fraction of a percent of salvation. If we could gather every good person who ever lived in the history of the world, and take from each one the best in his or her character, and combine these multiple qualities in one individual, that individual would still have to kneel at the cross and say, "Lord, be merciful to me a sinner."
—Martinez, A. (Adapted).

SATAN

678
President Theodore Roosevelt once owned a feisty little dog that was always getting into fights with other dogs and always losing. Once, after watching Roosevelt's dog pick a fight and then taking the usual beating, a friend said to the President, "That dog of yours isn't much of a fighter, is he?" To which Roosevelt replied, "On the contrary, he's a very good fighter, but he's a bad judge of dogs. He always underestimates his adversaries."

If you are serious about growth in your Christian life and ministry then, most assuredly, Satan is your most formidable adversary. Don't ever underestimate Satan! He's tough! And he's not about to underestimate you!

SECOND COMING

679

O Blessed Lord Jesus,
give us thankful hearts for You, our greatest gift.
Let not our souls be busy inns that have no room
for You and Yours,
but quiet homes of prayer and praise,
where You will find good company;
where holy thoughts pass among us
as we fervently watch and await Your coming.
So, when You come again, O Blessed One,
may you find all things ready, and your servants waiting
for no new master, but for One long known and loved.
Even so, come Lord Jesus!

SELF-CENTEREDNESS

680

In a magazine cartoon by Dave Berg, two young women are leaving church on a Sunday morning. One says to the other, "This morning's sermon about only thinking of oneself was really moving." The other replies, "It had quite an effect on me, too! It's the first time I didn't pray that I'd find a good man to marry!...Instead, I prayed that my parents would get a good son–in–law!"

681/SELF-CENTEREDNESS

Years ago, a doctor named Frederick Loomis wrote the following "prescription" to treat man's preoccupation with events from the irrevocable past:

> Moaning over something that cannot change is a confession of futility and of fear...The best way to break this vicious, morbid cycle is to stop thinking about yourself and start thinking about other people. You can lighten your own load by doing something for someone else.

By the simple device of doing an outward, unselfish act today, you can make the past recede. The present and the future will again take on their true challenge and perspective. As a doctor I have written this prescription for 'self-centeredness' medicine many, many times and nearly always it has been far more successful than anything I could have ordered from the drugstore.

682/SELF-CENTEREDNESS

A teenage boy applied for a job in a large sixteen-screen movie theater complex. During the interview, the manager outlined in great detail his expectations of the ushers who worked in his theater. A routine part of the interview included questioning the prospective usher about what he or she might do in the event of certain emergencies. The manager asked, "Suppose a fire broke out in the rear of the theater. What would you do?" "Oh don't worry about me," the boy replied with confidence. "I'd get out all right."

SELF-DECEPTION

683

Bob Butera of the New Jersey Devils tells the story of the coach who called his players together when they were trailing badly at the second intermission and said to them:

"Men, I don't want you to think of yourselves as losing—I want you to visualize this game as a tie." Fired up with this reinterpretation, the players went back in for the third period and got killed. As they were leaving the field, one of the players put his arm around the coach's shoulder and said, "Don't feel bad, coach—I want you to visualize this game as a win."

SELF-DESTRUCTION

684

The Bay of Naples, Italy, is the habitat of a jellyfish called medusa and a snail of the nudibranch variety.

When the snail is small, the jellyfish will sometimes swallow it and draw it into its digestive tract. But the snail is protected by its shell and cannot be digested. The snail fastens itself to the inside of the jellyfish and slowly begins to eat it. By the time the animal is fully grown, it has consumed the entire jellyfish.

Many of us are like that jellyfish. We feast on our own snail that eventually will consume us.

For some it's alcoholism. We start out as social drinkers. Then the desire for a drink grows and begins to gnaw at us, and we wind up being consumed by a thirst we can't control.

In other cases, it's hatred. Someone does something that we perceive as hateful, and we hate them back. We seethe inside, and eventually we are consumed by our hate.

Worry can do the same thing; so can greed. But for most of us it can simply be the aimlessness of our lives.
—*"Soundings" (Adapted).*

SELF-ESTEEM

685
Doctor Oliver Wendell Holmes, the father of the United States Supreme Court Justice of the same name, was a short man. One day he went to a meeting and found himself standing in a room full of tall men. This made him look even shorter. Someone remarked to Dr. Holmes that he must feel very small among these big people. "I do," said Dr. Holmes. "I feel like a dime among a lot of pennies."

SELF-HELP

686
At the "Detroit Round Table of Christians and Jews," Rabbi Israel Halpern told of a certain rabbi who wanted to take seri-

ously his call to make a contribution toward the improvement of the world:

> First he thought his mission was to improve the entire world—but that was far too vast a responsibility;
>
> Then he thought, "I can improve my disciples"—
> but even that was too awesome a task;
>
> Next he decided to improve his family. But again he realized that was too much;
>
> Finally, he understood what he needed to do: improve his own self! (And each of us has that good place to begin—with his or her own self.)

SELFISHNESS

687

It is an all-too-common failing to expect others to inconvenience themselves on our behalf and yet become quite upset when the shoe is on the other foot.

A cold wind was howling and a chilling rain was beating down when the telephone rang in the home of a doctor. The caller said that his wife needed urgent medical attention. The doctor was understanding. "I'll be glad to come, but my car is being repaired," he said. "Could you come and get me?"

There was indignation at the other end of the phone. "What," an angry voice sputtered, "in this weather?"

688/SELFISHNESS

There is an Oriental story about a man who cries out from the depths of hell, pleading for release. He is asked what good he had done in his life. All the man can remember is that, while walking in the woods one day, he saw a spider and did not kill it. At once the thin, silvery thread of a spider-web is let down to him in hell. Seizing it eagerly, he begins to be slowly lifted out of his misery. Whereupon, his fellow-sufferers, seeing him about to escape, clutch his garment and his feet, and all are being lifted up together. But the man, fearing the web might break, cries, "Let go! Let go!" And when they let go, the thread breaks, and all fall back into hell. Although the thread was strong enough to lift all together, nevertheless it could not bear the heavy burden of a selfish soul.

SELFLESSNESS

689

An English missionary to a country in Central Africa tells the touching story of a most unusual offering he once received in the native chapel:

> It was a bright Sunday morning—a most fitting day, I thought, to preach my sermon on the Transfiguration of the Lord Jesus. In the sermon, I told the members of the congregation to reflect the glory of God's love in everything they did, just as Jesus did in His life and ministry and death on the Cross. After the sermon, the collection plate was passed. A young native woman who had recently been baptized, had no money to give. Consequently, when the plate came to her, she quietly rose from her seat, placed the plate on the floor and stood on it. And, as she carried out that symbolic act of total commitment—total gift of self—I saw in her face a brilliant, dazzling reflection of the glory of God's love.

690/SELFLESSNESS

There is a beautiful story of the courtship of Moses Mendelssohn, the famous German–Jewish philosopher of two centuries ago. Moses Mendelssohn, a small hunchbacked man, fell in love with a beautiful and charming young woman named Frumtje, daughter of a prosperous banker. Several months after he had first met Frumtje, Mendelssohn visited her father and asked him how she really felt about the possibility of marriage. "Please tell me the truth," Mendelssohn insisted.

The father replied, "The truth is that the girl is frightened by you because..." Mendelssohn interrupted: "Because I am a hunchback?" "Yes," said the father, "because you are a hunchback."

Mendelssohn then asked to see the daughter on the pretext that he wanted to say farewell to her. He found her in an upstairs room where she was busy with some needlework. She avoided looking at him during the conversation (which Mendelssohn eventually directed to the subject of marriage). The young woman asked if he really believed that marriages were made in heaven. "Oh course," he replied. "And something very unusual happened to me. As you know, when children are born they call out in heaven, 'This one or that one will get this or that girl for a wife.' When I was born, my future wife was thus announced, but it was added: 'She will, alas, have a terrible hump on her back.' I shouted, 'Oh, Lord, a girl who is hunchbacked will very easily become bitter and hard. A girl should be beautiful. Good Lord, give the hump to me and let her be well–formed.'" Frumtje was deeply moved. She saw Mendelssohn in a whole new way, and so she became his faithful and loving wife.

SELF-RIGHTEOUSNESS

691

As they were leaving church one Sunday morning, a wife asked her husband if he had really listened to the sermon. "Certainly," he replied. "It was about the Bible story of the Pharisee and the publican. And it really got through to me—you know, where the publican goes into the temple, falls on his knees and humbly prays, 'Lord, be merciful to me, a sinner!' But also in the temple is the proud Pharisee who stands and says, 'Lord, I thank you that I am not like other men. I thank you that I don't do the evil things they do. And I especially give you thanks that I am not like that publican over there. He's a bad person—a no-good tax collector; but I'm a good and respectable person.'" There was a pause, then the husband added, "That Pharisee—he really was a low-down, self-righteous man. I thank God that I'm not like him!"

692/SELF-RIGHTEOUSNESS

Two brothers were nearing death. Envious of his brother, the older of the two asked God:

> Why has my brother been blessed with wealth and happiness and I with nothing? All of my life I never missed a single day without saying my morning and evening prayers. My Church attendance has been perfect. I have made not a single decision in my life without first calling Your Name. And now, as I am nearing my final days, I pray to You day and night. Yet I can hardly afford to pay my meager rent. My brother on the other hand drinks and gambles all night long. Not once have I heard him in prayer. Yet my brother has more money than he can count. So I ask you God not to punish my brother but to tell me why have You allowed him such wealth and happiness while I have been left with nothing?

"Because," God replied, "you are such a self-righteous pain-in-the-neck!"

693/SELF-RIGHTEOUSNESS

He was a convicted criminal and a rough-looking character. His fellow prison inmates nicknamed him "Spike." Just before his release from prison after serving a fifteen-year sentence, Spike had a long talk with the prison chaplain. He told the clergyman how much he had been looking forward for all those years to the time when he could hold up his head in society and live a good life. Among other things, the chaplain advised Spike to join the church nearest to his home as soon as he was released. It so happened that Spike found an apartment on the edge of the poorest section of town, yet very near to the richest section of town. It so happened also that the church nearest to the ex-convict's apartment was located on the edge of the rich area.

Spike called on the pastor of this fashionable church and told him of his desire to join. "My dear man," said the pastor, with more than a touch of superiority, "I do not think you would be happy here, though I appreciate your good intentions. Really, you would be most uncomfortable among my people and I am afraid it would be quite embarrassing to you and perhaps to them. I suggest you think it over and pray and meditate and see if God does not give you some direction."

A week later, Spike met the pastor on the street, stopped him, and said, "Reverend, I took your advice and prayed and meditated and finally God sent me word. He said I should not bother any more trying to join your church. He said He Himself had been trying to get in there for years without success."

SELF-WORTH

694

Have you ever felt like your life is not important? Consider the man who received a Ph.D from Oxford University. The thesis for his degree was titled: "The influence of the Motion of Fish's Tails Upon the Tides of the Ocean." That's right! And he proved, to his satisfaction at least, that the great tides of the world are influenced by the motion of fish's tails. You who think your life doesn't count—aren't you of much more value than many fish's tails? Do you think for one moment that the God Who created such a Universe in which every movement has meaning can overlook you, a person for Whom His only Son died, and in Whose fellowship you may live forever?
—Byrd, W.O., "On Earth Is Not His Equal." (Adapted).

695/SELF-WORTH

According to an ancient fable, there once lived in a small village a man whose body was so twisted and whose face was so disfigured that the townspeople laughed at him. The children teased him. The dogs barked at him. The man became so embittered that he left the village where he had been born and went deep into the forest, where he lived alone. There he found a measure of solace in the beauty of sunrise and sunset, in the soft sighing of the breeze in the trees, in the frolic of creatures of the forest, in the sweet songs of the birds of the air. Still the bitterness only softened. It did not go away. One day, a visitor came into the hermit's hut. As they sat down together to the evening meal, the hermit asked the visitor to offer a prayer. But the visitor said, "No, you are the master here. It is you who must say the blessing." And so the hermit, nervous at first, spoke his gratitude for the beauty of the forest and the wonder of nature and the nourishment they were about to share. Whereupon the visitor said: "You have forgotten one thing. You have neglected to thank God for yourself." The hermit looked away, saying nothing. The visitor continued: "You have retreated into the forest because you have despaired of your physical unattractiveness. You have forgotten that in the eyes of God, you are far more beautiful than all the trees and all the flowers and all the birds of the forest." The hermit could not forget those words, and when the opportunity came, he moved back to the town of his birth. Strange to say, the people of the community no longer laughed when he walked by. The children no longer teased him. And his heart sang with joy, for he realized that he was living in the same town, with the same people, even the same dogs, but all was different! All was different because he was different. He had learned to thank God for himself.

SERENDIPITY

696

A lone shipwreck survivor on an uninhabited island managed to build a crude hut in which he placed all that he had saved from the sinking ship. Each day he prayed to God that he would be rescued, and each day he searched the horizon for a passing ship that he might hail. One day, in the midst of his prayer, he was horrified to discover that his hut was in flames. All that he had saved from the ship to help him survive was destroyed. He looked up at the sky and shook his fist at God. "Why didn't you listen to my prayers," he screamed. "Is it that you don't care?" But within a few hours, to his amazement, a ship arrived. "We saw your smoke signal," the captain explained.

SERVICE

697
An eighty-five-year-old woman was being interviewed on her birthday. What advice would she have for people her age, the reporter asked.

"Well," said the old dear, "at our age it is very important to keep using all our potential or it dries up. It is important to be with people and if it is at all possible, to earn one's living through service. That's what keeps us alive and well."

"May I ask what exactly you do for a living at your age?"

"I look after an old lady in my neighborhood," was her unexpected, delightful reply.
—deMello, A., "The Heart of the Enlightened."

698/SERVICE
"Giving to others heals me, as the Indians healed themselves with herbs. They did not understand what the herbs did, how they operated. They only knew their healing powers. So with me. I do not want to know what there is about the process of giving that heals me. But it is my herb. And I must not try to pick it apart, but just use it and know what it does and be grateful."
—Deneuve, C.

699/SERVICE
Henry Ward Beecher once said, "Religion means work; it means hard work; it means work in a dirty world. The world has to be cleaned by somebody and you are not really called of God unless you are prepared to scour and scrub."

Put on Your Overalls!

700/SERVICE

There's a clever young guy named Somebody Else,
There's nothing this guy can't do.
He is busy from morning till way late at night,
Just substituting for you.

You're asked to do this or you're asked to do that,
And what is your ready reply?
Get Somebody Else to do that job,
He'll do it much better than I.

So much to do in this weary old world—
So much and workers so few,
And Somebody Else, all weary and worn,
Is still substituting for you.

The next time you're asked to do
something worthwhile,
Just give this ready reply:
If Somebody Else can give time and support,
My goodness, so can I!

—*Whitham, A.E.*

SHARING

701

"But someone may well say, 'You have faith, and I have works; show me your faith without the work, and I will show you my faith by my works.' You believe that God is one. You do well; the demons also believe, and shudder" (James 18-19).

The point of this text is that if we tell people we have faith, we can't expect them to believe us unless we demonstrate our faith through the kind of life we live—in other words, through our works. In this connection, it is interesting to note that the Greek word for "fellowship" is "generosity." To prove ourselves worthy members of the Christian Fellowship we must be sharers:

God calls it sheer hypocrisy
To say unto another,
"Be warmed and filled, my needy friend,"
And then not help that brother.

Our propensity not to share is illustrated in the story of a conversation between two farmers:

> FIRST FARMER: "If you had two fields, wouldn't you be willing to share one of them?"
> SECOND FARMER: "Of course!"
> FIRST FARMER: "And if you had two houses, you couldn't live in both, so you'd be happy to share the other, wouldn't you?"
> SECOND FARMER: "Oh, absolutely!"
> FIRST FARMER: "If you had two cars, you would be willing to give one to your neighbor who had none, wouldn't you?"
> SECOND FARMER: "Yes, indeed!"
> FIRST FARMER: "Suppose you had two horses, you would give one to your neighbor, wouldn't you?"
> SECOND FARMER: "Uh, no, I couldn't do that!"
> FIRST FARMER: "Why not?"
> SECOND FARMER: "Because I have two horses."

702/SHARING

"New Yorker" magazine ran a cartoon in which a bank loan officer is seated at his desk with his hands folded and a pompous look on his face. Walking away from the loan officer's desk, with his head down and a sad look on his face, is a man whose loan application has just been rejected. In the caption, the loan officer says to the rejected and dejected man, "Well, thanks anyway for sharing your financial plight with us."

Most of us have no problem sharing our troubles. Whether it's a financial crunch or a rejection of some kind, we're usually ready and willing to spread the bad news. But what the New Testament writers are telling us is that whatever is happening in our lives—good or bad, by our standards—our calling is to be ready and willing always to spread the Good News. Our calling is to share the Good News of the God who loves us and will never reject us!

SIBLINGS

703

Overheard on a school bus:

First Little Girl: "What's wrong?"
Second Little Girl: "My hamsters are fighting."
First Little Girl: "About what?"
Second Little Girl: "About everything!"
First Little Girl: "They must be sisters."

SICKNESS

704

An elderly woman was seriously ill and was told by her doctor that everything humanly possible had been done for her. "Now you must trust in God," the doctor said. To which the woman replied, "Has it come to that?" As a people of Faith, we must acknowledge that it always "comes to that." Consequently, as a people of Faith, "we begin with that." God is not a last resort!

SILENCE

705

An old New England farmer was known as a man of few words. He spoke very little and, when he did, the words seemed to come out rather grudgingly. But he was a good man, in his own way, and a good husband. One evening, after a long day's work in the fields, he enjoyed a particularly good supper his wife had prepared for him. And it seemed to soften him up a bit, for when he had finished eating, he gazed rather tenderly at his spouse and said, "When I think of what a wonderful wife you've been all these years, sometimes it's almost more than I can stand not to tell you."

706/SILENCE

"...no human being can tame the tongue" (James 3:8).

Shortly after being elected to the Presidency, Calvin Coolidge arrived in Washington, D.C., to attend a large dinner party. He found himself seated next to a prominent socialite who kept up a steady stream of meaningless conversation to which he never replied. (Coolidge was noted for his unwillingness to engage in small talk on such occasions.) Finally, the talkative socialite leaned over and confided to the President-elect that she had made a wager she would be able to get more than two words out of him. Coolidge immediately answered, "You lose!"

SIN

707

At a prayer meeting, several women were discussing the latest dieting craze. One asked, "Can breaking a diet ever be a sin?"

"It's not normally a sin," the prayer-leader volunteered. "We're all temples of the Holy Spirit. But if you want to be a cathedral it's up to you."

—Henrietta, M. (Adapted).

708/SIN

President Calvin Coolidge was noted for his brevity of speech. He never used three words when one or two would suffice. One Sunday morning, he went to Church without his wife who wasn't feeling well. When the President returned to the White House, Mrs. Coolidge asked what the sermon was about. "Sin," Coolidge said. "And what did the preacher have to say about sin?" Mrs. Coolidge persisted. "He was against it," her husband replied.

709/SIN

Several years ago a church group was picketing the stadium just before a Sunday game. When Tampa Bay Bucs coach John McKay showed up, the minister stopped him and said sternly, "Sir, don't you know that it is a sin to play football on Sunday?"

"Well," said McKay glumly, "the way the Tampa Bay Bucs are playing, it sure is."

SINCERITY

710
Most people will probably sign thousands of letters in their lifetime with the customary closing, "sincerely." But most of us don't know its origin.

Etymologists tell us the word sincere has it roots in the marble quarries of Rome. When Roman quarry workers found a flaw in a piece of marble, they would attempt to hide it by covering it over with wax. The "cover-up" became widespread and was eventually outlawed by the Roman Senate. They decreed that all marble must be "sine cera," or "sincerus"—meaning "without wax." This is the root of our word sincere meaning free from pretense or deceit.
—*"Soundings" (Adapted).*

"You have been obedient to the truth and purified your souls until you can love like brothers, in sincerity." (I Peter 1:22).

SOCIETY

711
There is a daily, syndicated newspaper cartoon strip called "The Small Society" in which the author seems to be telling us that our Society is coming apart at the seams. For example, a December cartoon shows a sidewalk Santa Claus standing next to his artificial chimney and ringing his little bell. Facing him is a little girl who says, "I don't believe in Santa Claus anymore." To which Santa replies, "That's okay, I don't believe in kids anymore."

A few weeks later, "The Small Society" depicted a father and son confrontation. The teenage son is slouched down in an easy chair, looking very depressed. His father seems concerned, trying very hard to communicate with his boy. He says, "Of course we all want a purpose in life…but I promise you that after awhile you'll be too busy making a living to worry about it."

As a Society, are we coming to the point where we don't believe in anything anymore? As a society, are we too busy to think about our true purpose in life?

SPEECH MAKING

712

"Where are you going?" the long-winded preacher asked a man who got up to leave during his sermon. "Out to get a haircut," the main said. The preacher asked, "Why didn't you get it before you came in?" The man replied, "I didn't need one then."

SPIRITUAL BODY

713

General William Booth who founded the Salvation Army and who personally ministered to thousands upon thousands of people, became blind in his old age. In a beautiful poem by Rachel Lindsey, William Booth is pictured marching into heaven to receive his new spiritual body and his new eyes. All is joy and peace as he opens those new eyes and sees the people he had helped during his life on earth. All is joy and peace as he beholds his Christ.

On one occasion, during the last period of his life, Booth's daughter, Evangeline, escorted him to a spot where she had a clear view of a glorious sunset. Evangeline wanted desperately to share the beautiful sight with him. "Can't you see at least a little of the light?" she asked. The old man replied, very quietly but with absolute conviction, "I cannot see the setting sun, but I shall see it rise!"
Thanks be to God who gives us our spiritual bodies that enable us, in the next life, to experience the warm, healing light of His Presence.

SPIRITUAL HEALTH

714

Dr. Arnold Fox is a member of the California State Board of Medical Quality Assurance. "It is my pleasure," he says, "to help give oral examinations to the mostly young physicians applying for licenses to practice medicine in California. These doctors have already been graduated from medical school, completed residencies in their various specialities, and passed the written examinations. As a group, they are highly educated, motivated, and intelligent.

"I've been curious to see how much they know about stress. At the last examination, I asked the doctors to pretend that they were examining me—a 50-year-old man complaining of fatigue. One of the most common complaints of stress is fatigue. 'What are the causes of fatigue?' I asked. 'Give me five or ten possibilities.'

"All these bright physicians quickly suggested heart disorders, lung problems, and all kinds of exotic diseases that the average doctor sees once in a lifetime. None of them seemed to know that depression is one of the main causes of fatigue.

"They were very concerned with the organs of the body, with the systems, tissues, and molecules. Not one even tried peeking into my spirit. No one asked me what I thought of life, if I loved my wife, if I felt harassed or unappreciated at work, or if I had good relationships with my children.

"Unfortunately, it's taking a long time for my fellow doctors to understand and appreciate the tremendous impact of the mind on the body. The medical system is making progress, but slowly. Doctors are still being taught the disease/drug equation: for every disease there is a drug, or will be soon.

"But we already have something more powerful than any drug ever devised, and it's exactly tailored to our needs: our spirit. Unleashed, the spirit can be a whirlwind of health, happiness, and success in life...

When your spirit is weak, you are filled with pessimism and gloom; you feel small and helpless; you wonder if it's possible to find any joy in life.

When your spirit is weak, life is a chore, not the pleasure that it can be.

I've delivered many babies: boys and girls, black and white, small and large. I never delivered a success or a failure in life. I never delivered a lawyer, a doctor, or a truck drover. Only babies. At the moment of birth they were all successful because they were filled with unlimited potential. Some were physically stronger than others, some had more innate wisdom or inborn courage than others. But all had unlimited potential as far as their spirit was concerned.
—Fox, A., M.D. "Making Miracles." (Adapted).

SPIRITUAL JOURNEY

715
"So, my dear friends, continue to do as I tell you...not only as you did when I was there with you, but even more now that I am no longer there; and work for your salvation in fear and trembling" (Phil. 2:12).

The journey toward spiritual fulfillment is often hazardous. It can be likened to the situation in which a person comes upon a great stairway. Anxious to know what lies at the top, the person begins to ascend the steps, one by one. But, with each upward step, there comes an eerie feeling—a sense of being unable to turn back. And suddenly the person realizes that each time his or her foot comes down on the higher step, the step below disappears—and the only way to avoid falling into the vast emptiness below is to continue, step by step, on the journey upward.

STANDARDS

716
Once, on a battlefield, the flag got far ahead of the soldiers. An officer called back to his superior and asked, "Shall we bring the flag back to the regiment?" "No," came the reply, "make the regiment catch up with the flag!"

The New Testament Standard is far ahead of most of the Church today. Although it is true that our Church membership is made up of persons in all stages of personal growth and development and commitment, nevertheless we musn't reduce our standards to conform to the lowest levels. Rather, we should constantly strive to "make the regiment catch up to the flag," so to speak. We must constantly strive to make the Church move ever closer to Christ!

STEREOTYPE

717
A teacher held an empty jar up to his class and asked, "What do you think is in here?"

"Nothing," was the reply from his students.

The teacher wrapped a band of paper around the jar. On the band was the printed label: SILVER.

"Now what do you think is in the jar?" the teacher asked.

"Nothing," again was the response.

"But it's labeled SILVER," the teacher reminded the students.

"It's just as empty as before," the class insisted.

The lesson was taught:

An incredible fact about man is his belief in the reality of mere labels, mere words. He thinks he actually becomes what he calls himself. Abolish labels. Be real.

Labels separate a person from himself or herself. Dropping the labels ends self-division and self-conflict.

STEWARDSHIP

718

A visiting preacher to a small country Church delivered a thirty minute sermon on "Gratitude". At the conclusion of the sermon, he said, "And remember, however small the gift, always be grateful to the Lord." Later, when it was time for the offering, an usher used the preacher's hat to take up the collection. When the hat came back to him, the preacher shook it carefully, but heard no sound. Then he turned it upside down, but nothing came out. It was empty! Seeing this, every eye in the congregation watched to see if the preacher would practice what he had just preached. Whereupon, the clergyman raised his hands to heaven, still holding the empty hat, and said, "I thank Thee Lord that I got my hat back!"

719/STEWARDSHIP

A troubled pastor told his congregation, "As you know, our budget has increased eighteen percent this year. Let me suggest that all of you consider giving one-tenth of your income. Your church is in real financial need. Quite frankly, it's fit to be tithed."

720/STEWARDSHIP

A young preacher despised making the annual appeal to his congregation for financial support more than any other task that he was asked to carry out. In fact he disliked the job so much that he couldn't even bring himself to use the word money in his appeal. One year he opened his stewardship sermon with the following:

> "I would like to remind you that what you are about to give is deductible, cannot be taken with you, and is considered by some to be the root of all evil."

721/STEWARDSHIP

In a Colorado parish, it was decided to pattern a Sunday service after worship services conducted in Colonial America. The pastor dressed in knee breeches and a long tail coat. The congregation was divided: women on one side, men on the other. At "Offertory" time, the pastor announced that the collection too would be patterned after Colonial times. He then asked all "heads of household" to come forward with their contributions and place them on the altar. Whereupon, all of the men rose at once. However, to everyone's amusement, many of the men crossed the aisle to the women's side—to get money from their wives.

722/STEWARDSHIP

The more you give,
the more you get.
The more you laugh,
the less you fret.
The more you do
unselfishly,
The more you live
abundantly.

The more of everything
you share,
The more you'll always
have to spare.

The more you love,
the more you'll find
That life is good
and friends are kind.
For only what
we give away,
Enriches us
from day to day.

— *Rice, H.S., "Just For You,"*

723/STEWARDSHIP

An agent from the Internal Revenue Service called a preacher and said, "One of your church members, Sam Harris, put down on his income tax return that he had given $300 to the church. Is that true?" The preacher thought for a minute and replied, "Well, if he hasn't, he will!"

724/STEWARDSHIP

An elderly man, soliciting friends for a religious organization, asked Oliver Wendell Holmes, then in his eighties, for a contribution. As Holmes was about to make out a check, he suddenly stopped and asked, "What are you going to do with the money?"

"Give it to the Lord, of course," the man replied.

"How old are you?" the jurist asked.

"Seventy."

"Well, in that case," said Holmes, "I'll give it to Him myself. I'll be seeing Him before you will!"

725/STEWARDSHIP

A young clergyman, fresh out of the seminary, thought it would help him in his career if he first took a job as a policeman for several months. He passed the physical examination and then took the oral examination to ascertain his alertness of mind and his ability to act quickly and wisely in an emergency.

Among other questions, he was asked, "What would you do to disperse a frenzied crowd?" He thought for a moment and then said, "I would take up a collection."

726/STEWARDSHIP

A congregation was meeting in church as part of a campaign to raise funds for needed building repairs. After listening to the pastor's emotional description of the dire condition of the church building and his stirring appeal for funds, the congregation was nonetheless surprised when the man known as the most miserly person in the parish rose and offered to start the fund with a fifty dollar contribution. As he spoke, a chunk of plaster fell from the ceiling and hit him on the head. The miser, a trifle dazed, rose again and said, "I'd better make that one hundred dollars." Whereupon, a voice rang out from the rear of the church: "Hit him again, Lord! Hit him again!"

727/STEWARDSHIP

Seeking to inspire his audience, a fiery evangelist thundered: "This Church must get up and walk." Whereupon, a voice from the congregation cried out, "Amen! Let her walk!" "This Church must get up and run," the preacher shouted. Again the voice from the congregation cried out, "Amen! Let her run!" "More than that," screamed the preacher, "This Church must get up and fly." "Amen! Let her fly!" the voice responded. "Brothers and sisters," the preacher continued, "it takes money to make a Church get up and fly!" "Amen!" said the voice, "let her walk!"

728/STEWARDSHIP

Members of an outdoor group went on a camping trip in the Canadian Rockies. One man became separated from his friends and couldn't find his way back to camp. Night fell and a severe storm broke. To protect himself, he crawled into a hollow log and went to sleep. When he awakened in the morning, he found that the log had become swollen from moisture and he was hopelessly stuck inside. He thought he would die trapped in the log. Like a drowning man, his whole life passed before his eyes. He thought of how he had been raised and nurtured by loving parents. He thought about the years of loyalty and support he had received from his loving wife. He thought about the joys he had experienced as a parent. He thought about the help and encouragement he had been offered through the years by his many friends. As he thought about these things, he began to feel more ashamed that he had never expressed a proper "Thank you" to his family and friends for all they had done for him. Then he began to think of his Church and the wonderful sense of community it had brought into his life. And when he recalled the size of his pledge for the next year's Church budget, he felt so small that he slipped right out of the log.

SUCCESS

729

A fisherman was lying on a New England river bank, lazily casting his line into the water. Now and then, he caught a silvery salmon. As he was hauling in a fish, a prosperously dressed businessman from a nearby town strolled over. "Don't you realize," he asked the fisherman, "that you could catch more fish if you put several lines into the water at the same time?"

"Why would I want more fish?" asked the fisherman.

"Well, if you had more fish, you would have more to sell, and you would make more money," the industrialist replied. "And if you made more money, you could buy a big fishing boat. Then you could open up a store and sell your fish to the whole town. After you opened one store, you could open a second, and then a third. You would have many people working for you. Eventually you could open a large wholesale fish market, shipping fish all over America. You could become a very rich man."

The fisherman looked unconvinced. "And then what would I do?" he asked the industrialist.

"Why, then you would be successful, and you'd have all the time in the world to do whatever you most enjoyed doing. You could just lie on your back, relax, and go fishing!"

The fisherman looked up at him and smiled. "But that's what I'm doing now!"

—Hyatt, C. and Gottlieb, L., "When Smart People Fail."

"For what will it profit a man if he gains the whole world and forfeits his life?" (Matthew 16:26).

"For where your treasure is, there your heart will be also" (Luke 12:34).

730/SUCCESS

"If you have a good name, if you are right more often than you are wrong, if your children respect you, if your grandchildren are glad to see you, if your friends can count on you and you can count on them in time of trouble, if you can face your God and say 'I have done my best,' then you are a success."
—*Ann Landers*

731/SUCCESS

"I have found the road to success no easy matter," said a modern business executive to an interviewer. "I started at the bottom. I worked fourteen hours a day. I sweated. I fought. I maneuvered. I schemed. I took abuse. I did things others might not approve of. But I kept on climbing the ladder." "And now, of course, you are a success?" prompted the interviewer. "No, I wouldn't say that," replied the business executive. "Just quote me as saying that I have become expert at climbing ladders."

It has been said that to succeed in this complex modern Age, a person has to keep his back to the wall, his ear to the ground, his shoulder to the wheel, his nose to the grindstone, and both feet on the ground. Undoubtedly that is a good formula for the kind of hollow, worldly success that consists only in becoming expert at climbing ladders. If you want to aspire to genuine success, with lasting value and ultimate meaning, you must do more than keep your ear to the ground, your shoulder to the wheel and your nose to the grindstone so that you can become an "expert at climbing ladders." If you want to achieve genuine success, you must keep your eye on the Lord and your heart in the Lord's service.

732/SUCCESS

The chief executive officer of a large corporation decided to take stock of his life by participating in a week–long spiritual retreat. At the final general session, each of the retreatants was asked to say a few words. When the businessman's turn, came, he rose and told of his long struggle to be a success. He told of long hours, tough competition, burning ambition, little time for his family. He enumerated the many rungs he had climbed on his way to the top. Then he said, "Now that I am there, it isn't what I thought it would be. I feel empty inside. It's lonely at the top. This week I have looked around and have come to the conclusion that I propped my ladder against the wrong building."

733/SUCCESS

Actress Nancy Walker, of "Rhoda" fame, tells the story of one of the most successful people she knows, an old man who cleans the streets of the Metro Goldwyn Mayer studio lot.

> This gentleman is one of the best and happiest human beings. To me he is the best because he does his job fully and brilliantly. Every day he gets to the studio early, immaculately dressed. He makes it his business to know everybody on the lot. He has eagle eyes looking around for any debris that would clutter up his workplace, and when you see him at the end of the day surveying the grounds, you know he feels he's done a good job. That street cleaner knows MGM is his studio as much as anyone else's, and he is proud to be able to keep its streets clean. In my view he is far more successful than many of the actors, who think success means having your own makeup man. The street cleaner believes what I have always believed: it comes from the work itself.

SUICIDE

734

The following true story, by Teresa Allen appeared in the Marin (California) Independent Journal:

> On a warm, clear day last summer, 28–year–old Kenneth Baldwin stood midspan on the Golden Gate Bridge and said goodbye to the world.

> Weeping with joy at the decision to kill himself, he gripped the guardrail, vaulted over the bar, and plunged more than 240 feet toward the frigid waters and what he believed would be certain death.
>
> "When I got on the bridge," he said, "I believed I had made the right decision and I felt more happiness than I had experienced for months. But I panicked when I pushed off and saw my hands leave the guard rail. I instantly knew I had made a big mistake, but there was nothing I could do but live through those agonizing seconds knowing I would be gone as soon as I hit the water."
>
> But Baldwin didn't die. Despite odds of 100–to–1 that he would survive the impact, Baldwin was not only alive and virtually unharmed, but treading water with renewed vigor for life. "I should have died, but I didn't. And today, all I know is that I'm thrilled to be alive. I feel almost blessed, like I'm a chosen member of a very elite club."

"...yield yourselves to God as men who have been brought from death to life" (Romans 6:13).

SUNDAY SCHOOL

735
A Sunday school teacher had been telling her class of youngsters about "heavenly rewards" and "crowns of glory" that awaited people who believed, and lived good lives. "Now tell me," she said at the close of the lesson, "Who will get the biggest crown?" There was silence for a moment, then one bright youngster piped up, "The one who has the biggest head."

Another Sunday school teacher asked one of his students this question: "Johnny, can you tell me what we must do before we can expect forgiveness of sin?" "Yes sir," Johnny replied. "We must sin."

Still another Sunday school teacher asked, "What do you think a land flowing with milk and honey would be like?" "Sticky," came the answer.

736/SUNDAY SCHOOL
A Sunday school teacher was telling the creation story to youngsters in her class. "God fashioned the heavens and the earth, and He created man in His own image," she said. "The man's name was Adam, and God put him in the Garden of Eden. But he seemed to be lonely, so God decided to give Adam a wife. When Adam went to sleep, God took out a rib from his side and made it into a woman named Eve."

After class, one of the little students had run hard all the way home and, as a result, felt a pain in his side. He quickly went to his mother and said, "Gosh, mom, I think I'm going to have a wife."

737/SUNDAY SCHOOL
Comedian Dick Van Dyke tells the story of a little boy who figured out how babies get their belly-buttons. "You see," the little boy said, "when God finishes making little babies, He lines them all up in a row. Then He walks along in front of them, pokes each one in the tummy with His finger, and says, 'You're done...you're done...and you're done.'"

738/SUNDAY SCHOOL
After hearing the story of Jesus being tempted in the desert by Satan, one little boy asked another: "Do you really think that there's a devil?" "No," the other boy answered, "I think it turns out just like Santa Claus. It's probably your father."

739/SUNDAY SCHOOL
Two little boys had just listened to the story of "Noah and the Ark." Their conversation went like this:

First boy—"With all that deep water around I'll bet Noah did a lot of fishing."

Second boy—"How could he? He only had two worms."

First boy—"Why do you think Noah lived until he was nine-hundred-years-old?"

Second boy—"He probably watched his diet."

740/SUNDAY SCHOOL
One morning, a Sunday-school teacher asked her students if they knew who had defeated the Philistines. After a few moments one youngster asked, "Are they in the American League or the National League?"

SUSPICION

741
A young theater-goer reported the following true account of an incident at a discount ticket sales outlet in New York City:

> A well-dressed young man approached the line, holding up two tickets for that night's performance of a big hit musical. They were, he announced, FREE to anyone who could use them. He explained that his two friends could not make the performance because their car had broken down, that the box office would not refund the money, that he hated to have the tickets go to waste and that perhaps someone on line would like to have them.

There were no takers, only suspicious eyes from the crowd. The man shrugged and walked away. A while later he returned. With a knowing look, he announced that he would sell the pair of $35 tickets for $10 each, and he sold them immediately.

T

TEENAGERS

742

Og Mandino recalls a television show he appeared on in Los Angeles. One of the guests was a famous author of romance novels. She was complaining about her two teenage boys. They were driving her bonkers—that was the word she used. Their rooms were always a mess and they both had stereos turned up very loud to different stations. Having just gone through seeing my youngest off to college, I told that mother, "The day's going to come when you're going to walk down the hall, past two very quiet rooms, and you're going to ask yourself, 'Where did they go?'" Then I told the audience, "Go home and hug your kids."

TELEVISION VIOLENCE

743

TV "has come a long way, baby," says comedian Joe Hickman. "Sex, violence, profanity, drugs, nudity, it's all acceptable now on TV—as long as they don't smoke cigarettes."

"The plain fact is that violence sells," points out United States Senator Paul Simon. "Programmers, producers and advertisers have discovered the axiom that violence is nearly a sure-fire ratings-booster. It moves the numbers upward. But I strongly believe a democratic, pluralistic society like ours can find ways to protect itself against undue emphasis on televised violence. It's time for the television industry to forge a partnership with America's families to scale back the atmosphere of violence that is erupting in our communities, on our Main Streets, even in our schoolyards."

TEN COMMANDMENTS

744
A Sunday school teacher had just finished teaching the Ten Commandments to her kindergarten class. Then she told the class to think about the rules they had to obey at home. "Can anyone think of a rule you have to obey at home that isn't on this list?" she asked. A little girl raised her hand and said, "Thou shalt not touch the answering machine."

745/TEN COMMANDMENTS
A woman went to the post office to mail the old family Bible to her brother. She told the clerk she wanted to insure the package. "Does it contain anything breakable?" the clerk asked. To which the woman replied: "Only the Ten Commandments."

746/TEN COMMANDMENTS
A snobbish lady at a fancy dinner told a fellow guest, Rabbi Stephen S. Wise, that she was a member of the Daughters of the American Revolution. "My ancestors witnessed the signing of the Declaration of Independence," she said. Dr. Wise replied, "This is very well. My ancestors witnessed the signing of the Ten Commandments."

THANKSGIVING

747
If you were raised in a family that incorporated prayer into your childhood routine, you may recall a time when it seemed that stretching out your night prayers was the only way to get around the command to "Go to sleep." One little girl became

an expert at this by developing an ever-growing list of "Thank-you-God" prayers. She would pray for every child she knew: "Thank you God for Alice; thank you God for Patty; thank you God for Bobby," and on and on. Then she would breath deeply and run through a list of the adults she encountered at school: "Thank you God for our principal, Mr. Baker; thank you God for Miss Nordell, my teacher; thank you God for Mrs. Frano, the school librarian." And on and on. She also had a catch-all list which included such items as, "Thank you God for the lady in the shoe store; thank you God for my birthday which comes in eleven weeks and three days." Of course there was a "Thank you God for Mommy and Daddy," and one each for "Alice's and Patty's and Bobby's Mommy and Daddy." There were nights, however, when this prayerful little girl was so tired she could hardly keep her eyes open as she groped her way into bed. On such occasions her anxiety for sleep moved her prayers to the opposite extreme. She would forget her long list of "Thank you Gods" and say, simply, "Thank you God, for God. Amen."

"Thank God for God, Amen!" Because God is God, we are worthwhile. Because God is God, our lives have meaning and purpose. Because God is God, we do not hope in vain for fulfillment. Because God is God, we are going someplace with our lives. Because God is God, the final victory over death already has been won. "Thank God for God. Amen!"

748/THANKSGIVING

A Thankful Heart:

Take nothing for granted,
for whenever you do,
The "joy of enjoying"
is lessened for you.
For we rob our own lives
much more than we know
When we fail to respond
or in any way show
Our thanks for the blessings
that daily are ours...

The warmth of the sun,
    the fragrance of flowers,
The beauty of twilight,
    the freshness of dawn,
The coolness of dew
    on a green velvet lawn,
The kind little deeds
    so thoughtfully done,
The favors of friends
    and the love they impart
    in a myriad of ways,
Expecting no payment
    and no words of praise...

Oh, great is our loss
    when we no longer find
A thankful response
    to things of this kind,
For the joy of enjoying
    and the fullness of living
Are found in the heart
    that is filled with thanksgiving.

—Rice, H.S. (Adapted).

749/THANKSGIVING

Several years ago, "Dear Abby" offered the following Thanksgiving message:

> Dear Readers: Today is Thanksgiving, so take a few minutes to think about what you have to be thankful for.
>
> How's your health? Not so good? Well, thank God you've lived this long. A lot of people haven't. You're hurting? Thousands—maybe millions—are hurting more. (Have you ever visited a veterans' hospital? Or a rehabilitation clinic for crippled children?)
>
> If you awakened this morning and were able to hear the birds sing, and use your vocal chords to utter

human sounds, and walk to the breakfast table on two good legs, and read the newspaper with two good eyes —praise the Lord! A lot of people couldn't. How's your pocketbook? Thin? Well, most of the living world is a lot poorer. No pensions. No welfare. No food stamps. No Social Security. In fact, one-third of the people in the world will go to bed hungry tonight.

Are you lonely? The way to have a friend is to be one. If nobody calls you, call them. Go out of your way to do something nice for somebody. It's a sure cure for the blues.

Are you concerned about your country's future? Hooray! Our system has been saved by such concern. Concern for honesty in government, concern for peace, and concern for fair play under the law. Your country may not be a rose garden, but it also is not a patch of weeds.

Freedom rings! Look and listen. You can still worship at the church of your choice, cast a secret ballot, and even criticize your government without fearing a knock on the head or a knock at the door at midnight. And if you want to live under a different system, you are free to go. There are no walls or fences—nothing to keep you here.

As a final thought, I'll repeat my Thanksgiving Prayer:

O, heavenly Father:
We thank Thee for food
and remember the hungry.
We thank Thee for health
and remember the sick.
We thank Thee for friends and
remember the friendless.
We thank Thee for freedom
and remember the enslaved.

May these remembrances stir us to service;
That Thy gifts to us may be used for others.
Amen. Have a wonderful Thanksgiving and may God bless you and yours.
Love, Abby

750/THANKSGIVING
Actress Helen Hayes was preparing Thanksgiving dinner when she warned: "This is the first turkey I've ever cooked. If it isn't right, I don't want anybody to say a word. We'll just get up from the table, without comment, and go down to the hotel for dinner." When she returned from the kitchen about five minutes later, all family members were seated at the dinner table—wearing their hats and coats.

751/THANKSGIVING
You may have seen a cartoon which appeared in one of the weekly magazines in which the President of the United States and his wife are conversing. The "First Lady" is asking her husband: "Do you think a Thanksgiving Proclamation can be enforced this year?"

752/THANKSGIVING
A young man was walking on the East Side of New York and accidentally fell into an open excavation which was being dug to lay the foundation of a new building. It was broad daylight, and the young man was perfectly sober. It was purely an accident; he walked too near the edge and fell in. As he was struggling up the side of the deep hole to get out, an elderly gentleman who had witnessed the accident came over, bent down, laid a fatherly hand on the young man's head, and said: "Don't be foolish, my boy, stay down there." The young man climbed out and said to the old man: "Do you really believe that conditions in the world are so bad that I should remain in that hole?" When the elderly gentleman replied that he honestly thought so, the young man gave him a very polite shove, and the last he saw of the old man he was sitting very comfortably in the bottom of the hole.

Now there is a lot to be said in favor of the attitude of that young man. The world is in a turmoil, but that is no reason for us to become cynical, and discouraged, and lose our faith in human possibilities.

753/THANKSGIVING

Give thanks to God for everything,
The sunshine and the rain,
The joy and the grief, the gain and the loss,
The pleasure and the pain.

For every good and perfect gift
Give thanks to God above.
He daily showers blessings down
In mercy, grace and love.

Give thanks when difficulties rise,
for God is ever near.
His purposes are for your good;
Someday He'll make them clear.
Give thanks, although your present test
Is difficult to bear;
A crown eternal may be yours
Forevermore to wear!

Give thanks to God, for He still reigns
And watches o'er His own.
He guards His children night and day,
Perhaps to them unknown.

—Clark, E.L.

THOU SHALT NOT STEAL

754

A psychiatrist whose specialty was treating people with kleptomania, received a telephone call in the middle of the night from one of his patients. "Doctor, you've got to help me. I'm on a business trip and I'm in my hotel room with this frantic urge to steal." To which the half-asleep doctor replied, "Just take two ashtrays and call me in the morning."

THIEVES

755
The following events have been verified by the Suffolk County (NY) Police:

> On a recent morning, a gentleman we shall call Mr. Smith, who resides in Long Island, tried to start his car. It was parked in front of his home.
>
> To his dismay, he discovered that the car's battery had been stolen. He notified the police who duly wrote up the report and suggested that he report the incident to his insurance company. Mr. Smith went out and bought another battery.
>
> A few mornings later, Mr. Smith discovered a brand new battery sitting on the hood of his automobile. Attached to it was an envelope, containing a note of apology: "Due to a medical emergency in the middle of the night, it was necessary to take your battery. Instead of waking you at the time of the emergency, I chose to explain my actions later. Please accept this replacement battery, and the gift enclosed, as a small token of my gratitude." The note was unsigned. And there in the envelope, were two tickets to a performance of the hit show "Evita," for the following week.

Mr. Smith was ecstatic—his faith in human nature had been restored. Next week, he and his wife drove to Manhattan. They went to dinner, then went to the theatre and saw the show, using the tickets from their unknown benefactor.

The Smiths returned home, tired but happy from their night on the town. They opened the front door, and discovered that their home had been broken into. Just about everything of value—silverware, jewelry, furniture—was gone!

"They do not expect another note," said the police report.

TIME

756

The clock master was about to fix the pendulum of a clock when, to his surprise, he heard the pendulum speak.

"Please, sir, leave me alone," the pendulum pleaded. "It will be an act of kindness on your part. Think of the number of times I will have to tick day and night. So many times each minute, sixty minutes an hour, twenty-four hours a day, three hundred and sixty-five days a year. For year upon year...millions of ticks. I can't cope with it."

But the clock master answered wisely, "Don't think of the future. Just do one tick at a time and you will enjoy every tick for the rest of your life."

And that is exactly what the pendulum decided to do. It is still ticking merrily away.
—deMello, A.

757/TIME

A class of high school sophomores was touring the Metropolitan Museum of Art in New York City where they stopped to view the magnificent collection of old Dresden China. The teacher noticed that two of her students seemed greatly fascinated by a large plate which displayed an enormous amount of detail. "Isn't the intricacy of the workmanship absolutely wonderful?" the teacher exclaimed. "Think of the time and effort that went into the crafting of that plate!" Whereupon, one of the two teenagers whispered to the other, "No wonder! They didn't have TV in those days. There was nothing else to do."

"...Walk with care: not as unwise, but as wise, making the most of your time" (Ephesians 5:16).

TRANSFORMATION

758
A theology professor in an America seminary was fond of telling his students about a certain man he had met during his sabbatical year of teaching in Africa. He would explain that the man was introduced to him simply as "After" (that's A-F-T-E-R). In the professor's words:

> When I asked about his strange name, he replied, "You see, that wasn't the name I was given when I was born. I changed my name. I changed it because everything that has happened in my life to make me feel worthwhile and to give me a sense of real purpose did so after I surrendered to Christ and experienced the power of God in Him."

759/TRANSFORMATION
A mother, wishing to encourage her young son's progress on the piano, took the boy to a Paderewski concert. After they were seated, the mother spotted a friend in the audience and walked down the aisle to greet her. Seizing the opportunity to explore the wonders of the concert hall, the little boy rose and eventually made his way through a door marked "No Admittance." When the houselights dimmed and the concert was about to begin, the mother returned to her seat and discovered the child was missing. Whereupon, the curtains parted and spotlights focused on the impressive Steinway piano onstage. To her horror, the mother saw her little boy sitting at the keyboard, innocently picking out "Twinkle, Twinkle Little Star." At that moment, the great piano master made his entrance, quickly moved to the piano and whispered in the boy's ear, "Don't quit. Keep playing." Then, leaning over, Paderewski reached down with his left hand and began filling in a bass part. Soon his right arm reached around to the other side of the child and he added a running obligato. Together, the old master and the young novice transformed an outrageous situation into a wonderfully creative experience. And the audience was mesmerized.

Whatever your life situation—however outrageous, however desperate, however mournful, however disappointing—Jesus whispers deep within your soul, "Don't quit. Keep on playing. You are not alone. Your life is secure in My hands. Together we will transform the broken patterns into a masterwork of God's creative art. Together, we will mesmerize the world with our song of love."

760/TRANSFORMATION

Once a man went to call at the place of business of one of his friends, a jeweler with a large clientele. The jeweler showed his friend a store of superb diamonds and other precious stones. Among them was a stone so lustreless that the friend said: "That one has no beauty at all." "Hasn't it?" asked the jeweler, lifting the stone from the tray and closing his fist over it. In a few moments, when he opened his hand, the stone glowed with all the splendor of the rainbow. "Why, what have you done to it?" asked the friend. The jeweler smiled. "That is an opal," he said. "It is what we call a sympathetic jewel. It needs only to be gripped with the human hand to bring out all its wonderful beauty."

To become the uniquely beautiful person God intended you to be, you must position yourself within the grip of the hand of God.

761/TRANSFORMATION

Hugh Martin, in "The Parables of the Gospels," tells the story of a rather rough, uncultured man who fell in love with a beautiful vase in a shop window. He bought the vase and put it on the mantelpiece in his room. There it became a kind of judgment on its surroundings. He had to clean up the room to make it worthy of the vase. The curtains looked dingy beside it. The old chair with the stuffing coming out of the seat would not do. The wallpaper and the paint needed renewing. Gradually the whole room was transformed.

When you put Christ on the mantel of your heart, your whole life is transformed.

TRAVEL

762

A 747 was halfway across the Atlantic when the captain got on the loudspeaker: "Attention, passengers. We have lost one of our engines, but we can certainly reach London with the three we have left. Unfortunately, we will arrive an hour late as a result."

An hour later the captain made another announcement: "Sorry, but we lost another engine. Still, we can travel on two. I'm afraid we will now arrive two hours late."

Shortly thereafter, the passengers heard the captain's voice again: "Guess what, folks. We just lost our third engine, but please be assured we can fly with only one. We will now arrive in London three hours late."

At this point, one passenger became furious. "For Pete's sake," he shouted. "If we lose another engine, we'll be up here all night!"

TRUST

763

Rosalind Russell (1912-1976), noted for her portrayals of witty, sophisticated career–women in scores of motion pictures, also won wide acclaim on the Broadway stage. But perhaps her greatest triumph was her gallant fight against arthritis and cancer. After her death, this poem was found tucked in her prayer book:

> Trust Him when dark doubts assail thee,
> Trust Him when your faith is small,
> Trust Him when simply to trust Him
> Is the hardest thing of all.

764/TRUST

A family moved into a new neighborhood and grandfather came for a visit. On the first day he took his granddaughter for a walk. They walked about fifteen minutes and the grandfather asked, "About how far do you think we are from home?" The granddaughter said she didn't know. "Well, what direction do you think we should take to get back?" he asked. "I don't know," said the granddaughter. "Sounds to me like you're lost," said grandpa. The granddaughter smiled and said, "I'm not lost, grandpa. I'm with you."

765/TRUST

In a busy Washington, D.C. Metro Station, a security guard observed a man asking a passerby for directions. "Can you tell me the way to the Washington Monument?" he asked. The passerby eagerly gave the tourist detailed directions with great clarity and precision, and then departed. The security guard was surprised as the out-of-towner approached him and asked the same question. The guard said, "I couldn't help hearing that man give you excellent directions." Without blinking an eye, the tourist replied, "I always get a second opinion."

TRUTH

766

Isidore Robey, the world-famous physicist, came to the United States as a small child and grew up on New York City's lower East side. In an interview he was asked how a poor immigrant boy was able to become one of the leading physicists in the world. He said, "I couldn't help it. It was because of my mother. My mother had a deep appreciation for the search for truth. And every single day when I came home from school, my mother would say to me, "Did you ask any good questions today?'"

U

UNDERSTANDING

767

A wise physician once said, "I have been practicing Medicine for thirty years, and I have prescribed many things. But in the long run, I have learned that for most of what ails the human creature, the best medicine is patient understanding of another's problems." When someone asked him, "What if it doesn't work?" he replied, "Double the dose."

VANITY

768

It was grandmother's 80th birthday celebration. The house was so invaded by family members that meals had to be served in shifts. Sleeping bags were spread out on stairway landings. The driveway was jammed with 12 cars, bumper-to-bumper, double-parked. The high point of the celebration was a Saturday evening reception and dinner at Church.

All afternoon, true to her form of a lifetime, vain, old grandmother conducted what amounted to a personal fashion show for the rest of the family. She tried on a new dress and asked everybody, "How do you like it? Should I wear this one tonight?" Then she tried on another and repeated the process. Then came the jewelry combinations and the shoes and the hairdo and all the rest. Until finally, when it seemed that grandmother had run out of things to show off, she appeared in still another new dress. "I got this one on sale," she said, "It's my burial dress."
—The Christian Century (Adapted).

VENGEANCE

769
A young man was bitten by a rabid dog. The victim was rushed to the hospital. As the doctor entered the emergency room he saw the patient feverishly writing on a legal pad. The doctor examined him and said he didn't think the injury would prove fatal, and that there was no need for him to hastily write out a will.

"Oh, this isn't a will," the young man replied. "I was just making out a list of people I want to bite."

770/VENGEANCE
A woman arrived at the Los Angeles airport and lined up to check in her bags for the flight to Miami. At the head of the line, a man with several suitcases was shouting angrily at the baggage clerk who had just told him there would be an extra charge because his luggage was over the weight limit. The irate man did his utmost to belittle and embarrass the clerk in front of the long line of passengers. When the woman reached the head of the line, she said to the baggage clerk, "I'm sorry that man was so rude to you. You didn't do anything wrong. And you didn't even answer him back. You acted like a perfect gentleman." To which the clerk replied, "Yes, thank you, I am a perfect gentleman." Then he smiled and, with a gleam in his eye, said, "That man is going to Miami and, he doesn't know it yet, but his bags are going to Albuquerque."

"You have heard that it was said, 'An eye for an eye and a tooth for a tooth.' But I say to you 'Do not resist one who is evil. But if anyone strikes you on the right cheek, turn to him the other, also'" (Matthew 5:38-39).

771/VENGEANCE
There is an amusing story that begins with a man reading the following classified newspaper ad: "For sale. 1991 Mercedes Benz 560 SL. $500.00." Although he was certain that there had been a misprint, nevertheless the man decided to answer the

ad. The seller was a middle-aged woman. She showed the car to the man, and it was a beauty: very low mileage, in mint condition. The man said, "It is a beautiful automobile and I would like to buy it, but the price—$500.00—what's the catch?" The woman answered, "There is no catch. You see, my husband is on an extended business trip. I know he is involved with another woman, but he doesn't know that I know. Three days ago I received a telegram from him. It read, 'Sell; the car and send the money.' So I am!"

VISION

772

When the great poet, Tagore, was working among the poor in the slums of India, he experienced what he thought was an overpowering vision of God. He was so deeply moved by this vision that he made immediate plans to leave the city and retire into the mountains of the High Himalayas. He felt that he needed a period of solitude in which to reflect on the vision and try to understand it more deeply. But as he walked out of the gates of the teeming city to go up into the uninhabited mountains, he looked at his people, and the vision left him. And Tagore remained in the city–with his people!

773/VISION

Adlai Stevenson once observed that the astronomers of the world cooperate with each other partly because there is no one nation from which the entire sky can be seen. Perhaps we, too, might look beyond our individual, narrow interest so that we can see the entire sky. And when we do, perhaps we'll be able to see that each of our stars can shine side by side—each illuminating, and not diminishing, the other.

WAR AND PEACE

774

"I'd like to believe that the people in the long run are going to do more to promote peace than our governments. Indeed, I think that people want peace so much that one of these days governments had better get out of their way and let them have it.

Every gun that is made, every warship launched, every rocket fired signifies, in the final sense, a theft from those who hunger and are not fed, those who are cold and not clothed. This world in arms is not spending money alone. It's spending the sweat of its laborers, the genius of its scientists, the hopes of its children. This is not a way of life, at all, in any true sense. Under the cloud of threatening war, it is humanity hanging from a cross of iron."

—Dwight D. Eisenhower

775/WAR AND PEACE

Two apples on a tree were looking down on the world. The first apple said, "Look at all those people fighting, robbing, rioting—they don't seem willing to get along with one another. Someday we apples will be the only ones left. Then we'll rule the world! The second apple replied, "Which of us—the reds or the greens?"

—Danbury Times (Adapted).

WELCOME

776

Lines inscribed on the porch of a parish Church outside of London:

To all who are weary and seek rest;
To all who mourn and long for comfort;
To all who struggle and desire victory;
To all who sin and need a Saviour;
To all who are idle and look for service;
To all who are strangers and want fellowship;
To all who hunger and thirst after righteousness;
And to whosoever will come:

This church has opened wide her doors and, in the name of the Lord Jesus Christ, says, to all of you —Welcome!

777/WISDOM

A clever young man tried to match wits with a wise old man. he held out his hands which he had cupped together. Then he said, "In my hands is a small bird. Tell me, wise man, is the bird alive or is it dead?" If the wise man were to answer, "Dead," the lad would open his hands and the bird would fly away. If the wise man said "Alive," the lad would squeeze his hands together, killing the bird. As the wise man pondered the situation, the young lad asked again "Is it alive or is it dead?" To which the wise old man replied, "The bird is in your hands."

WISDOM

778

Before he became President of the United States, James Garfield was the Principal of Hiram College in Ohio. Once, when he was serving in that capacity, the father of a student asked Mr. Garfield if the course of studies could be shortened so that his son might graduate sooner than scheduled. "Certainly," Garfield replied. "But it all depends on what you hope to make of your boy. Remember, when God wants to make an oak, He takes one hundred years or more. When He wants to make a squash, he requires only two months."

779/WISDOM
We should be careful to get out of an experience only the wisdom that is in it—and stop there; lest we be like the cat that sits on a hot stove lid. She will never sit down on a hot stove lid again—and that is well; but also she will never sit down on a cold one anymore.
—Mark Twain

780/WISDOM
By the time we reach kindergarten age, we already have been exposed to all the wisdom we really need in order to live good and meaningful lives. So says Robert Fulghum in his book, "All I really Need to know I learned in Kindergarten."

"Wisdom," he says, "was not at the top of the graduate-school mountain, but there in the sandpile at Sunday School. In that sandpile I learned such things as "Cookies and milk are good for you" and "Wash your hands before you eat." But, more importantly, I also learned such things as...

> Share everything.
> Play fair.
> Don't hit people.
> Say you're sorry when you hurt somebody.
> Don't take things that aren't yours.
> Hold hands and stick together.

Think what a better world it would be if people would only put into practice the wisdom learned in the sandpile! Think what a better world it would be if people were more willing to

share and play fair and say they're sorry when they hurt somebody and not take things that aren't theirs. And isn't it still true that no matter how old we are it is best to hold hands and stick together?
—Fulghum, R., "All I Really Need To Know I Learned In Kindergarten," (Adapted).

781/WISDOM
The young, newly promoted CEO of a bank made an appointment with the retiring CEO to seek some advice. "Sir," he began, "as you know, I do not have the outstanding qualifications you had for this job. And since you have been so successful as Chief Executive Officer of the bank, would you be so kind as to share with me some of the insights that have contributed to that success?" The older man replied, "Young man, I can answer you in two words: good decisions." The young CEO said, "Thank you very much, sir, but how does one come to know which is the good decision?"

"One word, young man: experience."

"But how does one get experience?"

"Two words, young man: bad decisions."

Devout Christians are often accused of being "brainwashed." And perhaps the truly dedicated Christian is brainwashed to a degree. But the important thing is that devout, dedicated Christians have chosen what they want to wash their brains with. And, more often than not that good decision is arrived at as result of the experience of making bad decisions.

782/WISDOM
I sat down to write,
and I asked myself,
"What shall I write?"

My heart said,
"Write about love."
But my mind said,
"Write about wisdom."
My heart did not argue with
my mind,
it merely embraced my mind
with love.
Then after a while
my mind spoke again and
said, "Love is wisdom."

—Freeman, J.D., "Love is wisdom, Love, Loved, Loving."

WORD OF GOD

783

A man whose wife was sick decided that he would do the cooking. He did quite well at it until one day he became very ambitious. He thought he would bake some bread. As often happens the first time around, he misread the recipe and he put two pounds of yeast in the dough. After faithfully following all the other instructions, he put the dough near the heat and waited. Some time later his wife called down from her upstairs bedroom: "Have you put the dough in the oven yet, dear?" Frantically, he replied, "Put it in the oven? I can't even keep it in the kitchen!"

That's the New Testament: The leaven bread of the Word of God, the Name of Jesus, you "can't even keep it in the kitchen." You can't even keep it in the church. It just expands into the world.

The New Testament Christians were so filled with enthusiasm and joy over the difference the Word of God in Jesus Christ had made in their lives that they literally could not contain it within themselves. Wherever they went, the joy spilled over and people suddenly paid attention.

WORK

784

While most nine–to–fivers wish their working week was a little shorter and their weekends a little longer, there's at least one executive who probably never exclaimed, "Thank God it's Friday!" In fact, a plaque hangs over the desk of this "workaholic" which reads:

THANK GOD IT'S MONDAY!

WORLD NEWS

785

The year is 2065. An astronaut has been stranded alone in a space station for three years. Then, one day, the astronaut receives a reply to his S.O.S. radio calls. The Captain of a nearby shuttle has dispatched a rescue craft to the space station. As the rescue vehicle docks with the space station, the officer in charge says to the stranded astronaut, "Captain sends his compliments, sir. Also these newspapers. Kindly read the news of the world as soon as possible and then inform the Captain as to whether or not you wish to be rescued."

WORRY

786

Once there was a handsome grandfather clock that became preoccupied with worry. It began thinking about the number of times it would have to tick: 2 times each second, 120 times per minute, 7,200 times an hour, 172,800 times a day, 63,072,000 times a year. When it realized that in the next ten years it would have to tick 630,720,000 times, it had a nervous breakdown. The clock went to a watchmaker for therapy. While under the watchmaker's care, the clock began to realize that all it needed to do was to tick one tick at a time. Soon thereafter it began to tick again, and continued ticking—one tick at a time—for one hundred years. Everyone loved that old grandfather clock.

787/WORRY

From a "Guideposts" article, Lee Weber writes:

> When I was a boy, my father always led the family devotions after supper. I can't say that we were happy about this. While the other kids were out playing baseball, we were stuck inside until our evening devotions were finished. One night, however, I learned a lesson that I've always remembered. The reading was about trusting God, and it pointed out that we have options: We can either trust God or worry. From a little book, he read a poem that went like this:
>
> The brindle cow would have lived 'til now,
> If only she'd saved her breath.
> But she feared that her hay wouldn't last all day;
> And she worried herself to death.

I don't know why it's so easy for us to worry, and so hard to trust; I wish it were the other way around. If you find yourself falling into this rut, remember that God is faithful. He never fails, and He is never late. As the old hymn says:

> If you trust and never doubt,
> He will surely bring you out.
> Take your burden to the Lord...
> And leave it there.

—*Weber, L.*

Index

(numbers refer to illustrations)

F

G

H

Q

R

S